Wilderness Kingdom

Chasse aux Bisons (1)
sur la terre des Pieds-noirs, (2)
Automne (3) 1847. (4)

(1) Bisons principalement, on 'exclut, ni les cerfs, ni les chévreüls, ours, cabris ou Gazelles, Grosses cornes, &c.

(2) des Pieds-noirs et des corbeaux leurs premiers voisins de l'ouest. les vues les plus belles appartiennent aux derniers

(3) automne - parceque les vignettes ont été dessinées en cette saison plus riche en couleur

(4) 1847 pendant la dernière Chasse de cette année - quoiquil y en ait de toutes les saisons et de plusieurs années

5 les vignettes et le texte placé en regard ne s'accordent pas toujours - raisons principales, avantages retirés des ordres chronologi.

WILDERNESS KINGDOM

Indian Life in the Rocky Mountains: 1840–1847

The Journals & Paintings of

NICOLAS POINT, S. J.

*Translated and
introduced by Joseph P. Donnelly, S. J.*

With an appreciation by John C. Ewers

Holt, Rinehart and Winston

New York, Chicago, San Francisco

Designer: William Nicoll

8 6 5 4 4 0 2

Printed in the United States of America

Foreword:

An Appreciation of Father Nicolas Point,

Pioneer Recorder

of Indian Life in the Northwest

An Appreciation of Father Nicolas Point, Pioneer Recorder of Indian Life in the Northwest

JOHN C. EWERS

Smithsonian Institution

Few of the hardy pioneers who entered the American West during the years prior to 1850 possessed that rare combination of skills which would have enabled them to record their experiences and observations in the Indian country in both words and pictures. Only one of their number accurately described and pictured Indian life among the tribes of the Northern Rockies in the present states of Montana and Idaho. He was Father Nicolas Point, S. J.

White settlement came late to that northern Rocky Mountain region. When Father Point left Westport by wagon on April 30, 1841, to

facing:
Grand Chief Eagle of
the Blackfoot tribe.

assist Father Pierre Jean De Smet in founding the first Catholic mission in the Northwest, there was not a single permanent white settler in the remote Rocky Mountain area. Many of the Indians whom Point came to know in the Northwest were old enough to remember the first American explorers to pass through their country under the command of Captains Lewis and Clark in 1805–1806. During the intervening thirty-five years they had come to know white men as beaver trappers and fur traders. These mountain trappers and Missouri River traders explored the high country in quest of beaver and erected some small, isolated trading posts in the Indian country. They furnished firearms, metal tools and utensils, blankets, beads, and other manufactured goods to the Indians in exchange for furs and buffalo robes, but they had no desire to acquire the Indians' lands or to civilize the primitive red men.

Father Point was a pioneer in the third wave

of whites—the missionaries who followed the explorers and fur seekers into the Rockies. Not only did he help to establish the first Christian mission among the Flatheads in the Bitter Root Valley just west of the main chain of the Rockies in 1841, but he also founded the first mission among the Coeur d'Alenes of northern Idaho in 1842 and initiated the first mission activity among the warlike Blackfeet in the valley of the Missouri east of the Rockies in 1846. He labored for six years as a missionary to these then remote and little-known tribes.

At the time Father Point left this region, in the spring of 1847, none of the Indians he had known had yet seen a white prospector, an agricultural settler, or a white woman in their homeland. None of these tribes had sworn allegiance to a European power. And they were not to negotiate their first treaty with the United States for another eight years. The buffalo, which was their staff of life, roamed in countless numbers over the plains east of the Rockies, for this was a full four decades before they were exterminated in that region.

As a zealous Catholic missionary, Father Point's first concern was with the saving of souls among the Indians he was called upon to serve. Yet from the time Father De Smet appointed him official diarist of the missionary party, before they left Westport for the mountains, Point carefully recorded his experiences and observations in the West. His writings were of two kinds. First he sought to chronicle the history of the mission work he undertook and to show the effects of Christian teachings on the minds and hearts of the primitive Indians. He described those events which appeared to him to be signs that God added his blessing to the efforts of the priests. These records reveal the anxieties as well as some of the satisfactions of the pioneer missionary to the Indians. They tell us as much about Father Point and his values as they do about the Indians among whom he labored. Perhaps these may be designated the subjective accounts of Father Point.

Much of this priest's writing, however, is of a different character, comprising a richly detailed description of Indian life and customs as he observed them. In the area of religion it must have been difficult for him to be wholly objective—probably as difficult as it would have been for a contemporary fur trader to evaluate fairly the bargaining methods of a lively competitor whom he was trying to put out of business. The Indians had strong, traditional beliefs and practices which did not coincide with the principles of Christian morality and the religious teachings of the priests. The red men looked to many of their "medicines" as sources of power which would help them to defeat their enemies, and Father Point soon learned that some of the most desperate warriors were eager to obtain Christianity as a new and more potent war medicine. Yet even in his studies of native religion, the priest made some very cogent observations—the most noteworthy in his analysis of the various functions of medicine in Indian life. Indeed, he recognized more clearly than have some modern anthropologists the important role of witchcraft in the primitive religious practices of these Rocky Mountain tribes.

Point had unique opportunities to observe many aspects of Flathead, Coeur d'Alene, and Blackfoot life over a prolonged period and at a time when—save for the Indians' use of the European horse and of manufactured trade goods—traditional customs were little changed by influences from the white man's world. In telling how the nomadic Indians moved camp, hunted, and fought their intertribal wars, his descriptions are especially rich. Father Point repeatedly accompanied Indian camps on prolonged buffalo-hunting excursions on the plains east of the Rockies, during which the Indians of his parties encountered and fought enemy tribesmen. Nor was he content merely to notice the Indians' actions during these hunts. He questioned them about why they acted as they did. Consequently, and even at this late date—eighty years after buffalo were exterminated on the northwestern plains—his writings provide new and fresh details of Indian hunting practices.

Father Point appears to have possessed greater skill as a draftsman than as a colorist. Some of his pigments are a little muddy, while his forms are rendered with precision and remarkable accuracy of detail. Surely his paintings are much more than the quaintly charming period pieces of a mid-nineteenth-century amateur artist. Father Point's miniatures, like his writings, reveal their creator's two primary interests—the Christianizing of the heathen Indians and the observation of Indian life. His religious paintings are filled with the holy symbols of his own faith. They appear to be carefully designed and rendered in the pietistic tradition of his native France. But they employ this Old World style to depict the introduction of Christianity among Indians of western North America in the mid-nineteenth century.

Many of Father Point's paintings, however, are completely free of subjective religious symbolism. They are first-hand graphic representations of the Indians he knew and of their customs. Those pictures in which the human or animal figures are rendered at large-enough scale to show details, become pictorial documents of great interest to historians and anthropologists. They cover a wide range of subject matter. I marvel at his ability to reveal so much in such small pictures.

A goodly number of Father Point's paintings are the only portrayals of places, people, and/or actions which several generations of historians have read about in the literature of the West. They have tried to imagine what these people and scenes must have been like, not knowing that they had been depicted faithfully by Father Point. It will be a revelation to these students to view such pictures as that of the two Iroquois, Ignatius and Pierre, in St. Louis in 1839, petitioning the Jesuits to send priests to their friends the Flatheads, in the far-off Rockies; or that little map of Westport, the historic staging area for parties of overland trail emigrants to the Far West, showing each house and naming the families who occupied them in 1840; or that only known view of Fort Lewis, built in 1845 as the American Fur Company's most remote trading post on the Missouri in the country of the Blackfeet. Equally unique are the little pictures of Indians trading at the post and of white *engagés* baling buffalo robes for shipment downriver to St. Louis.

Prior to the appearance of this book historians could not have known what one of the key figures in the history of the fur trade of the Upper Missouri looked like. Now they will see Point's portrait from life of Jacques Berger, who during the winter of 1830–1831 was the only man at Fort Union brave enough to try to search for the Piegan Indians and induce them to come to that fort to trade. Berger was successful in what his

fellows regarded as "the forlorn hope." And thus ended a quarter century of American failure to establish peaceful trade with the hostile Blackfeet, who had killed many Mountain Men and twice driven American trappers from the headwaters of the Missouri.

Father Point's little portraits of Indian chiefs should interest both historians and anthropologists. They include not only the earliest-known portraits of Flathead and Coeur d'Alene leaders, but also several of the Flathead chiefs who signed that tribe's first treaty with the United States in 1855—among them the head chief, Victor. The Blackfoot chiefs whose likenesses the priest captured on paper were no less important in the history of their people. Wolf's Son, chief of the Little Robes Band of the Piegans, was the first member of his tribe to be baptized, receiving the Christian name of Nicolas on Christmas Day, 1841, while on a friendly visit to the Flatheads west of the Rockies. Great Lake was the principal chief of the Piegans when Point painted him in 1846.

To those whose notions of the way Plains Indian chiefs dressed more than a century ago have been derived from museum exhibits and romantic illustrations, it may be a revelation to see some of Point's portraits of chiefs clad in semi-military uniforms of cloth and wearing plug hats or caps of white man's manufacture. But it was a common custom for Indian traders in Point's time to give "chief's coats" and fancy headgear to prominent leaders in order to obtain and retain the trade of the bands these Indians led. The guns, metal knives, Hudson's Bay blanket coats, cloth bandoliers, and lavishly bead-decorated skin shirts shown in these portraits should be further reminders to us that the Indians known to Point were not totally unsophisticated aborigines.

Point's numerous scenes of Indian life are equally revealing as accurate portrayals of tribal customs of the eighteen forties. Although they cover a wide range of activities, I find the scenes depicting camp movements particularly interesting, for they show in detail the objects and the actions which my elderly Blackfoot informants of the early nineteen forties described to me as typical of their tribe in the days of their youth. One Point painting shows a woman leading a horse bearing the sacred medicine pipe, which

Coups remarquables d'une chasse d'hyver. 1841 à 1842

Le 29 décembre. Selon la coutume le départ préparé [...] dès la ville ne commence à s'effectuer que dans l'après midi et par petits pelotons. La grande chasse étant de long cours les chasseurs y mènent avec eux tout ce qu'ils possèdent chaque loge compte ordinairement de sept à huit personnes, ce qui avec le bagage et les provisions faites ou à faire nécessite le service d'une vingtaine de chevaux. — Entre deux chaînes de montagnes qui tantôt se rapprochent pour faire voir de plus près ce que le désert a de plus grandiose et tantôt s'éloignent pour offrir à la vue une gradation de lointains variés à l'infinie serpentent une quinzaine de sentiers parallèles formés par la traînée des perches qui servent à soutenir les tentes. C'est ce qu'on appelle le grand chemin des chasseurs — Pour les diverses occupations, accidens rencontrés etc. voyez le 8e volume.

La présente chasse venant immédiatement après la réception du baptême par presque toute la peuplade devoit se distinguer des autres par la piété. Aussi dès le premier soir les chefs réunis pour la prière demandèrent que tout se fasse en voyage comme à Sainte Marie. En conséquence il est arrêté que deux fois le jour on se réunira pour la prière, après la prière on entendra une instruction précédée et suivie du cantique; que le matin au point du jour avant le départ pour la chasse et le soir avant de se coucher le gros on récitera trois fois en famille la salutation angélique ... qu'enfin les dimanches et fêtes seront chômés et célébrés le mieux que l'on pourra — on ne parle pas des prières de surérogation que chacun multiplioit et prolongeoit selon sa ferveur.

La grande chasse du bison offre des milliers de scènes toutes plus émouvantes les unes que les autres. Notre vignette ne représente qu'une seule des coups de chasse les plus remarquables au jugement des sauvages c.à.d les plus tragiques ou les plus comiques ils n'ont pas eu lieu tous le même jour, mais tous le même hyver ..... Ceux qui ont le plus enrichi leurs mantes se rattachent à des circonstances religieuses. La part de la Religion proprement dite a été au jugement de tous la plus consolante ....

REGINA COELI LETARE
Hommage à Marie
Retour à Ste Marie le jour de PAQUES

always headed the procession when camp was moved. Another picture shows a woman standing on an A-shaped horse travois in order to reach the upper part of the tepee to insert the wooden pins which hold the buffalo-skin lodge cover in place when a tepee is set up. These were all common scenes—Indian genre—among the Blackfeet and their neighbors in buffalo days. But I know of no other artist who pictured them from life in such detail.

So rich is this portion of the collection in its accurate renderings of Indian customs of more than one hundred and twenty-five years ago that it is difficult to select those of most significance. To me the little gems of this group are those which portray in semi-diagrammatic form how these Indians trapped wolves and eagles. Contemporary word descriptions of these actions can be found, but Point offers us a unique pictorial record, based upon his first-hand knowledge of Indian trapping methods of the eighteen forties.

Not the least interesting of the many pictures in this book are the eleven drawings made by Indians and gathered together by Father Point. Prince Maximilian and Carl Bodmer collected some Indian drawings on paper among the Mandans in 1834, but the ones reproduced in this volume seem to be the earliest from the tribes nearer the Rockies. One of these, a "letter" dated 1842, is in the traditional style of the crude picture writing which Indians executed on the inner surfaces of buffalo robes to record their coups earned in battle. In it the human form is represented in terms of a featureless knoblike head and rectangular body. But the other ten, drawn by a Blackfoot in 1846–1847, seem to show a break with the old tradition. The artist has been concerned with representing both the true proportions and the details of human beings, their costumes and accessories, while the subject matter provides a fascinating commentary on the Indian's view of the white trader. Perhaps this Indian artist was a protégé of Father Point. If so, the priest may be regarded as a teacher of the white man's artistic as well as religious traditions among the Blackfeet. And we should remember that these Indian pictures were made only fifteen years after Americans opened peaceful trade with the Blackfeet.

Surely Father Point's skill as an artist must have helped him to gain the friendship and confidence of the Indians—both adults and children —among whom he worked, so that his art and his missionary endeavors were not wholly unrelated activities. In less than nine months, as the first priest among the Piegan tribe of Blackfeet, Point baptized 667 Indians (nearly all children), translated the ordinary prayers into the Indian language, and held daily instructions in Christian doctrine in separate sections for men, women, and children. He must have been an extremely energetic man, this pioneer priest and painter.

Then on May 19, 1847, after six years among the Indians of the Rocky Mountain West, Father Nicolas Point packed his pictures and papers, bade good-by to his Indian and white friends at Fort Lewis, and boarded a barge for the first leg of his three-thousand-mile journey down the Missouri to St. Louis. He took with him a unique record of Indian life in the Northwest, which we are privileged to see and to read, faithfully reproduced in this handsome book.

facing:
Incidents during the winter hunt, 1841–1842.
The Latin inscription within the picture reads:
"Lead us on high." The figure 153
records the number of buffalo slaughtered.

CONTENTS

Amerique Septentrionale.

Comprenant les états unis, le Mexique et la nouvelle angleterre

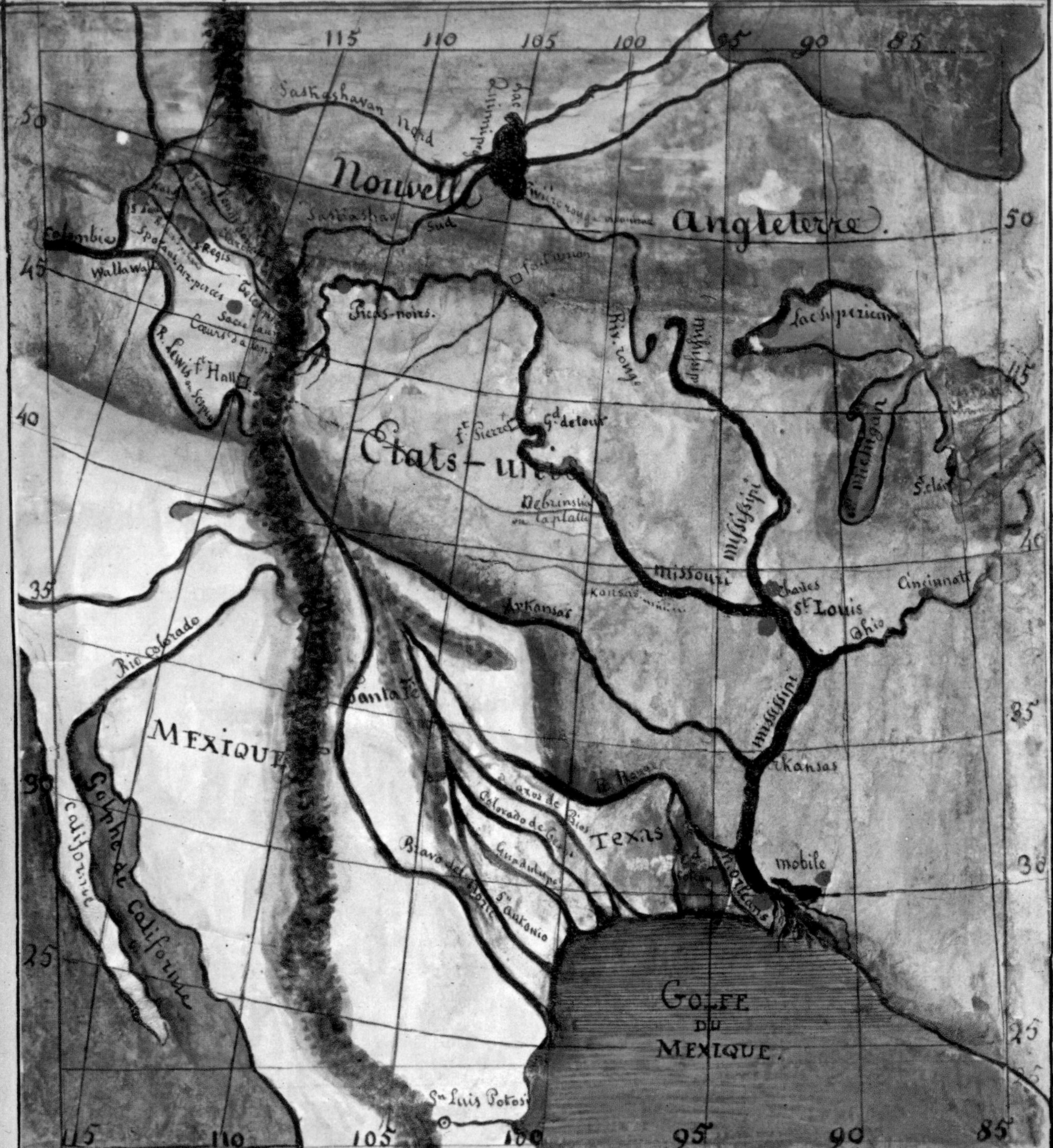

115
110
105
100
95
90
85
50
45
40
35
30
25
Saskashavan Nord
Lac Winnipeg
Nouvelle
angleterre.
Saskashav Sud
Colombie
Wallawalla
S. Regis
Pieds-noirs
R. Lewis
F.t Hall
Riv. Jaune
Missisipi
Lac Superieur
Michigan
S.t Clair
Etats-unis
F.t Pierre
G.d detour
Debrinsta ou la platte
Missouri
Kansas
Arkansas
S.t Louis
Cincinnati
Ohio
Rio Colorado
Santa Fé
Mexique
Golphe de Californie
Californie
Arkansas
Missisipi
Texas
Colorado de Tex.
Guadalupe
Bravo del Norte
S.t Antonio
mobile
n. orleans
Golfe du Mexique.
S.n Luis Potosi

Les points rouges indiquent les établissemens de la compagnie de Jesus
Le cours du Missisipi est de 5120 Kil.. (Embouchure decouvert par la Salle en 1582)
Si on le joint à celui du Missouri il est de 7000 kil.
La largeur du Missisipi à sa jonction avec le missouri est de 2400 metres – largeur ord.re de 900 a 1500 metr
Sa profondeur apres sa jonction avec l'ohio est de 30 a 40 metres
La vitesse ordinaire de son cours est de 3 Kil. à l'heure
celle d'un steemboat qui le descend de 19 Kil. a l'heure et seulement de 9 quand il le remonte
Le Missouri est navigable jusqu'a son confluent de la Riviere jaune. environ

. Residences
\+ Missions
* Colleges

EDITOR'S INTRODUCTION

Father Nicolas Point, S.J.

1799-1868

EVERYONE interested in the history of the development of the American West has some knowledge of the life and work of Father Pierre Jean De Smet, S.J., missionary promoter and diplomat to the Indians of the Pacific Northwest, whose efforts on behalf of the aborigines did much to enable

facing:
Map of North America,
including the United States, Mexico,
and New England [Canada].
Red dots indicate
locations of Jesuit establishments,
and the legend below
gives information on the discovery
of the Mississippi River
[misdated by Father Point];
its length, width, and depth;
the speed of its current (and that
of a steamboat traveling up-
or downstream);
on the Mississippi's joining
with the Ohio and Missouri, and of
the latter with the Yellowstone.

Americans to emigrate to the old Oregon Territory. Very little, however, has been published about his Jesuit companions, who carried on the gruelling missionary task of converting and civilizing the Indians once Father De Smet had opened the field. One of these missionaries, Father Nicolas Point, is a figure of historical importance in his own right. Though he received no formal training as an artist, he was the first to depict scenes from the aboriginal life of the native tribes among whom he worked. His drawings furnish us the only contemporary pictures of many of the early trading posts of the American Fur Company and similar organizations. Besides his drawings, Father Point left a mass of manuscript material concerning the Indians of the Rocky Mountain country, most of which has remained unavailable to historians. Before presenting Father Point's major work, *Souvenirs des Montagnes Rocheuses*, it is proper to review the essential facts of his biography so that the reader may know something about the man.

Rocroy, Nicolas Point's native place, is a small village located on the left bank of the Meuse River, about two miles from the present border of Belgium. Now an unimportant village of some two thousand inhabitants, the place has had its day of glory. Because it commands the Ardennes plateau, Francis I constructed a grim fortress there. During the Thirty Years War, Louis II, Prince de Condé, a stripling of twenty-two, fought an important battle against the Spanish at Rocroy on May 19, 1643. Jacques Bénigne Bossuet, Bishop of Meaux, court preacher to Louis XIV, gave a brilliant summary of that battle in the sermon he preached at Condé's funeral. Voltaire, in his *Siècle de Louis XIV*, devoted a lengthy passage to the same incident. Louis XIV considered Rocroy of sufficient strategical importance to order Sébastien Le Prestre de Vauban, a brilliant military engineer, to erect an imposing pentagonal fortress there, thus protecting the Ardennes.

Only the barest outline of the history of the Point family has come down to us. Nothing we know of Nicolas Point's early life indicates that his was a family of any importance.[1] Nicolas was born on April 10, 1799, the eldest, apparently, of several children. If he received any schooling before his eleventh year, the fact is not known. It would not have been unusual in that day for the child of poor parents to receive no schooling even in quite normal times. Point's early years coincided with the period of the French National Assembly's confiscation of ecclesiastical property. There was grand talk in the Assembly of a system of universal free education for all as a replacement for the schools confiscated from the Church, but nothing came of that. What little education Nicolas Point received as a child began when, at eleven, he was prepared by the local pastor to make his first Holy Communion. In the spring of 1810 one of the curés opened a school in Rocroy and continued it until 1812. Nicolas attended, learning, it is supposed, the rudiments of Latin and perhaps a little more. At the end of those two years, the boy's father seems to have died, for Nicolas was put to work as a lawyer's drudge and later as a clerk in the office of the local receiver-general. Young Point's future might well have been settled then and there had not Napoleon's last bid for power interfered.

The winter of 1813–14 was a decisive one for France. Intent on crushing Napoleon, the combined forces of Russia, Prussia, England, and Austria drove the French army out of the Germanies and into France. When Prussian troops, under command of General Gebhard Blucher, crossed the Rhine and entered the Ardennes plateau, the French Marshal Michel Ney (Duke of Elchingen) spent some time at Rocroy. There he met young Point and was so taken with the boy that he offered to adopt him. Madame Point, however, with the native shrewdness of the poor, declined the honor proffered her son, lest wealth and glory endanger the boy's soul. Whatever Nicolas thought of the offer was, perhaps, forgotten because of the immediate danger from the armed conflict being waged about him. When Rocroy was under bombardment, Nicolas was nearly killed while on an errand for his employer. That incident and one other are the only intimate details known of Point's early life. Once, when the Meuse was frozen, Nicolas ventured out onto unsafe ice, which gave way under him. He barely escaped the treacherous current of the river. One other fact of his early life is worth recording. From his childhood, the boy had some talent for drawing. In his memoirs, Father Point tells us that when, as a child, he showed an interest in sketching, his mother obtained the materials needed for him to indulge his talent. He soon made for her a copy of a picture of the Blessed Virgin, which she treasured all her days. Point was a self-taught artist, but his portraitures have character and his scenes have feeling. As a missionary, he drew to please and instruct, but he captured much of Indian life which would otherwise have been lost.

In 1815, when Napoleon was defeated, Point returned to school, taking lessons with a dozen other youths who aspired to the ecclesiastical life. During the next three years, while he was being drilled in fundamentals, he came upon a life of St. Francis Xavier which imbued him with a desire to become a missionary. Pursuing that vocation, Point offered himself to the Society of Jesus and was accepted on June 28, 1819, by Father Loriquet, rector of St. Acheul, a small Jesuit college located seven miles from Amiens.

Since the Society of Jesus had been restored in France only five years before, French Jesuits were few in number with only a small cluster of institutions under their charge.[2] Instead of beginning his novitiate at once, young Point was made prefect of discipline at St. Acheul while he was tutored in philosophy. Three years later, on September 23, 1822, he was sent to Montrouge where he was to undergo his novitiate. The next five years of his life are something of a mystery. Soon after entering the novitiate he was sent home because of an illness, sufficiently serious to raise doubts as to whether he should continue with the Jesuits. When Point's health was restored, he returned to the novitiate where, on March 9, 1827, he pronounced the vows binding himself to the Society of Jesus. Returned to St. Acheul, he resumed the duties of prefect of discipline while he studied theology. The quiet of academic life did not continue long, however, for France, along with other European countries, was being inundated by a wave of anticlericalism especially threatening the Society of Jesus.

European anticlericalism had its roots in the rationalist enlightenment of the eighteenth century. The rationalists were shrewd enough to perceive that they must control the education of youth if rationalism were to succeed. Since the strongest educational body in Europe was the Society of Jesus, that organization must be destroyed. Expulsion of the Jesuits from France in 1763 was not only a triumph for the rationalists, but it also allowed them to persecute the Church by heaping opprobrium on the Jesuits. After the fall of Napoleon and the restoration of the Bourbons, Talleyrand, himself a rationalist and renegade bishop, urged Louis XVIII to invite the Jesuits to resume their work in France. So violent was the opposition to their return that Talleyrand, who had successfully wormed his way through the whole French Revolution, fell from power in France. When Charles X succeeded his brother in 1824, he imprudently determined to restore the ancient regime. Of the many measures which irritated the rationalist bourgeoisie none was opposed more viciously than the monarch's recall of the Jesuits to France. Hundreds of books and pamphlets condemnatory of the Jesuits poured from the French presses. National and provincial legislatures rang with fulminating oratory against them. Because the Jesuits had accepted charge of a few minor seminaries, the Government instituted a most minute investigation of all such schools in France. Riots broke out in several places where the Jesuits were in residence. In 1828 a mob attacked St. Acheul, stoned the rector, and burned the place to the ground before a detachment of militia could arrive from Amiens to restore order. With the college in ruins, Point was sent to Brigg, where he finished his theological studies and was ordained to the priesthood on March 20, 1831.

Since the Jesuits were unable to work in France, Father Point was sent to Freiburg, in Switzerland, where he remained until 1832, assisting in the small college which the Society of Jesus conducted there. But opposition to the Society soon flourished so strongly in Switzerland that the college was closed and Point was sent off to San Sebastián, in Spain, where he functioned as vice-rector of the Jesuit college of St. Roch. Spain shortly followed the example of other countries and exiled the Jesuits, who were obliged to leave by 1834. During all his peregrinations Father Point nourished his ambition to be sent on the missions, and finally his desire was granted.

While most of Europe's countries were intent on expelling the Jesuits, the American hierarchy was only too anxious to procure them. Benedict Joseph Flaget, first bishop of Louisville, Kentucky, had, as early as 1828, appealed to Father Nicolas Godinot, major superior of the Jesuits in Paris, to send a band of the sons of St. Ignatius to establish a college in his frontier diocese. An unexplained failure of communications brought about an embarrassing situation. Hearing nothing from Paris, the bishop founded St. Joseph's College in Bardstown and turned it over to the clergy of his diocese. Unexpectedly a group of Jesuits reached New Orleans in 1831 and joyfully announced to Bishop Flaget that they would shortly arrive at Louisville to establish a college. Though the original opportunity was now unavailable, there was in the diocese a sketchy little school called St. Mary's, which had been started just ten miles outside of Lebanon, Kentucky. Its founder, Father William Byrne, who was anything but a schoolman, quite happily relinquished his claim to St. Mary's in favor of the newly arrived French Jesuits. In the summer of 1831 two French Jesuits, Pierre Chazelle and Nicolas Petit, arrived at St. Mary's. Since they did not speak English and had no experience with American boys, Father Byrne agreed to stay on for two years to acclimate them. To assist these Jesuits in Kentucky, Father Nicolas Point was sent to the United States from France. Leaving Europe on August 15, 1835, he did not reach New York until December 15, after a stormy crossing in a badly managed sailing vessel. Six months later, he reached Kentucky and began teaching at St. Mary's.

It is reasonable to assume that the plight of the French Jesuits isolated in the Kentucky wilderness was far from pleasant. Besides the language barrier, the priests had no understanding of that unique genus, *puer Americanus*, whose counterpart is met nowhere else in the world. Father Walter Hill, S.J., a student at St. Mary's just a year before Father Point arrived, relates in his reminiscences how very difficult the French Jesuits found it to manage their American students.[3] Somehow, in spite of the problems, the boys learned Latin, produced plays, declaimed elocution pieces and were led to appreciate the things of culture. St. Mary's continued under the direction of the French Jesuits for some time after Nicolas Point joined the faculty, but he remained there only a few months before being directed to open a new college in Louisiana.

When the first band of Jesuits from France reached New Orleans on their way to Kentucky, in 1831, Bishop Leo de Neckere of New Orleans, who also wished to open a college under the direction of the members of the Society of Jesus, boldly kidnaped Father Pierre Ladavière. By holding him "temporarily" in New Orleans, he hoped to procure from the Jesuits further recruits as well as permission to open a college in his own diocese. Bishop de Neckere had not obtained his wish before his death in 1833, and his successor, Antoine Blanc, continued to hold Ladavière. In 1836, Blanc packed himself and his kidnaped Jesuit off to France, there to plead his cause. When the French Jesuits pointed to their lack of men, the determined bishop took his case to Father John Roothaan, the Jesuit general, who ordered his French subjects to

denude themselves, if need be, to grant Bishop Blanc's request. Four French Jesuits were, therefore, released for the proposed school, but none of these was considered a capable administrator. Nicolas Point, who was already in America, had held the office of vice-rector in Spain. He was chosen to go to Louisiana and assume responsibility for establishing a Jesuit college in Bishop Blanc's diocese.

Because subsequently Father Point was not always understood by his superiors, it is significant to report the estimate of him recorded as he was about to begin an important new venture. Father François Renault, provincial of the province of Lyons, wrote to Father Roothaan that the Jesuits of France would sacrifice four priests for the new college, but:

. . . where is the superior? I do not see him anywhere this year, except at St. Mary's, Kentucky. Last year I sent Father Nicolas Point to that house; he is a man of men for a college, although he is drawn by preference to the missions, and the Indian missions at that, after the manner of Father van Quickenborne. In case of need, Father Point could be replaced at St. Mary's by one of the Fathers whom I propose today to your Paternity.[4]

At the age of thirty-seven, Point was considered by his superiors to be a good schoolman, a zealous priest, and a man of sufficient judgment and prudence to be unhesitatingly entrusted with a new venture. His health was seemingly stable and his ability to manage Jesuit subjects, as well as to deal with the general public, was judged to be above average.

Father Point left Kentucky for Louisiana in February, 1837, at just about the time Bishop Blanc with a band of French Jesuits arrived at New Orleans. In addition to Ladavière, the recruits were Fathers Jean François Abbadie, Joseph Chauvet, Paul Mignard, Joseph Seller; also a novice, Father Henri Duranquet, and a coadjutor brother, Joseph Alsberg. In seeking a site for the new college the Jesuits had several possibilities. Ten years before Bishop Dubourg, first bishop of Louisiana, had offered the Jesuits a tract of two hundred acres of land near Opelousas, Louisiana, on condition that a college would be established. In 1830, Bishop de Neckere had acquired at Iberville land which he offered to give the Jesuits. Several other opportunities were suggested by town councils, land speculators, and private persons. Father Point visited many sites and sent his companions to visit others. He finally settled on Grand Coteau, a hamlet some ten miles southeast of Opelousas. Whereupon Bishop Blanc donated to the Jesuits the two hundred acres purchased by Bishop Dubourg, including a small church and house as well as a log cabin which had been erected on the property. The bishop also promised to give the Jesuits ten thousand dollars toward the erection of another building. The Religious of the Sacred Heart, who had already built a school for girls near the bishop's land at Grand Coteau, offered to subscribe two thousand dollars as well as to provide clay for bricks. The members of the parish there agreed to furnish help in building. With the site for the college chosen, Father Point gathered his community together and took up residence in a log cabin at Grand Coteau in the spring of 1837. All set themselves to the task of readying the few existing buildings for the opening of the college.

Throughout the summer of 1837 Father Point and his companions were subjected to innumerable threats from the citizenry of neighboring towns. The newspaper in Opelousas ran a series of articles condemning the Jesuits as men unfit to breathe the pure air of Louisiana. Anonymous letters were sent, threatening to drive the priests out by force. Committees were formed to recruit armed bands to attack the Jesuits. The people of Grand Coteau, however, loyally pledged their support of the priests, and for a time the Jesuits were guarded around the clock. When it became evident that the priests intended to suffer their detractions in silence, the whole vigor of the attack slowly faded away. Even the editor of the Opelousas newspaper was shamed into silence. On July 31, 1837, he came to preside at the laying of the cornerstone of the new brick building under construction. His presence and his forthright address to the people of the neighborhood went far to dissipate any lingering animosity to the Jesuits at Grand Coteau.

Though the fine brick building was not ready, Father Point opened St. Charles College on January 5, 1838. Within a very brief time there were some sixty students enrolled. At first they were housed in the parish rectory and classes were also held there. The faculty consisted of the Jesuit Fathers Abbadie and Mignard who were aided by Father Duranquet, and Pierce Connelly, a former Anglican minister. His conversion to Catholicism was the talk of Philadelphia where his wife, Cornelia, belonged to an old, prominent family. There were two curricula offered at St. Charles College: classical and commercial. The first session lasted from January to October, 1838. During the term frequent contests were conducted to stimulate assiduous study by the students. At the close of the session a play, "Joseph Sold by His Brothers," was presented by the students in the presence of Bishop Blanc and many of the parents. Once, during the term an epidemic of yellow fever swept through the little school. Father Point was so seriously afflicted that his life was despaired of and the student body was summoned to receive his final blessing. Before the session ended, Point had recovered and was eagerly looking forward to a successful new academic year, unaware that there would be no new term for him at St. Charles. Orders which would change Point's future had already been issued by Father John Roothaan. As the Jesuit general viewed the efforts of his subjects in America, there appeared to be little isolated caches of men spread widely with no general supervision over them. It seemed more practical to gather all those working in the Mississippi valley under one central administration so that work and personnel could be more efficiently managed. A directive was issued on July 14, 1838, whereby all Jesuits west of the Allegheny Mountains would be the responsibility of Father Peter Verhaegen, superior of the Jesuits in St. Louis. He was directed by Father Roothaan to visit Grand Coteau and, if possible, to strengthen the college faculty with an addition of some Jesuits who spoke English and could teach it. The new administrative arrangement was announced to the Jesuits at Grand Coteau by Verhaegen himself on his arrival there in November, 1838, with Father Isidore Boudreaux, who was to become a member of the faculty at St. Charles.

The second session of the college, December 1, 1838, to December 10, 1839, brought with it an avalanche of trouble. The addition of seven Jesuits from St. Louis to the faculty occasioned friction between the native French and the American-born Jesuits. The enrollment gratifyingly increased to nearly a hundred, but there was constant difficulty with the boys and a rumor spread that the place was unhealthy. The new brick building was finished and occupied, though Father Point had encountered endless difficulties with contractors who would not complete their work or who flagrantly overcharged him. Another epidemic of yellow fever ravaged the students and faculty. Thus, in general, conditions seemed so unpromising to Father Verhaegen that in the spring of 1840 he decided to replace Father Point as superior at Grand Coteau. Writing of this decision, Pierce Connelly, professedly a friend of Father Point, commented to Bishop Blanc:

There is certainly a wonderful Providence in regard to it [i.e., St. Charles College]. In Father Point especially the more I know him the more I am astonished at our good fortune. . . . Father Verhaegen has given us a sad blow in the removal of Father Point, one who understood the necessities of the country and the means that should be taken to satisfy them. . . . He certainly has nothing to regret, his work here has been crowned with such a success as was beyond all hope—he has done what he had to do and well.[5] •

Father Point himself seems to have felt that his removal was a reflection on his personal ability and zeal. He wrote lengthy letters to the Jesuit general, Father Roothaan, attempting to explain his entire administration of St. Charles College. On the whole these letters have a plaintive character, which leads one to sense that Father Point sought to assure a good father that his child had tried hard even though he failed. Ever after Father Point suffered periods of melancholy during which he berated himself, wholly unnecessarily, for his failure at Grand Coteau. But the blunt fact was that he was removed and directed to report to St. Louis. It must have been with a heavy heart that he left Grand Coteau on July 21, 1840, even though the missionary career which he had dreamed of as a boy in Rocroy awaited him. His heart's blood had been poured into this first work. The gnarled old oak trees with their Spanish moss

are still at St. Charles and so are the nuns in their convent a mile away. But now Jesuit novices, and not schoolboys, inhabit Father Point's brick building.

Life moved quickly for Father Point during the following months. In St. Louis he found a bustling college in a busy city. Probably the school was in a mild ferment over the great, new venture which Father Pierre Jean De Smet, S.J., was about to launch. Missionaries in some numbers were being despatched to the Flathead country, a kind of never-never land with a fabled tribe of Indians whose representatives had traveled thousands of miles to beseech the Blackrobes to come to them. Since the story of the Flathead search for missionaries has intimate relation to Father Point's career, it is briefly repeated here.

In about 1816 a group of Catholic Iroquois, long settled at Caughnawaga opposite Montreal, migrated westward, seeking a new home. They drifted into the Bitter Root valley in the present western Montana, where they came in contact with the Salishan Flatheads, a native race whose moral standards were surprisingly high. The immigrant Iroquois intermarried with their new friends and soon instructed them in the basic truths of Catholicism. Knowing that the Indians had need of missionaries, the Iroquois and Flatheads despatched several expeditions to St. Louis, where they knew they would find their traditional spiritual fathers, the Jesuits. After several failures, one intrepid band finally reached St. Louis in 1831, where Bishop Rosati promised to do what he could for them. Four more such expeditions, the last in 1839, were undertaken before the Indians were finally assured that missionaries would be sent to them. Father Pierre Jean De Smet, a sturdy, determined Belgian, who had already labored among the native tribes in the present Kansas and Iowa, made a hurried trip to the Flathead country early in 1840 to survey the field. He was back in St. Louis on the last day of that year full of enthusiasm for the Flatheads. During his absence the personnel of the new mission had been selected. They were Father Gregorio Mengarini, a Neopolitan freshly arrived from Rome; Brother William Clessens, a twenty-nine-year-old Belgian blacksmith; Brother Charles

Huet, a carpenter from Belgium; and Brother Joseph Specht, a German tinner and factotum. Father Point was the second of two priests who were to accompany Father De Smet, the appointed superior. As the great venture was about to get under way De Smet described Father Point as "zealous and courageous for the salvation of souls as his compatriot La Roche Jacquelin." [6]

While final preparations for opening the new mission were being completed in St. Louis, Father Point was sent on ahead to Westport, Missouri, the staging area for wagon trains going west. Arriving there on November 1, 1840, he set about erecting a small church and gathering the residents together to instruct them. There were twenty-three families (twenty-five counting married members in separate homes), mostly French Canadian trappers married to native women. Though nearly all were Catholics by birth and baptism, hardly any knew the simplest truths of his Faith. Putting his artistic ability to use, Point decorated his little chapel with pictures of Christ, His Mother, and the saints. He made little pictures of holy scenes which he used as awards for those children who excelled in learning their prayers and their catechism. He instituted pious societies for the various age groups to induce them, by mutual good example, to lead better lives. For himself, he suffered from the cold, the poor food, and the wretched accommodations. By Easter of 1841, Father Point had wrought great changes in the moral lives of the people of Westport. Even the neighboring Kansa Indians came to visit him and his chapel, and they were greatly impressed. Soon, however, Father De Smet and his companions arrived, signaling the beginning of the journey to the Rocky Mountains. [7]

The six Jesuits left Westport on April 30, 1841, together with a rather large caravan led by John Bidwell, who was elected captain, and Thomas Fitzpatrick, an experienced Westerner who was captain of the missionary party and pilot of the expedition. The caravan consisted of seventy people of whom fifteen were women and children. Few immigrant caravans were better reported. Father Point was appointed official diarist of the Jesuit portion of the expedition, but De Smet and Mengarini also kept notes and wrote accounts of their journey. Several of the laymen, too, kept journals. [8] Because of this, we know in great detail how the missionaries lived, what they took with them, how they were treated by fellow travelers, and what they saw on the way. Since Father Point's own account of the journey is to be found in his text, the details need not be repeated here.

On August 15, 1841, an advance guard of Flatheads met the missionaries at Fort Hall on the Snake River whence they escorted the Jesuits to the Flathead country in the Bitter Root basin. On September 4, the Flatheads and the missionaries chose for their mission a site on the right bank of the Bitter Root River, about thirty miles north of the present Missoula, Montana. Father Point drew plans for a group of buildings, including a residence for the missionaries, a church, and utility buildings. The Indians set to with a will and helped prepare the new mission center. Father Point helped with the physical labor, but he also rendered valuable aid through his artistic ability. He entertained the Indians by his sketches of them at work and at play as well as by doing portraits of individuals. He also employed his talent to produce charts and scenes which would help the Indians to learn the truths of religion.

As the winter approached, the Flatheads were obliged to leave the mission to hunt buffalo so that they might feed themselves. Since the Indians had barely begun their religious instructions, they asked that one of the fathers accompany them in order to continue teaching them as well as to help them live up to the dictates of their religion. Father Point was assigned this arduous task by his superior, Father De Smet. From December, 1841, until April, 1842, in the dead of winter, he endured the cold, the hunger, the importunities of his neophytes and probably above all the loneliness of nomadic life. His personal example, as much as his instructions, caused the winter hunt to be religiously profitable to the Flatheads, who returned well prepared to be baptized. The hunt also offered Father Point the opportunity to encounter other tribes of Indians. Of these the Coeur d'Alenes seemed to offer the most fruitful field for the opening of a new mission.

After Father Point's contact with the Coeur d'Alenes during the winter, Father De Smet visited their village during the summer of 1842 and determined to begin a mission among them. In October, Father Point was sent to open the mission, which he called the Sacred Heart because he had placed the Coeur d'Alenes under that patronage. Father Point chose a site on the St. Joe River about a mile from the southern end of Lake Coeur d'Alene. However attractive it might have been in the fall, when the winter set in, the place was flooded and so unsuitable that the whole enterprise was abandoned in favor of a new site several miles from the lake. Introducing the Coeur d'Alenes to Christianity and a sedentary existence was far from the happy task that such work had been among the Flatheads. Having had little previous contact with white men, the Coeur d'Alenes were much more aboriginal in their habits than the Flatheads. The leaders of the Coeur d'Alenes opposed the missionary, making his life very unpleasant. Father Point encountered so many serious difficulties with certain of these leaders that he seems to have become greatly discouraged, thinking, perhaps, that he was a disgraceful failure.

By 1844 Father Point's health had begun to fail. He suffered a rather painful rupture and he often experienced great weakness of body, which was accompanied with distress of soul. In 1843, when there was question of appointing a bishop for the Oregon country, his name was submitted with that of Father De Smet as a possible candidate for the new bishopric, but the honor fell to neither, for François Norbert Blanchet, a French Canadian, was appointed. Quite likely, Father Point was totally unaware that he had ever been considered for the episcopal dignity. Sick and discouraged, he asked Father Roothaan to recall him from the Rocky Mountains and send him to Canada where he would be with French-speaking folk. The petition was forwarded in 1845, but Father Point did not receive an answer for two years. During that time, he continued to devote himself to the Coeur d'Alenes, with occasional absences to accompany the Flatheads on extended hunting expeditions.

From the beginning of the Jesuit mission effort in the Oregon country, the major obstacle to success had been the predatory and murder-ous Blackfeet, whose country lay athwart the road to Oregon. Determining to establish a mission among them, De Smet arranged a treaty between the Blackfeet and the Flatheads, using Point as the go-between. De Smet and Point left the Flathead mission of St. Mary's on August 16, 1846, and traveled to Fort Lewis, an American Fur Company trading post on the Missouri River at which the Blackfeet were wont to trade. Father Point spent the fall and winter there, evangelizing the Blackfeet as well as the personnel of the post. Before spring, he had baptized some six hundred persons, though less than thirty of them were adults. However, his efforts to gain the friendship of the Blackfeet for the other aboriginal tribes were highly successful. A lasting truce was arranged, which made possible the rather peaceful immigration of Americans to the Oregon country.

In the spring of 1847, Father Point's petition to Father Roothaan was favorably answered, and in March he left Fort Lewis on a barge bound for Fort Union. While on that journey he kept a diary which offers an intimate picture of life on a river barge. From Fort Union he took the steamer *Martha*, which brought him to St. Louis at the beginning of August. He departed at once for Canada, where he was stationed at Sandwich, now Windsor, Ontario, to rest. But the rest consisted of reorganizing the mission at Wikemikong on Grand Manitoulin Island, which lies at the western outlet of Georgian Bay.

Point sought to put into practice in his new mission all the institutions which had been so successful with the Flatheads. He introduced orderly cultivation of the soil by the Indians so that they would be self-supporting. He reorganized the educational system, introducing nuns as teachers. The parish buildings were repaired and a new stone church was built. Handling his own Jesuit subjects, Father Point was insistent that they must not be overburdened with work and that they must have regular periods for rest and rehabilitation. The years spent here were probably Father Point's happiest.

In October, 1855, he was directed to assume charge of the Jesuit mission of the Immaculate Conception at Fort William on Lake Superior. But he was so ill on arriving at Sault Ste. Marie that it was decided he must not go on to new responsibilities. Instead he was sent back to Sandwich where, until 1859, when that mission was closed, he did what light tasks his strength permitted. He was then ordered to take up residence at Sault-au-Recollet, near Montreal, where he was to retire from active work. There Point composed his *Recollections of the Rocky Mountains*, embellishing them with his drawings. He also helped in the parish and acted as chaplain to the nuns who taught in the school. Finally, in 1865, Father Point was sent to Quebec with orders to rest and care for his health. For the next three years he prayed, suffered, and prepared to die well. His last apostolic assignment was preparing small boys for their first Holy Communion and acting as confessor for the canons of Quebec's cathedral. On June 28, 1868, he became desperately ill; he rallied briefly, but on July 4 he died peacefully at eight in the evening. At the insistence of his penitents, the cathedral canons, he was buried in the crypt of the cathedral of Quebec.

To his dying day Father Point never forgot his "dear neophytes" of the Rocky Mountains. He wrote long letters to the Jesuit general, begging to be allowed to return to them. He importuned American governmental officials on their behalf, attempting to procure consideration and understanding for them. In his own introduction to his *Souvenirs des Montagnes Rocheuses*, he says that his purpose in preparing the manuscript was the hope that readers might learn from it what sort of people the Indians were and how much they deserved every consideration. It is quite likely that Point always blamed himself for having asked to be removed from the Rocky Mountain mission, thinking, perhaps, that he had chosen a less-than-perfect solution for his difficulties. He was repeatedly assured by Father Roothaan that such was not the case, that he was a much-loved son of the Society of Jesus and that he should put his mind at rest. Perhaps Father Point's most painful cross was the burden of bearing with the sensitive nature which God gave him. Artistic personalities are frequently misunder-

stood by their associates, and even have difficulty understanding themselves. In the full vigor of middle age he had often been at odds with his associates, especially with De Smet, who certainly never understood him. In his declining years Point was a gentle, kindly, patient man whom the young loved and understood.

Nicolas Point's manuscripts, as yet chiefly unpublished, are scattered through several archival depositories. The Jesuit archives in Rome are the depository of a collection of his letters, the baptismal records which he kept, some lengthy letters to the Jesuit general and some sketches. The archives of the Missouri Province of the Society of Jesus, in St. Louis, possess the Linton Album (really a record of De Smet's travels, which Point embellished), some of his letters and a few of his notes. The national library of Italy has the original manuscript of his journey on the barge from Fort Lewis to Fort Union. The most valuable Point manuscript, his *Souvenirs des Montagnes Rocheuses*, here presented in translation together with his paintings, is in the archives of the Collège Sainte-Marie, Montreal. The whole of this manuscript, both the art work and the text, is Father Point's own work. He is said to have taken great pride in his ability to write nearly perfect copper-plate script, which to him was as much a work of art as his drawings. One notes, however, that when he made corrections here and there the penmanship is somewhat inferior to the usually beautiful penmanship of the text as a whole. He often refers to himself in the third person.

Though the art critic may find Father Point's work somewhat primitive, one cannot but be attracted to the subjects which he portrayed. His scenes of Indian life captured for us a people whose whole way of life changed almost completely during the period Father Point was among them. Point's portraits of Indians have a strength and dignity which is nothing short of amazing. Thanks to Father Point, we have a pictorial record of a people and a way of life which has vanished forever.

An untitled decorative device
embodying the dove of peace and a small ship
in the background probably intended
to symbolize Noah's Ark.

Recollections
of the Rocky Mountains

Herein Father Point comments on the customs and morals of the Indians
before they were influenced by Christian ideals. His characterization of individual
tribes to whom he ministered is very revealing. He had little respect for the integrity
of the Coeur d'Alenes or the Blackfeet, but he considered the Flatheads
an excellent people, who well deserved the appellation "nation of chiefs."
His detailed observations regarding the term "medicine" and its various applications
are particularly valuable.

SO MANY INTERESTING accounts of the Rocky Mountains have already been published that the present writer, at first, thought that another might only detract from those now available in print. However, if these lines should serve no other purpose than to recall very pleasant memories, that, in itself, would make the effort worth while for the author. But a more worthy purpose will be served. By recalling interesting and edifying facts, now almost forgotten, and by supplying new details concerning persons already well known, interest and accuracy will be added to previous accounts. Also, those who read these memoirs may find in them one more reason for admiring the divine mercy in the salvation of souls.

These pages concerning the Indians are limited to only three tribes, for the author, during his many years among them, knew those three best. Among the Blackfeet and the Coeur d'Alenes there are many who are in no way inferior to the generally superior Flatheads. However, it would undoubtedly be correct to maintain that among the Flatheads one rather usually finds the virtues of modesty, frankness, courage, goodness, and generosity. On the contrary, the Coeur d'Alenes are noted for dissimulation, egotism, and cruelty. The Blackfeet are notorious for being bloodthirsty and are well known for their pillaging. These are the principal traits which have earned for the Flatheads the appellation of "the nation of chiefs," and for the others the opprobrious names still applied to them. Common to all three, with some exceptions among the Flatheads, is an unrelenting spirit of independence, laziness, a passion for gambling, cruelty to the vanquished, very little regard for women, forgetfulness of the past and improvidence for the future. While all of these traits were true of them before their conversion, since their baptism an admirable transformation has taken place in their entire manner of life.

Illustrations have been added to the notes in an attempt to make visible, as it were, the marvels of grace which were granted the Indians. These illustrations have the advantage of having been sketched on the spot, and, for the most part, at the very time the events depicted took place. Even as a child I felt compelled to reproduce on paper whatever struck my fancy. My mother, realizing that this instinct might be useful, procured the necessary equipment and encouraged my talent. God rewarded her care, as He did all her sacrifices during her widowhood to further the education of her children. The result was that all of us were attached to our home, removed from dangerous company, and attracted to the religious life. Twenty years after leaving my family I met a nun on the banks of a great river three thousand miles from my native land. She was my sister who entered the novitiate of the Sacred Heart [1] on the very day on which her brother entered the Society of Jesus. In speaking of those to whom we owed so much, she told me that our mother had, in her last moments, rested her eyes with great consolation on an image of the Blessed Virgin which I knew very well. This image, which she had venerated for thirty years, was one which I had painted for her. I am unable to express what I felt as I recalled this memory.

During the traveling season which followed the meeting with my sister I found myself deep in the Rocky Mountains, surrounded by scenes about which I had often dreamed as the beautiful ideal of all natural perspectives. The sight of these vistas awakened my early artistic interest and I found myself beginning to sketch mountains, lakes, streams, forests, flowers, the birds, and the beasts. Then I drew sketches of the savages on their way to battle or smoking the calumet. Finally I sketched landscapes, river scenes, Indian buffalo hunts, hunting feasts and, above all, religious scenes. The products of my brush, in many ways still very primitive, had at least the good effect that they contributed in some small measure to the innocent amusement of the company. Father Pierre Jean De Smet, then my superior, would often say: "Father, here is something beautiful; sketch it for me." I always complied, and I had my reward when, in 1862, he wrote to me: "The little sketches which you were so kind as to make for me are included in my album, together with others relative to the Rocky Mountains. I am very fond of them and they make a very pleasant memento, indeed."

At the end of a five months' trip on horseback, we had to turn our attention to the task of Christianizing the savages. One might think that then no further opportunity for sketching would arise. However, brief experience showed that the savages learned more quickly through their eyes than through their ears, whereupon I made a great effort to speak to them through pictures. In order that there might not be any lack of decorum in our instructions, silent preaching was elevated to the dignity of scenic representations. Some scenes showed the mysteries; others, the sacraments; some represented the precepts; others, prayers. Still others depicted the great virtues and the vices. Finally, there was one large scene, called the "Way of Heaven" because in it one saw, together with the important series of laws given to man, the succession of periods from the Old and New Testament, all of which summarized Christian doctrine. This method of instruction had two noticeable advantages. While the truths entered their souls through their eyes, the great virtues were infused into their hearts. The inspiration for these drawings came, for the most part, from the great religious ceremonies enacted before them and from the most noble actions of their great men. These pictures tended, naturally, to impress the Indians very vividly.

The most marked characteristics of the Flat-heads were a rare combination of goodness, courage, and generosity. There was not a single one of their chiefs who did not become staunchly and fervently religious. Many remained so, even during battle, showing mercy to the vanquished foe in the hope of saving souls. "I hope to count a great coup," remarked one of the youngest braves, "because to do good you must be listened to, and to be listened to you must be brave." Inspired by a similar spirit, a certain Pend d'Oreille lad, scarcely sixteen years old, joined the Flatheads, the better to profit by the presence of the missionary there. After having ventured forth as a member of a band of four braves to attack a party of forty Blackfeet, the young Pend d'Oreille asked to be baptized and did everything possible to lead other young braves of his tribe to do the same.[2] He was rewarded for his zeal by having the happiness of baptizing his own father, who was also his chief, when the latter was on the point of death.

Such incidents undoubtedly have their origin elsewhere than on earth, but it constantly remains true that, of all the means employed for the conversion of the savages, the most efficacious were certainly those which appealed to the sense of sight. Since most of the drawings then used, and others made later, were given away as tokens of friendship or gratitude, I had only a few sketches of the Blackfeet when I arrived at Fort Louis.[3] But since, fortunately, I had an opportunity to follow the Piegans on their great autumn hunt, and later to visit other camps of those who came to trade, I saw that my new companions were attracted no less than the other Indians to anything that extolled their persons or their customs.[4] Accordingly, I again took up my pencils and attempted to depict for them the more striking scenes from the hunt and the most sterling characteristics of their great men. This amazed them so much that any of them who thought he possessed some physical attribute which made him a particularly good subject lost no time in paying his respects to the Blackrobe in grand style. Hence the variety of types which are to be found in the pages of the first and second volume of this account. In return for their courtesy, they had the pleasure of seeing their portraits included among the great men of their nation. This was their sole reward, for the mission treasury had nothing to offer them.

In the spring of 1847, Father De Smet was expected to return with more missionaries as well as material help of all kinds. Wherefore, my superiors recalled me to Canada where there was need for missionaries to work among the Indians of the Great Lakes and upper Canada. During my twelve years of missionary work, whether among the islands of Lake Huron or on the banks of the upper St. Lawrence, my earlier attempts at art, so very poor as art but so rich in memories, were seldom unpacked. As for the persons still living who are represented in these drawings, I can quite truthfully say that they were never forgotten. Thus it was that, in 1860, when the Flatheads, whom I so fondly remember, were undergoing severe trials, I was on the verge of rejoining them, with the permission of my superiors.[5] But because of a serious illness I was unable to follow into the wilderness those sheep who had gone astray again, in spite of themselves. I was obliged to satisfy myself with bringing them to the attention of others who were able to help them. Once more I took up my brush and my pencil, hoping to aid them. This is why the present collection has assumed the singular form it now has. Should this collection be appraised by a connoisseur, he would say, I know, "This is the work of neither a painter nor even a doodler." And he would be right, for I have had no formal training in painting or sketching. But with this collection, such as it is, I do homage to you, dear reader, and were it to do nothing more than to give you an agreeable diversion from your serious occupations, I should be grateful to God for that. If it should, however, accomplish more, that is, if it should prompt you to do for our poor savages even the hundredth part of the good I wish for you, then, certainly, you would receive a hundredfold [blessing] in this world and in the next. If, on the contrary, my production only bores you, pray for me, as I do for you, in order that God, Who alone does not err, may judge both of us only in the light of His most sweet mercy.

Near the 47th degree north latitude, in the middle of a labyrinth of valleys formed by the great wilderness, is found the country of the Flatheads and the Coeur d'Alenes, and not far distant from there, on the descent toward the Missouri, that of the Blackfeet. The country of the first-named tribe is dominated by high summits and extensive valleys; that of the second-named, by steeply banked lakes and somber forests; and that of the third-named by rolling plains, sand hills, and ravines dug by streams. In the valleys there are edible roots in abundance, and in the lakes and forest, fish, aquatic birds, and deer. On the rising ground and in the ravines big game is plentiful. These factors have made the Flatheads a nomadic tribe, the Coeur d'Alenes a sedentary people, and the Blackfeet the mortal enemies of their neighbors. These circumstances also account for the differences which can be noted in the physical, industrial, and moral aptitude of these peoples. Much depends, too, on the character of their chiefs, on their more or less frequent contacts with strangers and on illumination in ways that are more or less extraordinary. Left to himself the savage has not been able to make any marked progress toward civilization. Still, however degraded he may be, when it is a question of passing from the most abject kind of natural life to the most noble supernatural life, the savage always offers less resistance than the man perverted by civilization.

What were these savages like before their conversion? How have they emerged from the deep abyss of misery into which they were plunged? What are they like today? These are questions which will be answered, more or less satisfactorily, by the observations we were able to make while among them.

The skin of the Indian is the color of copper; cheekbones are prominent; eyes are brown or black; hair is long and straight; stature is medium; legs are slim, feet are misshapen because of binding during infancy. Some distinguishing features are: canoemen have stronger arms; hunters are more agile on their feet, have sharper vision and more adroit hands; warriors are more courageous in battle, more polished in their manners and more eloquent in their speech. Young men, on the other hand, are preoccupied with nothing but their appearance and are more vain in this respect than girls. Girls and women content themselves with separating their hair in two tresses which hang over the shoulders.

Before the arrival of white men in their land, the aborigines lived entirely from their catch at fishing or hunting, or on roots. Their only clothing was the skins of animals. Their only weapons were the bow and arrow, the spear and the club. Their only shelters were earthen huts or rushes. Their only means of transportation were their own legs or their bark canoes. For making fire, they relied on striking two stones together or rubbing sticks together. To cook their meat, they used a stick thrust into the earth before a fire. Their only cooking utensils were woven from roots, and their only means of bringing food to a boil was by stones which had been heated in a fire.

In what consisted their moral aptitude? It was a vestige of natural law, whose author, end, and sanction they, of course, did not know, but which, nevertheless, sufficed to give their actions a kind of natural rectitude, which always prevailed except when, as in the case of the Coeur d'Alenes, who were less advanced than the others, the passions asserted themselves. They were somewhat cruel toward the infirm, but would have considered abandoning them a serious offense. Though given to very artful dissimulation, they distinguished this vice from gross lying, which they condemned. They cast longing eyes on the goods of others, but the faintest suspicion of robbery turned them against the thief. They were inclined to polygamy, but would have regarded themselves as abductors if they had taken women to themselves without first purchasing the right to do so. Finally, they were not too concerned about conjugal stability, though they never disrupted it unless doing so could be more or less speciously justified.

All of this held true, as we indicated, so long as their passions were not aroused. Once they became excited or the interest of their territory was jeopardized, all light seemed to be extinguished and their hearts were like a stormy night when all nature's elements become confused. For example, should a relative or friend commit an offense, one was not expected to place the blame on the guilty party, but rather to support him in the ensuing quarrel. According to this principle of conduct, a woman who said to her husband—be he thief, murderer or adulterer—"You have done wrong," gave her husband the right to reply, "Well, if you are not satisfied, you may go." And should the woman venture further comment, the husband had a right to order her to leave. Such dismissal was final and, moreover, so customary that it was nowise unusual to meet very young women thus dismissed three or four times by as many husbands. The effect of this practice was to inculcate in those women who wished to avoid the disgrace of dismissal a submissiveness that bordered on complicity, on the principle that might was most obviously the equivalent of right. In matters of inheritance, how often the rights of a distant, but rich or malicious, cousin prevailed over those of the widow and the orphan! In matters of war, there was no formal declaration. Any individual had the right to make war, even for the most trifling reason, and to make a war of extermination, mutilating, scalping, massacring women, children and old people. Exploits of that nature were considered acts of courage. Such was the force of these customs, and of many others, that, among the savages, anyone who made the slightest attempt to abolish them would have been the most imprudent of men.

If there was such confusion of ideas in matters of custom, what could be expected in matters of religion, where ideas are ordinarily even less clear? There was a veritable chaos, and for good reason. For just as weak eyes dazzled by the sun seem to see its images in the most insignificant objects long after the sun has disappeared, so these infirm intellects, having lost the idea of the true God, thought to see the divinity where its shadow scarcely even extended. As happens with those who become delirious, the weaker the foundation for faith the stronger the propensity to believe. They called "manitou"—that is, "spirit"—such apparently animated objects as the sun, thunder, and so forth, and the cult they practiced they called "medicine." Hence such frequently used terms as "medicine," "instrument of medicine," "strong in medicine," and so on.

What does the term "medicine" signify? It is the name given to the idolatry practiced by these savages, who know no cares other than the needs and ills of the body and, therefore, ask of their manitou only what is required to meet these needs and cure these illnesses.

How many different kinds of medicine are there? Only one, properly speaking, the object of which is the cure or removal of bodily ills. But there are many powers or virtues to which the term medicine is applied by extension. They may all be reduced to three: (1) Medicine of utility, or the power to acquire, with the least possible effort, the greatest possible abundance of things necessary for life, such as fish on the line of the fisherman, game in the path of the hunter, and so on. Included here is also the power to win at gambling or games. (2) Medicine of ostentation, or the power to dazzle the eyes of others by prestige, tours de force, sleight-of-hand tricks, and things of that sort. (3) Medicine of malice, or the power to do injury to the persons or fortunes of others. This medicine is held to be evil, even by the medicine men themselves. Consequently, it is more rare and, perhaps, morally less harmful than those appearing to be more innocent because invoked as a means of doing only physical injury. The first medicine—that of utility—on the other hand, by fattening the savage at little expense, encourages his laziness and the brute appetites. The second medicine—that of utility with respect to the winning of prizes or stakes—by making one family prosperous causes ten others to be poor, and makes everyone a slave to cupidity.[6] The third medicine—that of ostentation—by nourishing vainglory and self-importance perpetuates the stupid confidence of those who are a prey to it. Thus there are sloth, gluttony, lust, covetousness, envy, cruelty, vengeance, pride—in short, all the vices which characterize man fallen to the lowest level. They are the natural effects of the medicine. Who could fail to recognize the author of these vices by their signs? Some of the most reputable medicine men admitted after their conversion that much of what they used to foretell merely followed from natural causes or was only apparently mysterious. Still there were some things which could not be explained without assuming the intervention of some occult power, at least superior to that of man. Examples were the healing of certain wounds, the removal of plagues, knowledge of events taking place at great distances—all without any means other than a certain kind of feather or claw or some ridiculous contortion.

To what can these various powers be attributed? Perhaps to some venomous plant, such as those from which we extract poison? This is impossible, for the effects produced by these powers are entirely beyond the inherent nature of their instruments. Can they be attributed to the person of the medicine man, just as miraculous power is attributed to the person working miracles? This is even less possible, for the medicine man does not possess the least trace of such power, even accidentally. Could they not be attributed, as is the case with our relics of saints, to some material object having some relation to his [the medicine man's] person? This is also impossible, for besides the fact that their instrument has no relation to his person, except as deposit to depositary, there is also the fact that the instrument itself is not essentially material, as is a relic. Sometimes the instrument is nothing but a sound, a breath, or a simple sign. Is the instrument therefore something like our sacraments—a kind of sign, either material or immaterial? Some comparison (if such an execrable thing can be compared with what is most sacred) does indeed seem justified, especially since, of all diabolical tricks, none produces its effect so infallibly as does this one. This fact probably prompted the Apostolic Vicar of Columbia, Monsignor Blanchet,[7] to translate the word "sacrament" with the Indian term "medicine of the soul." But all comparisons are inadequate, especially in this case. Not only are the instruments of the medicine as numerous as the wanderings produced by the wildest of imaginations, but they also differ from sacramental signs in that each one had some special mediator, usually from among the lower animals.

What are these signs? Usually the hoof of a deer, a bear claw, a feather, the cry of some animal, some strange sound, an exhalation, a menacing gesture, a grotesque dance, a ridiculous contortion, and so on. And how are the signs applied? In a manner best calculated to degrade human nature. If, for example, the medicinal power is attributed to a bear claw, and is deemed applicable to the treatment of a wound, the medicine man hurls himself upon the poor patient as a bear upon its prey, imitat-

ing as closely as possible the roaring and the fury of this animal. If he is called upon to cure some internal malady, he sucks vigorously at what is though to be the part on the surface of the body corresponding with the internal malady. Then, like a man holding the malady in his mouth, he retires with violent gyrations, or vomits what he claims is the malady he has just sucked from his patient. If his medicine is that of a wolf, the medicine man, to give thanks to his wolf for a cure so marvelous but so perilous to him, begins to howl like a wolf. Obviously one could write at length about these things.

I will end my account with a short description of the most commonly practiced medical or surgical operation, that of "breathing." This operation consists in breathing or blowing on a wounded limb or on some part of the body thought to correspond to an internal malady. This is done with such comical seriousness and with such violence that one can avoid breaking out into laughter only by thinking of the soul of the dying patient. If the breathing is effective, if the patient recovers, the medicine begins to be respected and the medicine man himself achieves a good reputation. No matter how rarely similar cures succeed after that, the reputation of the medicine man is rapidly enhanced, until finally foolish credulity accords to the most dishonorable impudence the most coveted of titles, that of one "strong in medicine," which carries with it much more prestige than the title of "doctor." To be "strong in medicine" is to be at one and the same time a prophet, a miracle-worker, a kind of pontiff. Such a medicine man is the recipient of revelations. Prodigious feats are accomplished by him and his religious authority is virtually absolute. The foregoing justifies the conclusion that satanic power is firmly established here; human dignity is degraded, divine majesty is eradicated, and an untold number of souls are eternally lost. Such are the fruits of the perfidious work called "medicine," fruits which will perhaps become more evident in the course of this account.

This power can be acquired only through rigorous fasting, great mortification, long pilgrimages; during sleep, during a fainting spell, during a fit of delirium; arousing or satisfying some passion; and never without rendering homage to the real or pretended spirit which is the source of the power. But let us see how the candidate for "medicine" begins. He is still in that state in which he is wretched, ignorant, worthy of pity—I almost added good for nothing. This is roughly what one who is "strong in medicine" calls those who are not. As long as the candidate remains in this state of misery, it is easy to see by what temptation he is ordinarily assailed. If his temptation is stronger than usual or if the ambition of his father prompts him, the candidate will depart, traveling over hill and dale, like an errant knight. Where he is going, it is useless to ask, for he does not know himself. He will go where his impulses send him, but, melancholy as his temperament is at such a time, it can be guessed that he will most probably seek solitude. He penetrates the fastness of a somber forest, he scales a precipitous rocky slope, or follows the twisting shore of a lake. The majestic scenes around him penetrate his imagination, but do not elevate his thoughts above the objects he sees immediately about him. The sky is to him nonexistent; he thinks only of the earth and wants only the earth, since it is the earth that gives existence to everything anyone knows. Thus it is to the earth that he addresses his first prayers. If she remains deaf to them, he turns to a nearby tree, moved by a need to pray to a being more powerful than himself. Embracing the trunk wildly, he cries, "O you who are the most beautiful, the greatest, the strongest of all the children of the forest, take pity on an unfortunate one who has recourse to you." His prayer ends, but, his idea still remaining fixedly with him, he resumes his way and, unless he collapses from fatigue or want of food—for he is fasting—he continues to walk until he encounters something extraordinary, or at least, something which appears so to him.

Usually what he is in search of will present itself to him late in the day when the setting sun produces its most magical effects. It may be a deer, a bear, a beaver or some other animal, but of a color and a shape never beheld at any other time. Or it may be something which resembles a man, but which is not a man—a monster, a kind of giant, a colossus vomiting fire from its mouth. Or it may be a dwarf, so small as to be hardly distinguishable among the foliage, but so

agile that the swiftest chase will not overtake it. In any event, the man or the fantastic animal will articulate words that are in harmony with the desires of the searcher—or else he will disappear after an instant or two or reappear while the visionary is asleep or in a fainting spell (for excessive fatigue—if not other factors—sometimes reduce him to this state). If he is not more fortunate during this final stage than during the preceding ones, it is a sign that he was not made for medicine.

But it is rare that his luck is so poor. Let us suppose, in order to make more evident the kind of resources a "medical" head can lay hold of, that it has been the lot of our candidate to have only a third-class encounter. You can be sure that his genius for invention will be able to make up for all deficiencies. He will make certain of returning to his father's dwelling just when the time for serious talks has arrived. The first thing he will do upon arriving will be to fill his pipe. He will smoke in silence, like a man who has momentous information to communicate, until his audience, attracted by the smell of the calumet, has had time to assemble. Then, if the moment seems propitious, he will announce that he is about to speak. After completing his turn at the pipe, he will begin to speak.[8] Before announcing his great news, he will not fail to mention everything calculated to increase interest. At length he will describe what he has seen, while everyone listens eagerly. If he is naturally of a cheerful disposition, he will have seen a red sign, a green ram, a white deer. If his disposition is somber, he will have encountered thunder after a storm, which assumed the shape of a man and then changed into the likeness of a tree. If he is normally inclined to the whimsical, he will say that he saw a wolf which was so long that, while its tail was still in the country of the Nez Percés, its ears were in the country of the Coeur d'Alenes.[9] And so it goes. But what did the things he saw say to him? Oh, many great things! He was told, for example, what he must believe regarding their attributes, how he must pay homage to their powers, and what he might expect through their favors. Now the idea of favor is immensely appealing to the savage. Accordingly, at this word, some of his audience, wide-eyed and eager, ask what he received and what he was promised.

The speaker continues in grave tones: " 'Do not forget,' the red sign told me, 'that it is from me you have your power. Here is a feather to which I have given the ability to heal all burns, cuts, knife wounds, and so on.' 'Take this small bone,' the green ram told me. 'From it you will know the proper time and place to fish, to hunt, and to harvest fruit, and so forth.' 'See this tail,' the wolf said to me. 'From it you will know where your enemies are, what they are saying, what they are doing and what they are planning. Fear nothing; if your enemies attack your tribe, tell your people to follow you; go out bravely to engage your enemy in battle. Throw yourself into the thick of the fighting, for neither arrow nor bullet nor club nor any other weapon will be able to touch you.' 'Take this piece of red wood,' the thunder told me. 'With its help you will be able to recognize, immediately, other medicine men. If their strength is less than yours, you will be able to estimate, instantly, the amount of their power. You will be able to overawe the bravest men and crush them if they resist you. When your hour has come, you will die, but tell your children not to bury you, for you will rise again on the fourth day after your death.' As for the white deer, before speaking to me, he showed me an animal and an iron weapon of a kind I had never seen before. He called the animal a horse and the weapon a gun. Then, while presenting me with a deer's tooth, the deer said, 'Guard carefully the gift which I make, for if you keep it, you will have the first of the animals and weapons I

have shown you.' Then the deer added solemnly, 'You will soon witness great events; I see strange men coming from afar; they are white and their garments are black. I have spoken.' " Then the narrator is silent.

"My son," his father says, "these things which you relate to us, did you learn them while you were asleep or while you were awake?"

"Father," answers the young medicine man, "I was not asleep." And to support his statement, he allows his audience to have a glimpse of a medicine bag which suggests, forcefully enough, that he has not related everything.

Thus, these Indians were not governed by ignorance and passion alone, but by animals, or rather, through animals, by medicine men who used their authority to disparage the divine majesty. Add to these deplorable aberrations of spirit and of heart the scourges of all kinds which come in the wake of a war of extermination, and you will have some notion of the miserable state of these savages before the arrival of the missionaries. But these extreme evils were of some value in that they created in these unfortunate souls so strong a desire for some sort of change that at the first hint that there existed a better life, they gathered, like starved eagles, to learn about it. Within every nation the Lord has His chosen few. To some who are still living He partially revealed Himself, planting, thus, in the midst of their wilderness, landmarks intended to point to the way to His great mercy. In the following chapters, we shall see the principal agents of that mercy.

I

Historical Notes

*Father Point reviews the heroic efforts of several Indians
to persuade missionaries to come to them from St. Louis. He records his own departure
for Westport in the fall of 1840 and outlines his work there. A detailed account
of his journey to Fort Hall with Father De Smet and other missionaries is made colorful
by keen observations concerning plants and animals seen along the way.*

IN THE FIRST years of the present [nineteenth] century, the United States sent men to explore the area now known as Oregon. Mindful of the material interests of their country, they were not concerned with spiritual values. They did, however, introduce the aborigines to the notion of the existence of a spirit superior to all others, a spirit all men must worship. The explorers were followed by traders, who possessed little religious training. If, in their trading, they did not always give evil in exchange for good, they certainly never failed to exchange little for much. Their engaging manners and apparent good will toward the Indians made them welcome. Some of the traders, speaking respectfully of the religion they had learned in their youth, gave their hosts such an exalted concept of what they called the "French prayer," that not infrequently the Indians asked if they, too, might not become followers of that doctrine. Knowledge of the true God had not yet reached the Coeur d'Alenes when there arrived in their midst an Indian from the Red River.[10] A Protestant himself, he became a sort of apostle to the Spokanes and the Nez Percés.[11] Probably because he informed his teachers that they would be welcomed, Presbyterian ministers and their families soon came to settle there. These evangelists succeeded in establishing homes for their families, though they were not very popular with the Indians, many of whom disdainfully called the ministers "brothers of the long knives." [12] Some of the aborigines were attracted to the teachings of the Catholic Church merely because they disliked the Presbyterian ministers; but others, especially two named Ignatius, seriously desired to procure Catholic missionaries for their people.

The first of these two, known as Great Ignatius, was a native of the Iroquois village located at Sault-St.-Louis on the St. Lawrence River.[13] To procure Catholic missionaries for his adopted people, he undertook two expeditions to St. Louis, Missouri. On the first journey, three of his companions sickened and died; on the second, he and all of his party were massacred by the Sioux. His heroic death, far from discouraging the Flatheads with whom he had lived, increased their desire to obtain teachers to instruct them in the truths which Great Ignatius had explained to them. They despatched to St. Louis two other Iroquois who had long been their guests, in the hope that the compatriots of the Great Ignatius would, better than anyone else, be able to win a favorable response to their petition. Such perseverence deeply impressed both the bishop of St. Louis [Joseph Rosati] and the Jesuits in St. Louis, who had been brought there especially to work among the Indians. Therefore, Father Pierre Jean De Smet was sent to the Rocky Mountains to examine the disposition of these Indians and to discover what might be done to improve their spiritual condition. When he had reported the results of his investigation, it was decided that, the following spring, he and five companions, two priests and three brothers, would establish a mission in the country of the Flatheads. The priests were Nicolas Point and Father Gregorio Mengarini; the brothers were William Clessens, Charles Huet and Joseph Specht.[14]

I was sent to Westport to act as pastor there until Father De Smet returned.[15] I lived in a part of the village occupied by twenty-three families, most of whom were French *voyageurs*, their Indian families and their children, who were called *métis*.[16] Though all of the families were poor, they had built a small chapel and had frequently asked for a pastor. The ignorance of some, the drunkenness of others, and the love of pleasure of nearly all of them was more than enough to incite the zeal of a mission-

ary. I set to work with confidence, for, despite their faults, they had good will. This insignificant post could well become, in the eyes of God, a place of considerable importance, for Westport was truly the gateway to the West. This was the place where expeditions were assembled to depart for Mexico, California, and the Rocky Mountains. Before their departure, travelers often remained at Westport for several weeks in the spring, and often during the Easter season. If that great feast could be properly celebrated, how influential would Westport be on the travelers, and through them, on the Indians!

I arrived at Westport on All Saints' Day when winter was already making itself felt.[17] The cold, which lasts until Easter, is sometimes so intense that I have seen the wine freeze in the chalice, even between two mounds of glowing embers. In spite of the cold, the distance, and the poor roads, the chapel was constantly filled on Sundays and feast days, not only during Mass, but also at other services. To lend more dignity to my position, I decided to avoid being a burden to anyone. By dint of a little industry, many little gifts, given to me in Louisiana, became ornaments, pictures, statues and even a monstrance, so that by Christmas this little chapel enjoyed all the services which are available in a big city church. I even taught the children to sing, and the singing worked wonders.

But these poor people required a great deal more than singing lessons. Paradise, Hell, eternity, and even more, sacraments and the Church were all terms which virtually held no meaning for them. I gave them simple instructions, not hesitating to insist on the consequences of sin, of which St. Paul speaks, especially for drunkards. Above all, I began catechetical instructions, giving particular attention to the children with the best memories. They, in turn, could do for others what I had done for them. Some say that in America it is impossible to engender among children a spirit of competition such as exists in France or Italy. It is more difficult here, I admit, but by no means impossible. There is a certain amount of vanity everywhere, which, if properly directed, will always stimulate competition. I experimented along these lines in Westport, and my success far exceeded

*An imaginative representation
of the killing of Great Ignatius and his companions. Actually no white
men witnessed the event.*

*A prelude to Father Point's assignment as
missionary to Indian territory was this conference of Young Ignatius and
Pierre, Iroquois, with Bishop Rosati of St. Louis.*

my expectations. During the week, I conducted catechism classes for the children. On Sundays I did so for the entire parish, with everyone present. Seated directly before me were the very young and behind them, in order, were the First Communicants, then the children who showed marked perseverence, then the mothers, and finally the married men. During the week I passed out "good points." On Sunday I handed out crosses of merit to the best in each catechism class. Once a month I awarded little pictures to the one who had given the best recitations during the month. These pictures were placed in the most conspicuous place in the home and it was before them that the family gathered to say their morning and evening prayers. When the missionary visited the home, he never failed to glance approvingly at the little oratory. Thus, a laudable spirit of competition spread, not only among the children, but even among the adults.

Since the piety of the children depends, in great measure, on that of the mother, I established, for the married women of the parish, a pious association in honor of the Seven Sorrows of Our Lady. Soon after this, I established one for the girls, under the patronage of the Immaculate Conception. The girls were very modest and capable of true piety. (It was common in the country to indicate a young man's wisdom by remarking that he was "as undisturbed as a girl.") The fact is that among the twenty-three families of that community there was not a single girl of immoral character. This was an admirable thing in a country where dissolute men are common. Some of the girls, encouraged by the example of a pious widow, made rather charming artificial flowers for the chapel. As the season of Lent approached, I suggested the observance of the Forty Hours,[18] at which everyone, men, women, and children, volunteered to take a turn for an hour. During the three days there was someone constantly before the Blessed Sacrament. The novena to St. Francis Xavier, patron of the parish, was also well attended. At Christmas, two thirds of the parish received Holy Communion.

During the previous year, there had been parties every week. This year there were only one or two, which I tolerated lest by being too rigid I lose what had been gained. This is how things were done to make the [first] party as moral as possible. The old soldier of the Empire who accompanied Father De Smet on his return from the Rocky Mountains—whom the community thought I should, therefore, refuse nothing—was delegated to visit me.[19] He informed me that he had a favor to ask, but before doing so he wished to kneel and recite the Hail Mary for the success of his mission. Having said his prayer, he broached the subject of the party with full confidence. The second was a wedding party, regarding which so many precautions were taken that there seemed no reason to fear any danger in it. Even the young people did not wish to join in a party without having first asked my permission. In this younger group there was a charming Iroquois girl who had declined an invitation to the party lest she expose herself to an occasion of sin. To provide an excuse for her absence, she cut her hair very short, a sign of deep mourning among the Indians. But everyone insisted that she go, even her father, who threatened to lock her in the cellar if she did not go. To avoid disobeying her father, she agreed to attend, provided he went as her escort.

There were victories much more difficult of attainment. The Iroquois, who were drunkards, emerged from their wretchedness, only to fall back into it. How many remained sober for weeks at a time? Some promised, solemnly, not to drink for a certain period. Cases were cited of some who, at the end of the period, tested themselves and were able to withstand temptation. There were two cases of men who gave up liquor for good. The older of them said to me, "Father, if you remained here, I believe you would succeed in making something of me. But I fear the time when you are gone."

On the day before my departure, a Sunday, the mothers, members of the Society of Our Lady of the Seven Sorrows and the young members of the Society of the Immaculate Conception received Holy Communion, as did the children who had made their first Holy Communion three weeks before. Two of the younger group failed to make their first Holy Communion on the day appointed. One, out of forgetfulness, had drunk a few drops of water and the other had eaten a bit of fruit he had found on the way to church. But on the following day they made reparation for their lapse by presenting themselves at the door of the church, this time fasting, when the sun had scarcely risen.

On the day after this Sunday there were the blessing of rosaries, medals and images; distribution of catechism prizes won during the period since All Saints' Day; and, finally, the erection of a large cross in the cemetery. In the evening I witnessed the death of a man who had given to his wife and children the most beautiful example of faith and resignation during his illness, and whose final recommendations were an expression of the most tender confidence in the Blessed Virgin. The day before, for the first time, I had had the consecrated ground opened to receive the remains of the leader of my first congregation. The deceased, a woman, had, this year, had the consolation of seeing all her children receive the sacraments.

During my stay at Westport I was visited occasionally by Indians. Among these visitors was the grand chief of the Kansa,[20] about whom I shall speak in my account of my itinerary through the Rocky Mountains. Before him, three members of his tribe had visited me, one, the son of the chief and another, reputed to be the first of the braves in the tribe. All three were painted black and red, and wore bracelets, medallions, necklaces, and feathers in their hair. After giving each one a small present, I conducted them to the chapel. It appears that they had never seen anything like it. They advanced, retreated, stood still in their tracks, peering in front of them and behind, up and down, to the right and left. Most of all, they were unable to control their great astonishment at seeing the heart of the Blessed Virgin pierced with the seven swords and the head of our Lord crowned with thorns.[21] They pointed out to one another the features they did not understand. What seemed to impress them the most were the large tears flowing from the eyes of our Lord. They asked each other who this person might be. Then a woman who spoke their language told them that it was the Son of God, who wept for our sins. This seemed to touch them. These Indians belong to a tribe which is so ferocious that during the winter a party of its

members had massacred more than eighty women and children of a neighboring tribe.

The Osage Indians, about whom so much has been published in France, lived a distance of only two or three days' journey from the village of Westport.[22] Taken all together, they do not number over five thousands souls. They are an evil tribe, as are all those who are not Catholics, and live on the fringe of civilization. I inquired whether those who had visited France were still alive and learned that of the original six only three remained.

As Christmas approached, Father Allen,[23] missionary to the Potawatomi, made a trip to the Kickapoo territory with orders to close the mission which had been established there.[24] He asked me to accompany him. Going and coming, we lodged with an Indian called Wolf, a great friend of the French, who claimed ability to speak the French language. To show us how well he spoke, he continued to repeat what he had learned on his travels in the West: "*Merci, mon ami; bonne la vache, mon comarade.*"

As for the Kickapoo, they are a hideous nation in every way, especially with respect to religion. Our missionaries preached to them for five years, but on Sunday, at Mass, scarcely anyone came to the chapel built by Father Van Quickenborne, whom I met in Philadelphia.[25] He had barely made a beginning, preaching to the Kickapoo, when he was recalled to St. Louis. From there he was sent to the Sioux, only to die within the short space of three weeks.[26] He was replaced in both missions by priests from St. Louis, who had none of his background or experience. Today, both of these missions, among the Kickapoo and the Sioux, have been abandoned. The people in this area were convinced that things would have turned out otherwise if Father Van Quickenborne had been able to continue his work.

The Kickapoo are now under the care of a Methodist minister and a certain Kenekuk, a member of their tribe who calls himself "The Prophet." [27] By force of sheer effrontery and continued hard work, this man, really extraordinary for his kind, has succeeded in assembling some three hundred souls in a temple built for him by the United States Government. He claims to be a special emissary from God. The complete, fantastic story he tells of his birth and mission would be too long to recount in detail here. He descended from Heaven, he says, through a blue opening and, after having soared about through space for a long time, he tumbled down upon our planet. This is but one example of his teaching, which may serve as an example of his imposture. The whites, he says, will not be saved because they made all Nature grieve. They cut the grass with their great scythes, thereby injuring the grass so that it wept. They chopped down trees with their great axes, thereby injuring them and making them weep. They ran their great steamboats on the rivers and thereby injured the rivers so that they, too, wept. Rivers, earth, trees and grass all wept. The white man, ingrate that he was, thus made all of Nature mourn. Consequently, he would not be saved. For the Indians the practical conclusion was that, since they inflicted none of these injuries on Nature, they could hope for eternal life, regardless of their stupidity, their sloth, their thievery, their adultery, their murderousness. And for the most part they were given to these vices. As for Kenekuk, in his capacity of prophet, five wives are not too many for him. No one knows how many men his son has killed. Kenekuk's palace—for he is chief—is as filthy as a stable and his temple, which I actually saw, is just as bad. But the king-prophet has only to speak of his revelations and everyone listens with admiration. The authority for his divine mission is a piece of wood about two inches wide and eight inches long.

On May 1, 1841, Father Point left Westport to consume the last Host remaining in the tabernacle of this unfortunate mission among the Kickapoo. He arrived in the Kickapoo village about sunset. The first news he received as he dismounted from his horse was that about a mile away there lay an infidel on the point of death and therefore in grave danger of losing his soul. Father Point asked for an interpreter and quickly made his way to where the sick man lay. He found that the man had in effect despaired both of earthly life and spiritual life, for he was only able to pronounce the words, "Everyone is abandoning me." The missionary, approaching the man said to him, "No, brother, not everyone is abandoning you, for I, one of the

Blackrobes, come to help you, and I come, certainly, in accordance with the will of the Spirit who wishes to save you." At these words the dying man breathed more easily; confidence was reborn in his heart. The minister of Divine Mercy asked him those questions which any other would have asked under similar circumstances, and the responses of the sick man were most consoling. He was made to perform the acts required under such circumstances and, since he was about to die almost any moment, the missionary considered whether he should baptize him then and there. There came into his mind the recollection of what St. Philip had done on a similar occasion for the eunuch of the Queen of Candace, and he regarded this sudden recollection as the inspiration of the Holy Ghost. Immediately he proceeded to administer baptism. It was fortunate that he did, for by the next day the man had died, to enter, let it be hoped, into the life which never ends and which shall be eternally happy. Was this not the most beautiful bouquet a beginning missionary could offer to the Queen of Heaven on the very first day of the month consecrated to Her? How profound are the judgments of God! This day was also the last day of a mission which had but lately been flourishing, but which the scandals of a supposedly civilized people had plunged to the depths of the most complete demoralization.[28]

On May 10, we left Westport, taking with us all the supplies for our dear mission in five two-wheeled carts driven by two Canadians who were excellent wagoners, and three of our brothers, still novices at that difficult art. The three priests rode horseback.[29] On quitting Westport, which is separated from the river by a stretch of woods about two or three miles wide, we saw before us what the inhabitants of the region call the Great Prairie. What a beautiful perspective for a missionary! But especially for me, who for twenty years have seen nothing but the walls of a college. At the sight of the azure distances, so pleasing to the eye, I thought I could perceive what is most attractive about the beautiful ideal of the apostolic life. The verdure of the earth and the thousands upon thousands of small spring flowers helped support the illusion.

*A typical view of the western prairie country
in the vicinity of Westport, Missouri.*

*Two astonished Indians, on a visit to Father Point's chapel
at Westport, view a painting
of Christ crowned with thorns.*

From the very first day onward we saw Indians. The first encampment on the great plains always has something memorable about it. What we noted particularly about this one was that it coincided with the feast of one of our most celebrated missionaries, Blessed Francis de Geronimo.[30] In the following days—after having passed through the territory of the Shawnee,[31] and the Delaware, where the only noteworthy thing we saw was a Methodist college, which, for reasons easily understandable, had been erected in the midst of the best Indian territory—we arrived at the right bank of the Kansas River.[32] There we found two men who had transported part of our baggage by water, and two relatives of the great chief of the Kansa, who had come to meet us. While one of them aided the pack animals in crossing the river by swimming ahead of them, the other announced our arrival to the first of the tribes awaiting us on the other side. As soon as they learned that we would camp at a spot only six miles from their village, they left, full gallop, and disappeared in a cloud of dust. Scarcely had our shelter been erected, when the chief of the area, accompanied by six ranking warriors, came to pay his respects.

First of all, he had us seat ourselves on a mat which he spread out on the grass and then, drawing forth a large portfolio with great solemnity, he handed Father De Smet a document, signed by the President of the United States, which recommended his tribe to the good will of the whites. The calumet was not forgotten, nor, on our part, a present for the occasion, which earned for us the honor of having placed at our disposal the two warriors who had visited us at Westport. These two braves, one armed with lance and shield and the other with bow and sword, stood watch before our door during the three days we had to spend waiting for the stragglers.

Only on May 18 the American element assembled. The most remarkable traveler among them was Colonel Bartleson, whom the Americans had made their leader in their search for fortune in the much-vaunted territory of California. This man, already somewhat advanced in years, calm in temperament but enterprising in character, was kind to us during the whole trip. His maxim in religious matters was that one should either have no religion at all or adhere to the religion of those with whom it was necessary to live. This was hardly our attitude toward religion. Nevertheless, through the maintenance of mutual respect, the most perfect concord reigned between him and us right up to the end. The rest of the travelers were a composite of all ages, languages and denominations. Some were traveling in pursuit of purely material interests, others for pleasure, and still others, of the age of the prodigal son, only to relieve their families of their unfortunate presence. Although their views differed, as we have just seen, all agreed on one point, namely, that they must try not to perish on the journey. This kind of agreement facilitated the establishment of good discipline.

In these immense solitudes it was necessary to have an experienced guide. The choice fell not on the colonel, who had never crossed the mountains, but on the captain Father De Smet had engaged.[33] He was a courageous Irishman, known to most of the Indian tribes as Tête Blanche (White Head). He had spent fully two thirds of his life crossing the plains.

The missionaries and their party were regarded as the first body of the vanguard. Each day the captain gave the signal to rise and to depart, ordered the march and the stops, chose the spot in which to camp, and maintained discipline. Whenever possible, camp was pitched on the wooded bank of some river so that there would be no lack either of drinking water or of wood for cooking. First, the captain would mark a spot for our tent; then the vehicles would be arranged one beside the other in a circle or in a square, more or less regular according to the nature of the terrain, but always in such a manner as to provide the pack animals a secure enclosure for the night. For added security, everyone picketed his own animals at a sufficiently great distance from the others, and on tethers long enough to permit them, without doing injury to themselves, to supplement by grazing what they had been fed in the evening. From the moment when the camp retired until the break of day, all the travelers, including the priests, stood watch according to roster, in order to guard against a surprise attack. Our little army of seventy persons, of whom more than fifty were able to bear arms, would, with a little prudence, be more than adequate for the long journey before us.

On May 19, while the rest of the party continued toward the West, Father De Smet and Father Point bore off to the left to visit the first village of the Kansa. Seen from a short distance, their dwellings bore a striking resemblance to the large mounds which cover our fields after the harvest. There were only about twenty of these dwellings irregularly placed, but each one of them covered a circular area about 120 feet in circumference, easily space enough to shelter thirty to forty persons. According to these figures the total population of the village should have been from seven hundred to eight hundred persons, an approximation justified by the total population of the tribe which was fifteen hundred for two villages. These dwellings, which were of an altogether unique kind, combined utility and comfort with solidity. From a circular wall, which rose perpendicularly to about the height of a man, sprang poles terminating in a central opening that served both as window and chimney. The door opened on the side most sheltered from the wind. The fireplace was located within the four columns supporting the rotunda and the beds were ranged in a circle about the wall. In the space between the beds and the fireplace stood some of the persons inhabiting the dwelling. Others were seated or reclined on animal skins or rush mats. It seemed that these mats were considered the most presentable; at any rate, a carpet of this sort was given to us as we entered.

It would be difficult to give an account of all the singular things we saw during the half hour we passed in the midst of these strange figures. A Flemish painter would have found a treasure there. What struck me most were the strong character written on the faces of some of those about me, the artlessness, the attitudes, the facility of gesture, the vivacity of expression, the singularity of their dress and, most of all, the great variety of occupations. Only the women were working and, in order not to be distracted from their tasks, those who had children still unable to walk had placed them, strapped to a kind of board, large enough to prevent injury to their limbs, either in a corner

or at their feet. Some of the men were preparing to eat, which was their principal occupation when they were not fighting or hunting. Others were smoking, sleeping, talking, laughing, or were occupied with plucking the hair from their faces, including the eyelashes and eyebrows. Still others were attending to their hair, an occupation they seemed to find most pleasing. Contrary to the habit of other Indians who preferred to wear their hair long, these shaved their heads, leaving only a stiffly frizzled tuft on top. To be thus decorated was, they thought, to have the most beautiful adornment the human head could carry. Their favorite ornament was the feather of an eagle, if it was at all possible to procure one, because this was the symbol of courage. Sometimes the feather stood above the head like a plume, sometimes it lay along the nape of the neck and sometimes it fluttered about the temples like a weathercock.

While the head man of the lodge smoked the pipe of peace with Father De Smet, I could not take my attention away from a dandy who kept looking at himself [in a small mirror] in order to give to his plume the proper graceful twist but was unable to attain the degree of perfection he appeared to seek.

Soon I became aware that I, myself, was becoming the object of attention, almost the occasion for hilarity on the part of the Indian children. For some days I had given no attention to the matter of shaving. In their estimation, the acme of beauty was the complete absence of hair from the chin, the eyelashes, the eyebrows, and the head. This was only a minor part of their grooming, but the trouble they took to achieve the ultimate perfection in this detail of appearance is only a small indication of their vanity. If you wish a picture of the supremely self-satisfied Kansa in all his glory, you must imagine an Indian with vermilion circles about his eyes; blue, black, or red streaks on his face; pendants of crockery, glass, or mother-of-pearl hanging from his ears; about his neck a fancy necklace, making a large semicircle on his breast, with a large medal of silver or copper in the middle of it. On his arms and wrists he would have many bracelets of brass, iron, or tin. About his middle would be a girdle, a belt of garish colors from which hung a tobacco pouch decorated with beads, and cutlass scabbard striped in various colors. And on top of all this would be a blue, white, green, or red blanket, draped in folds about the body according to the caprice or need of the wearer. This, then, would be the finery one would see on the most envied of the Kansa tribe.

In matters of dress, manner of speech, manner of acting, praying, and waging war, the Kansa very closely resemble the Osages, neighbors with whom they maintained friendly relations. The Kansa were quite tall and very well shaped. Their physiognomy, as I have already remarked, was quite virile. Their abrupt, guttural language was remarkable for its long and sharp accentuation of inflection. But this did not prevent their singing from being most monotonous. To their strength, shrewdness, and courage, they added good common sense, something lacking in most Indians. They used the rifle in their wars and hunting, just as the white man did. This, of course, gave them a marked advantage over their enemies.

Among their chiefs were some men of true distinction. The best-known of them—because Captain Bonneville's purported memoirs mention him at length—was White Feather.[34] The author of *The Conquest of Granada* presents White Feather in a most flattering light. It is said that this man was endowed with an intelligence, a sincerity, and a courage not of the usual kind. He had been well acquainted with M. Lecroix, one of the very first Catholic missionaries to visit this part of the West.[35] White Feather had a high regard for the missionary and for all whom the Indians called the Blackrobes. His attitude toward Protestant missionaries was quite different. To them, he manifested neither affection nor any regard. On one occasion, when one of the Protestant missionaries was talking to him about conversion, he said, "To change religions is a good thing, provided one changes the beliefs he has for those which are better. For my part, the only true religion I know is that which the Blackrobes teach. If you wish to convert me, you must leave your wife and put on the habit which the Blackrobes wear."

The Kansa, and their neighbors, the Pawnee, had recently waged a war of extermination.[36] The winter before, eighty Pawnee women and children had been massacred. Although the Kansa were vindictive and cruel toward their enemies, they were not strangers to the most tender sentiments of friendship and compassion. At the loss of someone close to them they were sometimes utterly disconsolate. And what would they not do to express their grief! But I should like to be able to convey a picture of the reverential surprise and sweet compassion which I saw appear on the faces of those who visited my little chapel in Westport at the sight of Our Lady of Sorrows and of an *Ecce Homo*, especially when the interpreter made them understand that this Head, crowned with thorns, was really that of the Saviour, and that this Heart, pierced by the seven swords, was that of His Mother, and that these ignominies and cruel sufferings had been borne for our sins. As we left the village of the Kansa, we passed over the desolate fields which the United States had cleared, enclosed, and sown for them.

The terrain between Westport and the Platte is one of endless undulations which bear a perfect resemblance to those of the sea when it is agitated by a storm. We found, on the summits of some of them, shells and petrified remains such as are found on some of the mountains of Europe. I have no doubt that sincere geologists would find there, as elsewhere, certain indications of the Deluge. A

facing:
This plan of Westport, Missouri, locates the mission church and the homes of the Catholic residents of the village in 1840. The column at the upper left-hand corner lists the names of twenty-five families. The text of Father Point's journal refers to twenty-three families, the seeming discrepancy probably due to the fact that individual members of certain families— a married son or daughter, perhaps—lived in separate houses. In the few months of the missionary's stay in the little settlement he managed to effect great changes in the moral lives of the people and even to impress the neighboring Indians who came to visit him and to see his chapel.

Plan de Westport (Missouri)

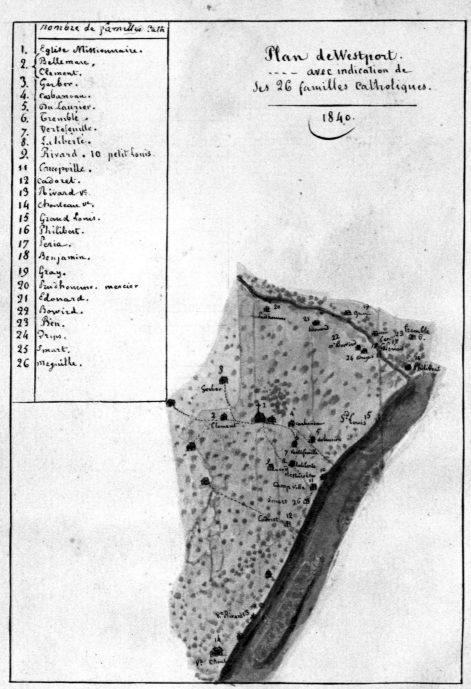

nombre de familles Cath.

1. Eglise Missionnaire.
2. Bellemare, Clement.
3. Gerber.
4. Cabaneau.
5. Du Laurier.
6. Tremblé.
7. Vertefeuille.
8. Laliberté.
9. Rivard. 10 petit Louis.
11. Guespville.
12. Cadoret.
13. Rivard Vve.
14. Chouteau Vve.
15. Grand Louis.
16. Philibert.
17. Peria.
18. Benjamin.
19. Gray.
20. Prudhomme. mercier
21. Edouard.
22. Bowird.
23. Ben.
24. Deps.
25. Smart.
26. meguille.

Plan de Westport.
---- avec indication de
Ses 26 familles Catholiques.

1840.

fragment of stone which I have saved seems to contain some.

As we left Missouri behind and penetrated farther west, the trees became less tall and more sparse and the forests less extensive, because of the smaller amount of water which nourished them. On the banks of rivers there was only a thin fringe of timber growth and rarely anything resembling a full-grown forest. In the vicinity of streams there were only willow thickets. And where water was lacking, one searched in vain for anything except grass. This connection between trees and water was so obvious that our pack animals, after only a week on the plains, would, especially after a long march, become excited and double their speed at the sight of trees in the distance.

After two or three days we observed two Indians to our left. One was draped in an American flag and the other had a scalp attached to his horse's bridle. What we beheld boded nothing good for the fate of our [recent] hosts. But when the captain inquired about the results of their expedition, they informed us that they had not even seen the Kansas and that they were very hungry. We gave them, and about fifteen others who had followed them, something to eat and to smoke. They ate, but they did not smoke and, contrary to the custom of other Indians, who, after one meal, wait for another, they took their leave with an air which seemed to indicate that they were not satisfied. The abruptness of this departure, the rejected calumet, the poor success of their expedition, the proximity of their tribe, their well-known inclination for easy pillage, all combined to convince us that these Indians might attempt something, if not against our persons, then at least against our supplies. But, thanks be to God, our fears were groundless. After their departure, not one returned.

During the first days of June we found ourselves on the banks of a river which, it is said, does not have an equal anywhere in the world. The Indians called it the Nebraska or the River of the Deer. The French *voyageurs* called it the Platte, and Father De Smet, in his first description of the Rocky Mountains, called it "the most marvelous and useful of rivers."

Next to the Missouri, which is for the West what the Mississippi is for the North and South, the most beautiful rivers of this area are the Kansas, the Platte, the Sweetwater, and the Green. The first, which empties directly into the Missouri, is quite remarkable for the large number of its great tributaries. Between the Kansas and the Platte we counted eighteen tributaries, which presupposed a large number of springs and, consequently, a very compact soil. The contrary is true in the vicinity of the Platte. Even on the buttes, which run parallel to the low shore for some distance, there are neither springs nor woods, since the soil, practically all sand, is so porous that water runs to the lower level of the valleys almost as soon as it falls. Hence the neighboring plains are very fertile and especially beautiful in the spring because of the great variety of flowers which grow there. By picking fifteen of each variety, I was able, on the eve of the Feast of the Sacred Heart, to fill an entire basket to honor this great day. The most common of the flowers is the *epinette des prairies*, a small five-petal flower of yellow color.[37] The plains on which they bloom, when seen from a distance, seem to have no green at all; all is a yellow-gold, similar to the color of the narcissus in northern France. Beside *la Cheminee*, the *pricleper* [prickly pear?] together with the *turnsol*, is dominant.[38]

The prettiest of them is the *Cactus Americana*, which had already been domesticated in European flower beds. I never saw anything as pure and vivid as the bloom of this charming flower. All shades of rose and green decorate the exterior of the blossom, which, like that of the lily, widens at the top. The flower, surrounded by a great many thorns, is only two inches from the earth and grows naturally only in the desert. Thus it, more than the rose, could be the symbol of the pleasures of this world. The most elegant flower is something like the European campanula, but surpasses it by the gracefulness of its form and the delicacy of its colors, which vary from pure white to dark blue. The noblest of them, found only on the mountains, is the "Needle of Adam." Its stem is about three feet high. Halfway up the stem begins a pyramid of blossoms matted closely together, shaded lightly with red, and narrowing to a point at the top. Its base is protected by a kind of tough, long and sharp leaf. From the roots can be made soap, often called Mexican soap, and, in times of emergency, this root might also serve as food.

We saw three other remarkable flower varieties, so rare that, even in America, their names were not generally known. The first one, whose bronze leaves are arranged something like the capital of a Corinthian column, we named the *Corinthienne*. The second, something of a straw color, which, because of the arrangement of its stem and branches reminded one of the dream which caused Joseph to be hated by his brothers, we named the Josephine. The third, which had around a yellow disk, shaded in black and red, seven or eight stems of blossoms, each one of which might have been a beautiful flower in itself, was named *la dominicale*, not only because it appeared to us to be the mistress of all the flowers found in the area, but also because it was first found on a Sunday.

The sight of the Platte, always beautiful, is sometimes admirable. In spite of its beauty, the river bore a very common name because the poor *voyageurs*, unable to think of a comparison for something of which they were ignorant, named objects for the first thing which came to mind. This did not prevent such names from being very apt in certain instances. Thus, the river which the Indians called the Nebraska was named the Platte by the French because of its width. In some places it is as much as six thousand feet wide. It is, however, no more than six feet deep and in some places only a foot. Once the deceptive character of the river is recognized, it can be said that there is nothing more gracious or more varied than the perspective it presents, at any rate toward midstream. But aside from prairie flowers, one saw on its banks only a stubble of forest and a few small bushes. Larger vegetation has sought refuge from the autumn fires on the islands which dot the river.

In spite of repeated warnings from the captain, a young man of the party chose to go hunting for buffalo. He fell into the hands of a party of Indians who began by appropriating his gun and horse and ended by responding violently to his remonstrances. Very angry and chagrined by his misadventure, he returned to the camp and gave the cry of alarm. It was toward evening. The campsite had already been chosen and the horses unsaddled when the cry reached our ears. In an instant the horses were rebridled, resaddled, remounted, and ranged in a battle line. It was the colonel who had ordered this maneuver. Women and children were placed between two lines of wagons. The men who were able to bear arms were drawn up on the right and on the left. In the distance one could see various detachments of Indians assembling. The young man wanted to pounce upon the robbers without delay, killing everyone and smashing everything if his property was not returned. Already he had charged with raised gun and at such speed that he failed to notice that his hat blew off. Fortunately, he was pursued by our captain, a man of good sense as well as of spirit, who had a great deal of experience behind him. By great good fortune, he was readily recognized by the Indians because of his white hair. And very soon there was no question of fighting, but only of friendship, provided restitution was made. Our young man learned that, even with the Indians, calm reason accomplishes more than force or anger.

These Indians were Cheyenne in search of adventure.[39] They were reputed to be the bravest Indians on the plains. When they camped about twenty paces from us, we thought only of exchanging tokens of confidence. Lances were planted in the ground; shields were hung on them, and the braves divided into several groups. They conversed, listened, and asked questions, laughed and smoked the calumet in our honor. Generally speaking, the physiognomy of the Cheyennes had about it something less harsh than that of the Kansas. I noticed one whose expression was so gentle and serene that I could detect in it nothing of the savage. As for dress, this was still according to the Indian manner. Their hair was dressed with a sort of red earth; faces were painted blue, red, white, yellow, or even black; garments were decorated with porcupine quills and glass beads; hair was spread fanwise on the shoulders, flat on the brow and hanging in long braids. The head was adorned with two feathers, extending vertically above the eyes. The chief was invited to eat with us, but, in the evening, at our request, he consigned his men to their camp. The next day and for several days after, until we reached the river, they followed us.

You kill a certain number of buffalo, skin them, arrange the skins in the form of a canoe by stretching it over poles, and then seal the openings with the tallow of the animals. You load into this vessel as much as you wish and then, by using a pole or even by getting into the water yourself, you propel it toward the other bank.

This time we came off with less trouble than usual, for our guides had discovered a means of crossing. But it required the most extreme caution, especially with the cattle, which were more difficult to drive than the horses. While the driver lashed away at the beasts from his seat, others, on horseback or wading on foot on either side of the wagon, shouted and whipped them, to keep the vehicle in motion as well as to prevent it from being turned aside. For greater security a number of ropes were tied to the top of the wagon and held taut by men placed at some distance in the river to help preserve equilibrium. The water and the cattle roared, the horses neighed, the men shouted in an earsplitting fashion. I have never heard such an uproar. Nevertheless, strange as it may seem, the crossing was made almost without mishap.

The most sorely inconvenienced members of the expedition were the poor dogs. How they ran to and fro on the bank! How piteously they yelped! Most of them remained on the first bank all night, not daring to swim across. Finally, the example of the more daring ones prompted the others to venture into the treacherous element and with great effort they all had the good fortune to be able to rejoin the camp. What courage can be inspired by the love of the fatherland!

Of all the many knolls to be found in the vicinity of the Platte, the most interesting one was commonly called The Chimney. After this one came The Castle, The Fortress, and so on. They are all, however, much more beautiful from a distance than close at hand.

Everyone has heard of the rattlesnakes and mosquitoes which have been mentioned so frequently in accounts by the first missionaries in America. I will, therefore, mention them only to thank God publicly for the protection he gave us from the former and for the patience he gave us to endure the latter. On the feast of St. Francis Regis, the wagoners, without once leaving the trail, killed a dozen rattlesnakes with their whips.[40] The menacing heads of these reptiles, and their rattling tails always warn one of their hostile intentions. Next to the more destructive winged insects, the small, inoffensive ant is very common. At almost every step, one found anthills of several feet in diameter constructed, not of grain, as in our European fields and gardens, but out of small pebbles. This observation would seem to necessitate a modification of that opinion which holds that ants exercise foresight in storing food and in constructing their dwellings. The grain, which ants collect in Europe, could well serve to feed them during the winter. But does it really serve that purpose as directly as the other? This seems to me scarcely probable, especially since provisions of another nature can be found in their individual cells. At any rate, the wonderful instinct with which God has endowed them for the continual preservation of their species is admirable. Why are these hills composed of tiny globules, and why are the globules arranged in little mounds? Why are the mounds given a specific inclination, and why is the entry always made on the side opposite to the prevailing wind? All of these things point to some kind of wisdom in these tiny heads.

In his account of the missions in Paraguay, Muratori remarks that the hummingbird sings like a nightingale.[41] He professed to be amazed to find that such a tiny body could emit such a surprisingly loud sound. Unless the hummingbirds in South America differ from those I saw, one must hold that only by a kind of analogy did that noted author add pleasing song to the undoubted beauty of the hummingbirds' plumage. This minute *chef-d'oeuvre* of elegance nourishes itself only with the honey it finds in the blossoms of flowers. It draws the honey out by means of its tongue, which it can extend after the manner of bees. While partaking of the honey, the bird stops in flight and appears to be humming as a bee does among flowers. But if one listens intently and looks closely, one discovers that the humming sound comes from the extraordinarily rapid beat of the tiny wings.

Father Point called this his "first sight of the Rocky Mountains."

I do not know how the prairie dog got its name. In shape, size, color, agility, and timidity, it resembles a squirrel more than a dog. Some think it to be a kind of marmot. Each single family of prairie dogs has its own burrow. On the prairies, families are so very numerous that they form villages. These villages differ from those of the beaver in that, instead of being on a stream's bank, they are located as far from water as possible. It is said that the prairie dog feeds only on grass roots and drinks dew. A tradition of travelers in the West, which borders somewhat on the fantastic, has it that the prairie dogs sometimes leave their burrows en masse to form a general assembly. When a prairie dog hears or sees something hostile, it scampers into its burrow and from there gives forth a piercing cry which is repeated from burrow to burrow, putting the entire colony on the alert. Since it is naturally very curious, however, in a few minutes it pokes its nose out of its hole. The hunter chooses that moment to shoot it. This requires a great deal of skill, for the small animal, endowed with great agility and piercing sight, ordinarily does not expose more than the top of its head.

What is said about the strength of the beaver's four small teeth is very true. I have seen trees, more than two feet in diameter, cut in two by these apparently feeble instruments. I do not know if what is said in addition to this is true. Some hold that before felling the trees which are to serve in the construction of their dams they examine, among the trees suitable to this purpose, those which lean toward the spot on which they are to be used. If none of the trees offers this advantage, they wait until a good wind comes to their assistance and, while the wind is bending the tree, set to work and soon have the tree toppling.

There is a kind of frog which differs essentially from those we see in Europe, in that it has a tail and lives in arid places which are stony and hot. I have heard it called a salamander.

On June 28 we left Fort Laramie to continue westward. Before us lay the Black Hills.[42] As we advanced, the shade of the vegetation became increasingly somber, the form of the hills much more rugged, the face of the mountains more towering. The general impression was one not of decay but of age or, rather, of the most venerable antiquity.

The most remarkable landmark in this beautiful solitude is Independence Rock, so-called, not, as would seem to be the case, because of its isolation and the extraordinary strength of its position, but because the Americans who named it arrived in its vicinity on the day on which their separation from Great Britain is celebrated. It is probable that, having thus named the rock, they inscribed their names on it, together with their birthdates. Hence its nickname, "The Great Register of the Wilderness." We ourselves arrived on the morrow of a similar day, that is, on July 5. According to custom, each one of us wrote down his name [on the rock], following the Name one pronounces only with a reverent inclination.

At the foot of this colossus runs the small, peaceful river called the Sweetwater. It is distinguished by its limpidity and its numerous twists, an indication of the evenness of its bed. But higher up, near its source, its aspect is altogether different. There one sees it leaping or, rather, one hears it rushing through a long crevice filled with rocky fragments—a blackish mass and a horrifying sound, which have earned for it the name "Devil's Door." It could have been given a more cheerful name, for if its precipitous passage suggests Hell by the horrors it conceals, it resembles the path of Heaven by the shades of rose and blue it displays from a distance. It was impossible to rest one's gaze on it without thinking of happiness.

Buffalo are so plentiful in the area that a single member of the party killed eleven of them within a few hours, satisfying himself with bringing back only the tongues.

Two long months had passed since our entry into the wilderness, but at last we were arriving, if not at the end of our journey and of the greatest perils, at least at the Rocky Mountains to which our most ardent prayers had so long transported us. A celebration was held in camp in honor of these mountains. Why are they called rocky? Because they are composed of granite and flint. Some travelers have given them the more pompous name of "Backbone of the World" because they are the principal chain which divides the North American continent lengthwise. This great chain is buttressed on the west by the Cordilleras and on the east by the Wind River Range. It was toward mid-July that we crossed the highest ridge of the latter. Behind us we had the tributaries of the Missouri; before us lay the rivers that empty into the Pacific. What a magnificent view! But who could describe the majesty of the wilderness as we then saw it? At this sight, a single need filled our souls, that of exclaiming like the King Prophet, "From the rising of the sun until its setting the name of the Lord is admirable." And we carved into the bark of a cedar which overlooked all this majesty the ever-adorable Name at which every knee in Heaven, on earth, and in Hell bends. May this blessed name be for those who pass after us a sign of hope and salvation!

Descending from these heights, we first followed, and then crossed, Little Sandy Creek and Big Sandy Creek. For three days our column floundered through the sands. There was neither good pasturage for the animals nor game to be shot for the men. We thought about the eleven buffalo tongues at the Sweetwater River.

By July 21 we were on the banks of the Green River. All about us was luxuriantly green; we reveled in the abundance. It was there that, nine years earlier, Captain Bonneville had reached the point beyond which he could not proceed. It was there that we met the vanguard of the Flatheads and also a party of French Canadians returning from California. In response to the question, "What news?," the latter painted a picture so little encouraging that many of our party thought only of taking advantage of the opportunity to turn back.

To the great satisfaction of those who were in need of rest, we remained on this spot for two days. We were able to say Mass, and all who were Catholic assisted most piously. On the day on which our parting took place, two persons who had frequented our bivouac, our hunter and a young Englishman, both came to bid us good-by. The Englishman was a Protestant, but notwithstanding his religious principles, he promised that if Providence should ever bring us together again, he would be happy to show us his gratitude for the services we had rendered him. I have retained this beautiful reflection of his: that one must travel in the wilderness to learn how attentive Providence is to the needs of man. What became of him? I learned that he was able to pass safely through the danger of the return journey, but that his companion, without having had time to repent, was killed by an Indian woman who was an enemy of his family.

As for the travelers returning from California, many acknowledged that they had more than one duty to fulfill, and all promised to fulfill them—but next year. Unfortunately for most of them next year never came. Two weeks had not passed before they were attacked and killed, some by Sioux, others by Arapahoes and Cheyennes. Among them was the greatest blasphemer of the party. Their leader had been one of the first to fall, struck by a stray bullet. He had made his fortune and had anticipated spending his remaining years resting from his adventures. In all matters one should profit by favorable opportunities.

Meanwhile our column was winding its way through a labyrinth of mountains. Once, when we had traveled from sunrise to sunset only to end up in a blind alley, we had to retrace our steps, surrounded by Indians seeking to kill and plunder. On August 10, after a long march across an open plain, we arrived, by skirting Bear River, at the most beautiful campsite that we had seen. Limpid springs, refreshing fruits,

game in great abundance, the most varied and picturesque views, all seemed to invite travelers to make this their winter quarters. There were some who thought seriously of doing this, but not all deemed it advisable. Since the small size of the group would not make a safe stay here possible, the march was resumed through a narrow pass which opened out into a plain stretching as far as eye could see.

It was there that the missionaries left the rest of the group, turning off to the right, while the Americans bore off to the left. We had lived together for three months amidst the same perils and were as of one fatherland. Farewells were sad. Many prejudices had disappeared during the journey. But, since most of them seemed firmly attached to error, there seemed little hope that we should see each other in the true fatherland.

During the following three days we had to march until nightfall to find spots suitable for for camping. On the evening of the third day we were still marching, having already spent eleven hours on foot. We were advancing toward the end of a narrow pass which seemed destined to be the end of the world for us. To the right and left towering mountain peaks arose. Before us there was an opening, for a river ran in that direction. But the gorge seemed so narrow and the river so swift that it appeared wellnigh impossible to drive our wagons through. Nevertheless, our competent driver, refusing to retreat before any obstacle until it was proven insurmountable, stopped the wagons while he went ahead to explore. Between the shoulder of the rugged mountain and the bank of the torrential river there was barely enough space to keep us from falling. An hour later we were only a few miles from Fort Hall, giving thanks to God for the constant protection He had graciously accorded us.[43]

jour de l'assomption de la T. S. Vierge vers le coucher du Soleil, par le plus beau temps du monde, et tous pleins de
et de santé, nous arrivames au fort Hall, où nous fumes reçus en amis par le Capitaine Hermetinger. Quoique protes-
ce brave écossais ajouta aux mille services qu'il nous rendit la promesse, de nous recommander à tous les forts ou maisons
de traite de sa compagnie. Nous retrouvames là le R. P. de Smet, arrivé de la veille, il étoit au comble de la joie, car il
voit nous présenter l'avant garde de nos futurs neophites; sous quels plus heureux auspices pouvoit-on se rencontrer! aussi
la joie de se revoir fut elle de part et d'autre profondément sentie. Celle du Tête-plate est peu demonstrative, mais à la ma-
affectueuse dont ils nous serroient la main, il étoit facile de sentir que leurs coeurs étoient contents. que n'avoient ils pas fait pour
tenir des Robes-noirs! que d'instances! que de voyages! que de sacrifices! ils nous voyoient enfin, et avec les secours, dont
jusqu'alors ils n'avoient eu que l'esperance, aussi ne sachant comment exprimer leur bonheur, ils gardoient le silence; silen-
purement qui ne venoit ni d'un défaut de coeur, ni d'un manque d'esprit; Les Têtes-plates concoivent et sentent vivemen
ceux là étoient des hommes d'élite. Je ne suis qu'un ignorant et un méchant disoit le chef de la députation, cependan
Je remercie de tout mon coeur le Grand Esprit de ce qu'il a fait pour moi; je ne veux plus vivre que pour prier, je pr
rai jusqu'à sa mort. Ce chef s'appelloit Oulstilpo. Voyez son portrait N° et sa biographie avec celle de ses compa
Ils nous apprirent que depuis le départ du P. de Smet les Têtes plates n'avoient cessé de prier pour son heureux re
que leurs freres étoit toujours dans les mêmes dispositions. que la plupart savoient par coeur les prières, qu'on l
avoient enseignées; que deux fois les jours ordinaires, et trois fois le dimanche, la peuplade faisoit la prière en commun
que cinq ou six enfants baptisés étoient partis pour le ciel, qu'une petite fille de 12 ans, se voyant sur le point de mo
avoit demandé le baptême, que Pierre l'iroquois l'avoit baptisée sous le nom de Marie et qu'au moment de sa mort elle a
éta Oh! que c'est beau, je vois Marie ma mère. Voyez page

avertissement Dans l'explication des vignettes qui suivent jusqu'à sa page on reconnoitra ce qui a été publié p
R. P. De Smet, ce qui n'est pas étonnant, vu que les écrits du célèbre missionnaire qui se rapportent à la 1ʳᵉ année
reduction des Têtes-plates procédent de la même source que les lignes que nous écrivons ici; un journal de la mi
Quant aux variantes et aux erreurs qui s'y sont glissées, elles sont le fait des copistes ou des traducteurs, le P. De Smet
ayant pas toujours eu le loisir de revoir les épreuves.

II

The Flatheads, the Coeur d'Alenes, and the Blackfeet

This is Father Point's own record of his work in evangelizing the Flatheads, partly at St. Mary's mission, and partly during a winter hunt. In October, 1842, he left them to open the mission of the Sacred Heart among the Coeur d'Alenes. Though this tribe, a rather unprepossessing lot, were "inclined to everything base," he found a few of them to be staunch characters. Even for the "bloody Blackfeet," whom he visited in October, 1846, he finds some extenuation.

THE FLATHEADS

ON THE FEAST of the Assumption [August 15], toward evening, we arrived at Fort Hall, where we were cordially received by Captain Aermetinger.[44] Though a Protestant, this worthy Scot, besides the many other useful services which he

facing:
The missionaries, on arrival at Fort Hall on August 15, 1841, were joyfully greeted by an advance party sent to escort them to Flathead country. Below is a reproduction of a page of the journal text.

rendered us, promised us that he would strongly recommend us to all the forts and trading posts of his company. We found Father De Smet at Fort Hall, where he had arrived the evening before. He was overjoyed to present us to the vanguard of our future neophytes. Under what more auspicious circumstances could we have met? There was mutual and profound joy at this encounter with one another. Though the Flatheads were less demonstrative at the meeting, it was easy to tell, from their manner of shaking hands, that they were, indeed, delighted. What had they not done to procure the services of the

Blackrobes! What distances they had traveled! What sacrifices they had made! We were among them, at last, to bring them the "prayer" they had so ardently desired. Not knowing how to express their happiness, they maintained silence; a silence which assuredly did not spring from lack of heart or of spirit. Flatheads have vivid imaginations and intense feelings, and these, before us, were the elite.

"I am only an evil and ignorant man," said the leader of the delegation, "but I thank the Great Spirit, with all my heart, for all He has done for me. I earnestly wish to live now only to pray. I shall pray until my death."

This man's name was Oulstilpo. These men informed us that, since the departure of Father De Smet, the Flatheads had not ceased to pray for his happy and safe return. Their brothers were still of the same mind, and most of them knew by heart all the prayers they had been taught. They said, further, that the tribe joined in common prayers twice on ordinary days and twice on Sundays. Five or six of the children who received baptism had departed for Heaven; and a girl of twelve years, seeing herself on the point of death, had asked to be baptized. Pierre, the Iroquois, had baptized her, giving her the name of Mary. At the moment she died, this girl said, "Oh, how beautiful! I see Mary, my Mother."

Leaving Fort Hall on August 18, the first step we took under the guidance of our good friends almost ended tragically, but by the grace of God, it only gave us further proof of their devotion to us. During the crossing of the swiftly running Snake River, one of our lay brothers, unable to manage the mules at that point, was carried to a spot so deep that the entire wagon might have been submerged. This would have been the end of the driver if our courageous Flatheads had not immediately plunged into the water and kept the wagon afloat. In spite of all their effort, three mules were drowned and one of our brothers who, to avoid shipwreck, had taken refuge at the bottom of his wagon, would have met the same fate, had it not been for the levelheadedness of our hunter, who, at the risk of losing his life, rode out to him and let him get a hold on his mount. The brave Sepelchimean, the best swimmer in the group, worked so hard to save the treasures

of our chapel that, when he reached shore, he collapsed from exhaustion. Fortunately, his strength did not abandon him before all had been brought to safety. On this day, as a result of certain difficulties which we had not anticipated, we had set out without the customary recitation of the *Itinerarium*.[45] After this telling lesson, we never again failed to do so.

Some days later, we perceived a group of Indians a short distance off. A cry arose: "The Blackfeet, the Blackfeet!" Two of the Flatheads seized their arms, mounted their horses, and rode off at full gallop to reconnoiter.

An hour later they reappeared at the head of a group of twelve Indians armed for war. They were not Blackfeet, but members of a tribe still more to be feared, in view of the fact that recently they had violated the rules of hospitality toward nine Flatheads who escaped being killed only by fighting off the entire village. For this crime, the brother of their chief had been killed by a Flathead chief named Michael, who now found himself face to face with the treacherous chief himself. But this was not the time to ask him the reason for his conduct. The Bannock were received as friends, though the Flatheads did not wish to smoke with them.[46] Two or three days later, the camp, of which this group had been only scouts, joined them. We profited by the occasion to make them see that the spirit of vengeance was not that of the true "prayer," as the Flatheads called religion.

On the second Sunday after the Assumption, the day on which the Church celebrates the Feast of the Immaculate Heart of Mary, our little vanguard consecrated itself to this Heart, so pure, so tender, and so generous, which had already been for them a source of grace, and which would become, for the entire tribe, a still more abundant source of blessing and consolation.

The evening of this day was remarkable for the great quantity of fish which we caught on lines in a small river running on the left side of the altar. In less than an hour we caught more than a hundred. The best catch—one which seems hardly probable, but, nevertheless, is actually quite true—was two fish on a single hook. This seemed prophetic, considering what was to come very shortly. One must have traveled a long time in the wilderness, exposed to privation and danger, to understand the joy which spreads through the heart of a missionary at even the slightest occurrence which bears relation to his ministry.

On August 30, after having picked our twisting way through a long mountain gorge to which we gave the name *Defile des Pères*, we emerged onto a broad plain and saw, on the horizon toward the west, the camp of the Flatheads. As we drew closer, we saw a succession of outriders coming from the camp. Titiche Loutso presented himself. He was distinguished from the others by a long red ribbon which almost gave him the appearance of a Marshal of France. As a warrior, he was certainly one of the handsomest men in the Rocky Mountains. In proof of his respectful attachment to the superior of the mission, he had sent his best horse and had forbidden anyone to mount it before its delivery. A short time later we saw a tall Indian running toward us at full speed, crying, "Paul! Paul!" And it was indeed Paul, the guide of the camp. Paul, one of three adults who had been baptized the year before, we had thought was absent. But now, by a singular disposition of Providence, he had arrived and would have the pleasure of himself presenting to his tribe those who had come to devote themselves to its happiness.

Toward sunset Father De Smet and his companions were surrounded by their dear converts. Among the children, the youths, the old men, the middle-aged ones, the mothers carrying their tiniest infants, it was a question of who would get to shake hands with us first. They all seemed to be of one heart and one soul. By sunset this scene had something moving and magic about it. Only a mother knows what she feels at the return of a long-absent son. Does she know what a missionary experiences when he sees himself, for the first time, surrounded by a numerous family, whose members he has never seen before, but who are, nevertheless, completely devoted to him?

Since it was already September, it was important to choose, before winter, a site for the future reduction, where temporary shelters could be erected, and to construct, as all fervently desired, a house of prayer. If all this were to be accomplished, no time could be lost.[47]

Therefore, we resumed our way, guided by the small group which had been our escort until then.

On September 24, we emerged from the gorge called Hell Gate onto a broad plain, bordered on the north by the country of the Pend d'Oreilles and on the west by that of the Coeur d'Alenes. But finding nothing there to suit our purpose, we turned south through a gorge, at first narrow, but then ever widening. A day later, the third day of our search, we had still found nothing by evening. But arriving at the foot of the largest mountain in the vicinity, we were agreeably surprised at the richness of the vegetation stretched out before us. This luxuriance was due to two streams running north. This large valley, protected against the Blackfeet on the south by a chain of mountains, was sheltered from the rigors of the north by another chain of mountains on whose slopes grew forests, so necessary as a source of construction materials. Between these two ranges ran the river of the Flatheads, called the Bitter Root River. Everyone thought we would be able to find nothing better anywhere else. It was there that we pitched our tents, intending to lay the foundations for our future reduction, which we began by erecting a large cross. I shall always remember the worthy old man Simon, who, in spite of the weight of years, had come to meet us at Fort Hall. While the cross was being hewn, he was seated on the trunk of a tree, obliged to support himself with his stick as a result of the fatigue caused by our last short march. His eyes were fixed on the Tree which saves the world, and which would soon open to him the true fatherland. Seeing him, it was easy to divine to what he had attached his heart. He was, I believe, the first to be buried in the shadow of this cross, after having given, during the little time remaining to him, every sign of being a fervent Christian.

What should be the name of this first reduction in the Rocky Mountains? It was recalled that almost all the principal events in our long voyage had coincided with some Feast of the Blessed Virgin. This was an inspiration to everyone and, in one voice, we said, "It will be called St. Mary's." We shall see that the Divine Mother did not leave this manifestation of devotion unanswered. May the memory of Her

Domine

Salva nos perimus

Dévouement d'un Tête-plate et d'un métis pour sauver un de nos frères

Partis du Fort Hall le 18 août, le premier pas que nous fîmes sous la conduite de nos meilleurs amis, faillit nous êt[re] funeste; mais graces à Dieu, il ne nous donna qu'une preuve de plus de leur dévouement à notre égard — En passage d'une rivière fort rapide (La rivière aux Serpens) un de nos frères ne pouvant plus guider ses mullets fut entraîné dans [un] endroit si profond que tout l'équipage eut de l'eau par-dessus la tête. c'en était fait de leur conducteur si nos courageux Tê[tes-] plates ne le fussent immédiatement jetés à la nage pour tenir à flot la nouvelle gondole malgré tout leur effort [trois] mullets furent noyés et l'un de nos frères qui pour éviter le naufrage s'était réfugié au fond des sa charrette eut le même sor[t] sans le sang froid de notre Chasseur qui au péril de sa vie alla lui présenter la croupe de la monture. Pour sauver le butin qui renfermait toutes les richesses de notre chapelle, le brave Sepelchimean qui était le plus fort nageur fit tant de ses pi[eds] et de ses mains qu'à peine qu'il toucha le rivage il tomba d'épuisement Heureusement quand ses forces l'abandonnèrent le tout [était] en sûreté. Ce jour là à cause de certains embarras que nous n'avions pas prévus, nous nous étions mis en route contre no[tre] coutume sans avoir récité l'itinéraire — depuis cette bonne leçon, nous n'y manquâmes plus

Quelques jours après on apperçoit des Sauvages à peu de distance, on s'écrie: les Pieds-noirs! les Pieds-noi[rs]
à ce cri deux Têtes plates saisissent leur arme, montent à cheval, et partent au grand galop pour aller reconnaître l'en[ne-]
mi — au bout d'une heure ils reparurent à la tête d'une douzaine de Sauvages armés en guerre ce n'étaient pas
des Pieds-noirs mais une espèce de gens plus à craindre encore vu que tout récemment, ils avaient violé l'hospitalité à l'égard
de neuf Têtes plates qui n'échappèrent au massacre qu'en se défendant contre un village entier ...... Dans cette circonstance le
frère du chef fut tué par un chef Tête-plate nommé Michel, et Michel se retrouvait en face du Chef de la trahison ...
... mais ce n'était pas le moment de lui demander raison de sa conduite ... Les Banacks furent reçus comme des amis; espen[dant]
les Têtes plates ne voulurent pas fumer avec eux. — Deux ou trois jours après le Camp dont ceux ci n'étaient que les éclaireu[rs]
se joignit aux nôtres ... Nous en profitâmes comme nous devions pour leur faire voir que l'esprit de vengeance n'était pa[s]
celui de la vraie prière (Religion)

The sacrament of baptism was administered to the Flatheads for the first
time on December 3, 1841. The Latin text above the chapel in the illustration is translated:
"May all things be made new"; that framing the Indian gathering reads:
"Thou shalt cleanse me and I shall be whiter than snow."

facing:
The heroic efforts of courageous Flatheads saved one of the lay
brothers from death by drowning when his wagon was almost submerged
in a swift-running river. The Latin text within the picture reads: "Lord, save us; we perish."
The journal text of the page on which the illustration
was mounted is also reproduced here.

blessings live forever in the hearts of Her new children.

When the hunters returned from their summer hunt, the cross was already elevated above the site of their future reduction, and their chapel was also rising. At the sight of the work going on, which had for the Indians all the interest of a novelty, and which promised so much for their future, there was a universal joy in the camp. Everyone gave his warmest and heartiest approval, especially to the choice of site. For it was then that they remembered a prophecy made some months before by the young child who died after having been baptized. It was Pierre, the Iroquois, who first remarked to those who, at that moment, were gathered about him, "Do you remember what little Mary said just before her death?"

"Perfectly," they replied.

Although still very young, this child had, during Father De Smet's first stay in the Rocky Mountains, heard enough about our sacred religion to desire baptism before she died. Having fallen ill and knowing that her death was near, she had Pierre, the Iroquois, come to her and said to him, "I am going to die. I want to be baptized." Having instructed her as well as he could, Pierre baptized her, giving her as patron the Queen of Heaven. As for her, believing as she did with a firm faith that death would open Heaven to her, she did not fear the approach of death, but rather rejoiced because of it. She prayed and sang with such fervor that her diminutive voice dominated all the others. Finally, as if in ecstasy, she cried, "Mary! Oh, how beautiful! I see Mary!" A short time later she added, "I am returning to tell you that those for whom you wait are the true Blackrobes. You must listen to what they say." Indicating with her hand the spot where the cross was later to be erected, she said that on that site would be built the house of prayer. Then she expired.

The enemy of God and of men had not viewed with pleasure the approach of so great a day, and God permitted him to try us. To mention these tests in only a word, the men whose help was most valuable to us under the circumstances fell ill. These were the interpreter, the prefect of the church, and the sacristan. On the very eve of the feast, a hurricane discharged its fury on the area and even upon the church itself. The windows of the church were blown in; three cabins became the plaything of the winds; and huge trees were blown down. But by the grace of God and through the fervor of these new children of the faith, nothing could prevent their little sanctuary from being adorned in the very best manner. The moment which seemed about to end in grief became instead a moment of glorification.

On December 3, the Feast of Saint Francis Xavier, 202 catechumens were gathered in the nave of the chapel to receive holy baptism. They had been sufficiently well instructed and could answer intelligibly all the questions put by the priest. I shall never forget the tone of these answers. Except for time taken for dinner, the ceremony lasted from six o'clock in the morning until nine o'clock in the evening. It was noticed that the Great Chief, who had been baptized two years earlier and who was almost a nonagenarian, wished to be present from the beginning to the end of the ceremony. What was still

more remarkable was the apparition of St. Francis Xavier seen by a catechumen of the tribe of the Crees, a man named Michael.[48] The event was related by him with such simplicity that it was impossible to be at all suspicious of deceit. The person, so said the Indian, was standing, elevated above the earth to the height of the altar on the epistle side, and was wearing over his cassock a surplice and a stole, and had on his head a hat such as the Fathers wore.

Hardly out of his infancy, a little Flathead of an angelic beauty, sweetness, and piety was most desirous of being baptized, but had such a poor memory that, in spite of all his efforts, he had been unable to learn what was rigorously required for the reception of this favor. And the second administration of the sacrament was to take place the following day, that was Christmas Day. This pious child said to himself, "I shall go to find Jean. Perhaps he will be able to teach me what I must know."

He rose, went into Jean's wigwam, and a few minutes later emerged in perfect command of the prayers. But it was neither Jean, Jean's brother nor Jean's mother, who had taught him, for they were no better instructed than the others. He had a teacher greater than all the instructors in the world, the Queen of Heaven herself. Here is the story, as the child repeated it on several occasions, without ever once contradicting himself:

"The moment I entered Jean's wigwam, I saw, above the fireplace, a very beautiful person. I do not know whether it was a man or a woman, for the person wore garments such as I had never seen before. Beneath the feet of this person there was a snake, and, beside the snake, a kind of fruit I had not seen before. Around this person, there was a very bright light. The person looked at me in a kindly manner, and in that instant my mind became clear, my heart became warm. I have no idea how all of this came about, but suddenly I knew my prayers. Then the person disappeared. This person told me that she was happy that our village had chosen to be called the name St. Mary's."

The veracity of the child's story is attested by the incontrovertible fact that, when he returned to his own wigwam, he could recite all the prayers with the greatest ease. Needless to say, on Christmas Day, he was admitted to the sacrament without difficulty. The child received the name of Paul at his baptism. He was called Little Paul, to distinguish him from Great Paul, who was known also as the Great Face.

We may recount here the edifying death of Pierre, the first baptized great chief of the Flatheads. It can be truthfully said that his death was like the evening of a beautiful day. Even before his baptism, while still a pagan, he never acted contrary to what he considered to be good. At his baptism, he said, "When I did what was wrong, it was because I was in error." And when this man, so righteous in all vicissitudes of life, arrived at the end of his glorious career, at the invitation extended to him to confess the sins he had committed since his baptism, he responded in a kind of astonishment, "Sins since my baptism! How could I have committed any, I who daily besought my children to refrain from sin." He received the last rites in full possession of his faculties and in the most edifying of dispositions. As he had requested, he was wrapped in the prayer flag, that is, in the flag which was raised every Sunday to announce the Day of the Lord, and his mortal remains were interred at the foot of the cross which had been erected the day the Flatheads took possession of this land in the name of the Saviour of men. Near this grave, thus guarded, were interred, during the following few months, the remains of six or seven others who had died at various ages.

In December, the Indians departed for the winter hunt. Preparations had begun the previous evening, but it was late afternoon before they started. Since these hunts were long affairs, the hunters took with them everything they possessed. Each wigwam counted usually seven or eight persons, and these, together with their provisions, required the use of about twenty horses. Some fifteen parallel trails, formed by dragging wigwam poles, wound between two chains of mountains which sometimes drew together to offer at close range a view of what was most majestic about the wilderness, sometimes separated to reveal a series of infinitely varied and distant perspectives. This is what was called the great hunting trail.

This hunt, following as it did immediately upon the reception of baptism by almost the entire tribe, was distinguished from others by the piety with which it was conducted. Thus, from the first evening the chiefs assembled for prayer asked that the expedition be dedicated to Mary. It was accordingly agreed that twice a day all would assemble for prayers. After prayers, they would hear an instruction, preceded and followed by hymns. Every morning, at sunrise, before leaving for the hunt, and every evening, before retiring, they would recite the Angelic Salutation three times, together with their families.[49] And, finally, it was decided that on Sundays and feast days there would be religious services, as circumstances permitted. There was no mention made of superogatory prayers, which each one was free to multiply and prolong according to his own devotion.

The great buffalo hunt offers many scenes, one more extraordinary than another. (The illustration on page x represents only one such scene.) These, according to the Indians, are the most remarkable events on a hunt; that is, the most tragic or the most comic. Not all the events depicted took place on the same day, but they did occur during the same winter hunt. Those which brought the greatest success are associated with religious circumstances.

The nomadic life of our neophytes was not without its attractions. But it was full of perils because it took them into enemy territory, and it was fraught with inconveniences because of the hardships imposed on the aged and the very young, who had to be carried from place to place. It was also dangerous to the morals of the Flatheads, since it brought them into contact with strangers unsympathetic to religion. A third danger arose from the Indian's rapid transition from dire poverty to great abundance. Therefore, it was our first concern to introduce them, little by little, to a much more sedentary existence. This could be done only by substituting the fruits of agriculture for those of the chase, the innocent pleasures of the fireside for those offered by the varied life of a hunter. Above all, religion had to assume an important position in their lives. Hence, the construction of a chapel first; then the cultivation of fields.

Consécration
au cœur immaculé
de Marie

Le second dimanche après l'assomption, jour où l'église célèbre la fête du cœur immaculé de Marie, notre petite avant garde se consacre à ce cœur si pur, si tendre, et si généreux, qui a déjà été pour eux une source de grâces, et qui deviendra pour toute la peuplade une source plus abondante encore de bénédictions et de consolations ___ La veille de ce jour fut remarquable par la grande quantité de poissons, que nous prîmes à la ligne, dans ce petite rivière, qui coulait du côté de l'évangile ___ En moins d'une heure nous en prîmes plus d'un cent. le plus beau coup, et le moins vraisemblable quoiqu'il soit vrai, est celui où un seul amorçon en prit deux à la fois ___ C'était comme une prédiction de ce qui devait arriver sous peu ___ il faut avoir longtemps voyagé dans le désert au milieu des privations et des périls pour comprendre la joie que répand dans le cœur du missionnaire les moindres traits qui font allusion à son ministère.

NOTRE DAME DE LA PRIERE

The brightly illuminated wigwam in the center of the picture above indicates where Little Paul saw the vision of the Blessed Virgin. The Latin inscription translates as "Our Lady of Prayer."

facing:
In words and in color Father Point records the consecration of his little group to the Immaculate Heart of Mary. The symbolic pen-and-ink sketch at the bottom of the page shows a little girl's Guardian Angel leading her away from sin, portrayed as a serpent.

Early in the spring, we began to put our plans into practice. The first great feast, Christmas, had been celebrated before the winter hunt. The first great feast after the winter was that of Easter. During the three months of the winter hunt, while the Indians were storing their victuals, those at the mission, assisted by our brothers, had begun to make a farm and even to lay out a village, surrounding the area with a strong enclosure. One may well imagine the great satisfaction felt, on the evening before Easter, when everyone assembled in the chapel, for the first time, to sing the *Regina coeli*.[50]

With the approach of the Easter season there arose the necessity of fulfilling an important obligation.[51] Considering the excellent disposition of our neophytes, this would not be a difficult matter. Except for those who had died during the winter, no one had as yet received Holy Communion; nor had anyone since his baptism received the sacrament of penance. Hence, all were obliged to prepare themselves to receive two new sacraments. More instructions were, accordingly, given, and we witnessed a renewal of the fervor and assiduity which the Flatheads had manifested in preparing for baptism.

It may be said that this month was observed with as much ceremony and in as edifying a manner as is witnessed in the most fervent parishes of Europe. During the singing, all the voices did not always harmonize, but there was, nevertheless, always one heart and one soul in the three services held daily in the chapel. At the end of the month, a small wooden statue of Our Lady, made by one of the missionaries, was carried in triumph by the tribe to the very place where their patron had appeared. Needless to say, after Our Lady, the person present who received the most attention was the one to whom Mary had deigned to appear. After the erection of the little monument, there was established a kind of pilgrimage in the name of Our Lady of Peace. Thereafter, no one passed that way without saying an Ave Maria. And every evening, everyone knelt to recite three Ave Marias.

Occupied as we had been during the winter hunt in preparing for baptism certain members of other tribes, who had followed us in the hope of sharing the happiness of the Flatheads, it had been impossible to prepare the latter sufficiently well to receive the sacraments of penance and Holy Eucharist. When all had returned to St. Mary's, the occasion was very favorable, since provisions had been stored up in sufficient quantity to feed the people until the summer hunt, which would not take place until July. Everyone devoted himself to his new instructions with fervor, all the more because reception of baptism had made obligatory the performance of the Easter duty. But the grace of baptism had been so abundant in all cases that this new task was a pleasure more than anything else. Sincere submission of spirit and heart to the new mysteries they had to believe, and to the practices, came so easily to them that when they were asked whether they believed this or that truth, their answer was, "Yes, Father, we believe that firmly." And when the question of confession arose, many wished that it might be public.

Pentecost Sunday of 1842 was the most beautiful day that had ever shone on the village of St. Mary's, for on this day its elite received, for the first time, the Bread of Angels. Apart from the moment when they actually received the sacrament, the most impressive one was, perhaps, when the missionaries, dressed in surplices, came to meet them. With the crucifix leading the procession, and with all that might solemnize the ceremony, they assembled, before proceeding to the chapel. The silence was so profound, their meditation so deeply religious, and their pace so solemn, that it was impossible not to be very deeply moved.

For lack of a monstrance, it had been impossible to hold a Procession of the Blessed Sacrament on the Feast of Corpus Christi, but by the time the Feast of the Sacred Heart arrived, this obstacle had been removed by the industry of one of the missionaries. Despite our poverty, the procession was magnificent; in harmony, at least, with the spirit of the Indians, which one of our great writers has called "simple and pompous." An outdoor altar, adorned with fresh greenery and flowers, was erected on the spot where stood the monument commemorating the appearance of the Blessed Virgin. There, under the eyes of its august patron, the tribe, for the first time, received the Benediction of the Blessed Sacrament, a privilege it enjoyed thereafter every Sunday after Vespers. The practice of devotion to the Sacred Heart was already familiar to many. To increase this devotion, as well as the devotion to the Immaculate Heart of Mary, we founded four societies in which the best from among the fathers and mothers and from among the young people of both sexes were soon enrolled. The great chief of the tribe was the prefect of the Society of the Sacred Heart; his wife was the president of the Society of the Immaculate Heart of Mary and their children were at the head of the other societies. All were elected by majority vote. Proof that merit alone was the determining factor in the elections is the fact that the head of the men's society also became grand chief, succeeding the one who had died the preceding winter. Would that in civilized societies all elections could be made in this manner!

The first desire expressed by the Flatheads, after their baptism in the winter, had been to have one of the three missionaries with them during the hunt which followed.[52] After what had been done with so much devotion on their return to St. Mary's, could it indeed be otherwise? The same missionary was commissioned to accompany them again. But since his own mount had been left dying from overwork in the Blackfoot country, another, and much better one, was placed at his disposal. While they were preparing to leave for the summer hunt, a large deputation of Blackfeet returned the abandoned horse to the missionary. This was remarkable, for it was, perhaps, the first time the Blackfeet had made restitution of anything. They offered, in the name of their chief, to return the horse on condition that the owner accompany them into their camp, which was located not far away. Since the Flathead party was to leave on the hunting expedition the next day, he was unable to accede to their desires. Nevertheless the horse was brought to St. Mary's some time later. When it beheld its master, the poor animal came galloping and prancing, as if to say that they were both very happy to see each other. After this, who could still say that animals are mere machines?

The summer hunt was more like a pious pilgrimage than a hunt of the ordinary kind, for it was, indeed, singular in all respects. To show how piously the Indians lived, attention may be drawn to the numerous communicants each Sunday. On the Feast of St. Ignatius, July 31, the chiefs and the elite of the braves were the first at the Communion rail. At the end of the hunt, an old woman was the only one who had not gone to confession. But Heaven, no doubt wishing to make an example, permitted the old woman to suffer a fall from her horse when it failed to halt in the descent of a mountain slope. She fell only a few steps from the confessor and suffered a broken leg. This so opened her eyes to her fault in not following the example of the rest that, on the spot, before rising, she wanted to go to confession. The last day of the hunt, after eleven hours of traveling across the mountains, there were confessions which lasted a great part of the night. On the following day, Communion was distributed.

THE COEUR D'ALENES

TOWARD THE END of October, 1842, Father Point departed from St. Mary's for the mission of the Coeur d'Alenes, accompanied by three chiefs and several members of that tribe.[53] Arriving at the plain called Hell Gate, he sent people to procure some domestic animals for the new mission. In the interval, he baptized a half-breed woman who had been instructed by Louis Brown. This young Canadian showed an inclination to accompany the missionary, under an arrangement which involved very little expense. He was, therefore, taken along, because he combined religious zeal with some knowledge of agricultural matters. With this re-enforcement, and a half-breed Indian interpreter who spoke Flathead and Nez Percé, the little expedition pushed their way into the somber gorge which separated them from their destination. For ten days, the group wound their way through dense forests, across the sides of mountains, and sometimes through the current of a river so tortuous that, in less than eight hours, they were obliged to cross it forty-four times.

The protection of Heaven saved our horses from many a tumble, and our packs from many a soaking. The little company finally arrived in the territory of the Coeur d'Alenes without mishap. The date was Friday, the fourth of November. Since the first Friday of every month is especially consecrated to devotion to the Sacred Heart, and, since the mission which was about to open had already been placed under the powerful protection of the Sacred Heart, it would seem superfluous to note that on dismounting from our horses, our first act was to renew that consecration. Hearing these poor converts expressing their sentiments and mingling their voices with the voices of those who had come to their aid, one would have said that the presence of their Divine Protector was already revealing itself in a perceptible manner.

What profound misery reigned among these poor people! What poor huts of straw and bark! Around them was the smell of animals, the remains of fish, and other filth of all kinds. Inside the huts bundles of roots were thrown in

top row:

Young Ignatius, an Iroquois,
staunch friend of the Flatheads, for whom he
helped to obtain missionaries.

Francis Oulstilpo, the Flathead
chief who escorted the missionaries from Fort
Hall to the Flathead country.

Adolphe, or Red Feather,
a capable young Flathead chief.

Moses Titiche Loutso,
considered the bravest Indian in
the Rocky Mountain country.

bottom row:

Victor, the Great Chief of the Flatheads.

Michel Ensila, called Little Chief.

Joseph Pepelchimo,
a young warrior with a reputation
for outstanding courage.

a corner, skins of animals hung from a pole, and fish were being smoked over a fire. What about the people? Dirty faces, hair in disorder, hands serving as comb, handkerchief, knife, fork, and spoon. While eating, foul sounds came from the nose, the throat, from the mouth; in fact, from any part of the body capable of producing them. This gives some idea of the visible squalor, but it is a feeble image of the pitiful state of their souls. For even at this time there still prevailed an idolatry which went so far as to render homage to the vilest of animals. There was a shamelessness of habit which knew no check other than caprice or passion. There was an addiction to gambling which absorbed even the time needed for sleep. They emerged from their sloth only when the pangs of hunger made themselves felt. Finally, there was a constant inclination to dissimulation, to gluttony, to everything base. These formed a part of the spiritual misery in which the Coeur d'Alenes had stagnated until now. Fortunately, even at the bottom of this abyss, an indefinable need to have recourse to a higher power had always made them attentive to the slightest word which might teach them something.

Seeing these poor creatures inhabiting a country whose capacity to produce a hundredfold required only the sweat of their brows, it was not difficult for me to assign the real reason for their misery. The goal to which our efforts must point was, therefore, to instruct them and teach them to enjoy work through help, encouragement, and recompense. To accomplish all this, we had to gather in one place the widely scattered families, that is, establish what our Fathers used to call a reduction. But to unite a people scattered over twenty-seven different points, to make reason dominate the tribal instinct so strong among the Indians, to prod into action an inveterate laziness, to satisfy an almost insatiable appetite—all these, without counting the redoubled efforts of Hell which would have to be overcome, were so many obstacles to the forming of a community. Nevertheless, because the chiefs could not overlook the fact that all their interests hinged on this plan, they agreed on one point, namely, that without favoring any one person it was necessary to select a site which would be most advantageous for everybody. Only five locations

were worthy of consideration. On the first one there was an abundance of wood, good soil, and plenty of water, but because of the annual spring floods it was impossible to find a place where anything could be built to advantage.

On the second site there were well-wooded mountains, fertile valleys, and a large field of camass. At either extremity of the plain was a lake on which large numbers of water fowl congregated. To the south was a gentle slope— the only suitable building site for a village, but it offered neither spring nor fertile soil. And besides the river was a great distance away. Though nothing was decided, the old chief there received us hospitably and, although the sun was about to set, gave orders to two of his men to fetch the chiefs of the Grand Lake.[54]

While awaiting the arrival of these chiefs, we went to visit a fourth chief, called Gabriel.[55] His land was nine or ten miles away, separated from us by a mass of mountains. The only means of communication between the two places was a pathway so rough and tortuous that at first it seemed the new site would be no better than the others. But when we arrived at a point from which we could behold all the beauties and advantages of this area, we were very agreeably surprised. Imagine to the south a horizon of mountains, even the lowest of which reaches into the clouds; to the east, distances which blend into the blue of the sky; to the west, waters losing themselves at two points in somber mountain gorges; in front of us, a river whose steep bank formed a peninsula sufficiently extensive to serve for the establishment of a farm. Between the river and the elevation on which we stood jagged rocks formed a grotto covered with greenery. Great stones stood vertically in huge shattered blocks of all shapes, and

facing:

*The Indians gathered around the
missionaries on the evening of their
arrival at the Flathead village.
The cart in the lower left-hand corner
is one used by the missionaries
to transport baggage.
The white horse was a gift
to Father De Smet.*

Le 30 août après avoir serpenté dans une longue gorge de montagnes à laquelle nous donnames le nom des défi
lées, nous débouchames dans une large plaine, à l'horizon de laquelle s'appercevoit du côté de l'ouest le camp des Têtes
plates. à mesure que nous nous en approchions davantage on voyoit se succéder à de courts intervalles de nouveaux courriers
qu'il s'étoit présenté. Titiche Houldo distingue les autres par un large cordon rouge qui lui donnoit presque l'air d'un
maréchal de France. Voyez son portrait. (liv. 2 N°) Comme guerrier c'est assurement l'un des plus beaux hommes des mon
tagnes rocheuses. En preuve de son respectueux attachement au supérieur de la mission, il lui avoit envoyé son plus beau cheval
et défense à qui que ce fût de le monter avant sa remise. — Peu de temps après on apperçut dans le lointain un sauvage
de haute stature encore recourant vers nous à toute bride, en même temps des voix crièrent: Paul! Paul! et en effet c'
Paul le conducteur actuel du camp, Paul, l'un des trois adultes qui avoit reçu le saint baptême l'année précédente
qu'on croyoit absent; mais qui par une disposition toute particulière de la bonne providence, venoit d'arriver pour a
le plaisir de présenter lui-même à la peuplade, ceux qui venoient se dévouer à son bonheur — Vers le coucher du So
le P. de Smet et ses compagnons étoient environnés de leurs chers Néophites: les enfans, les jeunes gens, les vieillards, les
do l'âge mur, les mères portant leurs plus petits enfans sétoit à qui viendroit le plutôt nous serrer la main. tout ne for
qu'un cœur et qu'une âme . Au coucher du Soleil cette scène avoit quelque chose d'émouvant et de magique . Une m
seule comprend ce qu'elle éprouve au retour d'un fils longtemps absent — Sait elle ce qu'éprouva un missionnaire en se voyant
la première fois environné et pressé par une nombreuse famille, qui ne l'a jamais vu et qui cependant lui est déjà toute dé
vouée

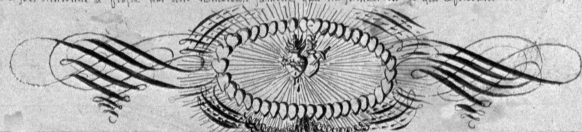

Memoriam fecit mirabilium suorum

communion générale le jour de l'assomption 1842
la Maternité divine

moriatur
Anima mea
morte justorum.

The death of Pierre, the first great chief of the Flatheads to be baptized
was "like the evening of a beautiful day." The Latin inscription translates:
"May my soul die the death of the just."

facing:
Holy Communion on the day of the Feast of the Assumption, August 15, 1842.
The Latin text reads:
"He made a memorial of His wonders."

at the foot of this severe beauty was a generous spring which gave the vegetation an appearance of freshness ordinarily found only on the banks of rivers. In the vicinity there was all the wood needed for fuel and construction. Also nearby was a quarry which looked as if it might contain limestone, soapstone, and whiting. All acknowledged unanimously that this site was ideally suited to our needs. And we were overjoyed when Father De Smet gave the same appraisal of the location.

The good old Ignatius, upon learning of this decision, was so disconsolate that he appeared to lose heart. "What!" he said, bursting into tears. "I who am on the point of death hoped the word of God would find its abode in my lands, and here it is leaving already." His sobs were redoubled, followed by cries so piercing that the hardest heart could not but have been touched. But since the common good required that the resolution of the majority be followed, we did all we could to console him and, with the help of

*Holy Communion on Pentecost Sunday, 1842, at St. Mary's.
The Latin words in the picture are from a hymn and
translate:"He has become the food of the wanderer."*

*facing, top:
In the process of building St. Mary's mission
the Flatheads learned some of the skills of civilization.*

*facing, bottom:
The first shrine erected among the Flatheads
in honor of Our Lady. The Latin text reads: "Hail, Queen of the Sea,"
the opening words of a well-known hymn.*

God, we succeeded in making him see that, by reason of the proximity of the place chosen, it would be easy for him to be carried there.[56]

The would-be grand chief of the Grand Lake arrived. I say "would-be," for in reality he was only a chief required by circumstances, not to say an illegitimate one. His name was Stellam, which meant Thunder, a name deriving no doubt from the extraordinary force of his lungs, to which he gave vent in his harangues. For several reasons he was jealous of the chief whose territory we had just visited, but most of all because the conduct of the latter was a living reproach to his own, which was anything but ordered. He was accompanied by a man named Montesat, "Mountain Ox." Despite this rude name, the physiognomy of this person was rather prepossessing, and his manner was conciliatory. But he acted only under the direction of Stellam. Thus, it seemed scarcely probable that they would look with favor on the choice that had been made. Unable to deny the reasonableness of the choice, they contented themselves with the promise that we would spend the

Ave maris stella

*The first procession of the Blessed Sacrament among the
Flatheads at St. Mary's. The Latin words translated: "Praise the Saviour,
O Sion," are from a hymn usually sung during such a ceremony.*

*facing:
This unique map shows the land and rivers
surrounding St. Mary's. The key at the lower right identifies
the various mission buildings.*

winter with them, and bound themselves to
accept any decision we should make. We sub-
scribed voluntarily to this arrangement because
the territory of Gabriel would not immediately
furnish subsistence to all of us. Nevertheless,
before their departure it was easy for us to see
that sincerity was not their prime virtue. What
confirmed our suspicion was the fact that Stellam had been shameless enough to insinuate
that, in order to merit his protection, we would
have to do nothing less than make a distribution

of all the powder and tobacco we had. He
claimed that Father De Smet had promised
these things during his visit to the Spokanes.
But to give a better idea of the kind of man with
whom we were dealing in the person of this
chief let me go back a little.

A dozen or so years ago the Coeur d'Alenes
still had only very obscure ideas touching the
Divinity, the future life, the existence of the
soul, and so on. The only evils they recognized
as such were stealing, lying, and fighting

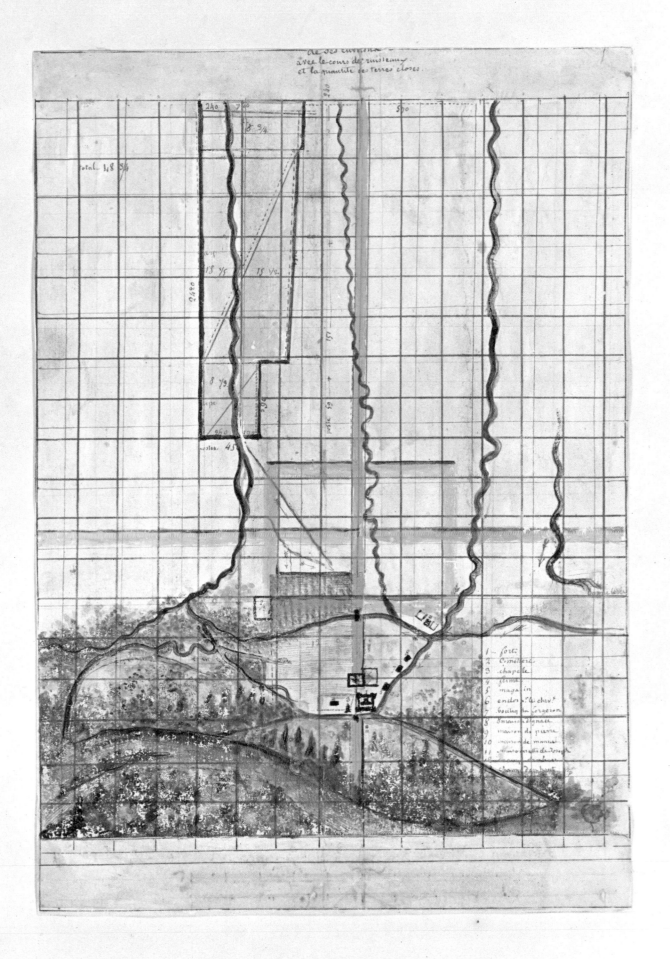

de ses environs
avec le cours des ruisseaux
et la quantité des terres closes.

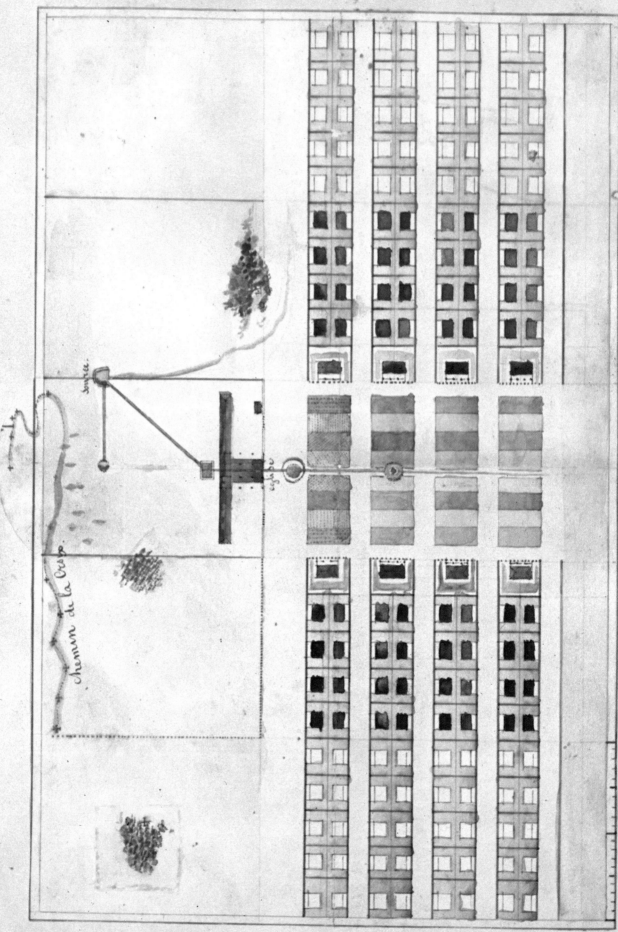

chemin de la Crép.

source.

église

Plan du Village des Cœurs-d'alénes.

The Latin text within this illustration
of the first summer hunt in Flathead country reads:
"He nourished those who revered Him."

facing:
*Called by Father Point the "plan of the
Coeur d'Alene village," this was probably his proposed layout
for the Mission of the Sacred Heart.*

among themselves. These rudimentary notions of morality they held only because they had received them from their fathers. At that time a Spokane by the name of Gueri, who had come into contact with the Protestants on the Red River, returned to his tribe with a few beginnings of religious ideas which, even though mixed with error, excited their curiosity. A Coeur d'Alene, who had heard the account of the traveler, imparted the news to his people among whom it spread far and wide with the rapidity of lightning. A large number of Coeur d'Alenes, curious to learn from the mouth of the man himself what they should believe of this news, assembled for this purpose in the land of Temisposomen.[57] Stellam went too, less for the purpose of adding to his religious knowledge than to do there as he always did, namely, to play the role of objector. He did worse than that. In the middle of the meeting he went so far as to say to the narrator, "So, young man, you expect us to believe this?" Before leaving he painted his body with bizarre figures and let it appear that he had cast a spell on the meeting.

*Those "strong in medicine" can hold red-hot
stones in their hands or between their teeth and plunge their
arms into boiling water without feeling pain.*

*One becomes a medicine man only after making a pilgrimage during which
he prays fervently, fasts from four to eight days, and eventually receives a "sign"
from a bear, a red deer, a green ram, or perhaps even from a monster.*

*Étienne Silimoulkelsimm,
a relative of Ignace.*

*Ignace Temisposomen, first
Coeur d'Alene chief to receive baptism.*

*Gabriel, Great Chief
of the Coeur d'Alenes.*

*Michael,
a Coeur d'Alene chief.*

However convincing he may have been, the fact is that as soon as he had left an epidemic broke out which, in a short time, took many lives. This is recounted to show the haughty and proud character of this chief. But Divine Mercy can draw good from evil. Here is what I heard from the very mouth of an old man who barely escaped being a victim of the epidemic. "During a fainting spell," he told me, "I beheld a light coming from Heaven and a globe of blue descending toward me. At the same time I heard a voice which said, 'Say to your brothers that their prayer is evil, that henceforth they are to place their confidence only in Him who has created the world and in Jesus Christ, His Son, who has redeemed it. Cast your idols on the mountain that extends into the lake. Address your prayers to Jesus Christ and have confidence, and the plague will cease.' "

It is possible that all this was the effect of an imagination still shocked by the news of the preceding day. It is even probable, since the sick man was in a sort of delirium. But when the vision occurred, it is certain that, scarcely had he obeyed the voice he heard, when he arose full of vigor. He made a tour of the stricken camp, recounted what had happened to him, persuaded all to do as he had done, and all the others also recovered their health.

The impeccable morals of this good old man, and the piety which moved him to shed tears as he recounted this, do not permit one to cast the least amount of suspicion on what was witnessed only by him. All the rest is attested to by so great a number of living witnesses that it would be impossible for any man of good faith not to believe it. What is also incontestably true is that, for a time at least, all superstitious practices ceased. They probably would have ended permanently had not the unhappy Stellam reinstated them, following a convocation of medicine men.

On November 13, 1842, a memorable day for the Society of Jesus,[58] we departed for the lands which were to be for us the theater of great trials as well as great consolations. Before the departure, our guide repeatedly asked the interpreter what the Blackrobe would give him for having come to meet him. It was observed that the luck which always attended him and his people in gambling would, this time, bring in nothing less than robes, blankets, hatchets, rifles, and even horses. He obviously expected some reward, equal, at least, to that which he would have realized from his gambling. Our departure on that day, for the purpose of spending the night on a beach not far distant from his territory, could be explained only by a desire on his part to share our supper, rather than have us share his. All of this caused more than one of the missionary's companions to ask just what sort of man we were obliged to deal with.

Early on the morning of November 14, we reached Stellam's country. His people flocked around us to shake hands. Because snow was falling heavily, we cut these ceremonies short in order to bring our packs under cover as soon as possible. We debarked near the spot where the lake empties into the Spokane River. The waters are teeming with fish which are caught, until January, by means of a trellised barrier extending from shore to shore. It is, in part, due to the ease with which food can be produced that the Coeur d'Alenes are so lazy and display other vices resulting therefrom. But everywhere there are good practices and good people. Here the catch from fishing or hunting is distributed at the lodge of the grand chief to all hungry mouths, whether the recipients have helped bring it in or not. A hunting or fishing expedition is never undertaken before the leader has invoked the assistance of whatever power he places his confidence in. Formerly he would trust in one of his manitous. Today, by the grace of God, Who has finally been revealed to these poor idolaters, it is to the Creator of Heaven and earth, to Jesus Christ, or to the Blessed Virgin that they address themselves. This year, for the first time, in spite of what has been said of the apostate chief, the invocations to obtain success or the thanks given for aid received were addressed to the true God.

On the first Friday of December, exactly one month after the consecration of the place to the Sacred Heart, the august symbol of our Redemption was erected not far from the church, on the same shore where the great fishing parties had assembled. During the ceremony, which was most edifying, the Coeur d'Alenes came respectfully to kiss this Tree, each saying, "Jesus, I give You my heart." At the same time

Pierre Ignace Montelsolem,
second chief of his locality.

Paulin,
a Coeur d'Alene chief.

Louis Joseph,
a Coeur d'Alene orator.

Paul, a son of Louis,
the mission interpreter.

The Great Toque, calumet
bearer, also one "strong in medicine."

Great Lake,
Great Chief of the Piegans.

Wolf's Son, chief of the Little
Lodge band of the Piegans.

Horse Hair Collar,
Chief of the Blackfeet.

*Favorite pastimes of children playing
on ice were sliding or a game called spinning tops.*

*The game of lacrosse originated among the Indians,
here pictured trying to hit the ball as high and as far as possible.*

*The game pictured here involves guessing
in which hand one's opponent holds an object. It requires
practice, keen observation, and skill.*

*A game called roulette was popular with young
people because it required strength and agility.*

the priest chanted and the entire tribe repeated, "*O crux ave, spes unica*" . . . "Hail, O Cross, our only hope." And remarkable as it may sound, from this day on there was no further question either of gambling, at which so much time had once been spent, or of those diabolical visions formerly so frequent, or of the medicine lodges where so many abominations had been committed. Noisy invocations of the manitous gave way to the cult of true prayer, the singing of sacred hymns, instruction in the word of God, and the thousand echoes of these lofty mountains announced the triumph of the Cross.

It seemed that all blessings, even temporal ones, should now descend upon these new children of the faith. But, to the great surprise of those who prayed so well, the opposite appeared to be the case. The Cross, instead of being a blessing for the fishermen and hunters, seemed to drive away the fish and the animals which, in other years, had been so abundant. And already there were rumors abroad, adroitly calculated to supply the spirit of falsehood with the means of regaining its worshipers. It became necessary to find a victorious answer to the question of what was the cause of a result so contrary to our expectations. The missionary could only attribute it — at least in some cases — to secret opposition to the public cult. This opposition had to be overcome for the glory of God and for the good of souls. The missionary dwelt on the sinfulness of hearts that forget, on the effort made by the evil spirit to hold them in his net. Reviewing the events between the serpent in Paradise and the temptation of Christ in the desert, he brought out vividly the ruses and the malice of the one whom Scripture calls the father of lies, stressing the severity of divine justice against those who lend an ear to his deceitful promises. From then on, every day, medicine sacks, an animal's tail, a feather, or some similar object—which, until then, had received the veneration due only to the Sovereign Master—were brought to the missionary's lodge to be thrown into the fire.

This lasted until Candlemas, a day which will always be memorable.[59] Only then could one say, "At last the tree of death has been cut down, even to its very roots." Then the Cross appeared powerful!

To give credit to their sacrilegious practices, until recently supported by hard-felt want, all the medicine men, recalling the time of their supposed efficacy, were pleased to repeat, "One day, after having invoked our manitous, we bagged one hundred eighty deer."

"And we," replied the true believers, "by the power of Him Who created and redeemed the world, have, almost without the aid of our bows or guns, in less than six hours bagged as many as three hundred."

The last medicine lodge kept by the Coeur d'Alenes may give some idea of what one is like. The grand officiating priest was the youngest of the medicine men, but, since he was the richest and the most generous, the others were willing to cede him the honors. In order to live up to the exalted idea of his merit, he began by decorating, as well as he could, a lodge capable of holding all the believers of the tribe. At about the height of a man, there is a sort of grille on which he arranges the objects relating to his medicine. Then he asks the eight people having the most striking appearance to seat themselves at either extremity of the lodge, four men on one side and four women on the other. Their duty is to assist the grand priest in his functions. The simple attendants are placed in two lines running the length of the lodge. These arrangements having been made, the grand master, his head decorated with elegant feathers and his body streaked with various colors, opens the session with a mysterious chant. After this, at a signal from the master, several cry out, "Kill the fire! Kill the fire!" At these cries, an indescribable confusion ensues, which does not end until the master pronounces the sacramental words, "My medicine is hidden." Then the fire is rekindled and the search for the medicine begins. In the midst of the milling about, begin the fainting spells, delirium, visions, revelations. What has the great manitou revealed? It is very cold, but, regardless of this, it is necessary to swim across the river and return with a certain kind of wood. Or stones of a certain kind are to be heated to red heat in the fire, extracted with the bare hands, and held between the teeth while one walks around the lodge. All these things are done. Then a voice cries, "The hunt has opened." Everyone leaves the lodge and makes a common invocation. The voice cries again, "Before taking the first shot, turn the rifle toward the sun. If the first animal killed is

*Among the Indians this sport—horse racing—
was as different from ours as they are from us.*

*Bloody conflicts were rare among members of
the same tribe but frequent between tribes.*

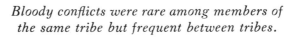

*After this heavenly vision there followed
a conversion—as complete as it was sudden—of
an Indian previously the slave of every vice.*

*Even before conversion, this family was noted for
its intellectual, moral, and religious disposition.*

a male, it should be brought into the lodge head first; if it is a female, the rump should be first." Thus prepared, it is said, the results of the hunt were abundant.

Gambling and idolatry had given way before grace, but a more powerful enemy, polygamy, still remained to be vanquished. For, deprived as they were of the light of faith, these poor blind souls were no less dissolute in their morals than insensate in their beliefs. Thus, to leave one woman in order to take another, or to keep several at one time was so common among them that, in return for a trinket, a father did not hesitate to deliver his daughter into the hands of a man who already had several wives. The subordinate chiefs, especially, had set the example for this shameful traffic. Montelsolem had three wives, one, the former wife of his own brother, and the others her daughters, whom she had given him. Stellam, at the time, had only one wife, but her youth attested to the fact that she was by no means the first. Besides, in exchange for a horse, this man, who was as greedy as he was shameless, had just agreed to the marriage of his niece to a wretch who had already taken and dismissed several others. His brother had seven wives. From this it is evident that if polygamy was not held in honor by the Coeur d'Alenes, at least it was widely practiced. To lead such people to the sacrifice required by reason, it was necessary to have recourse to every species of dispensation and indulgence. In spite of this condescension, it would be difficult to form an idea of the pain it cost most of them. Two days after Christmas the principle polyga- mists heard again from the mouth of the mis- sionary the only conditions under which they would be admitted to baptism, and the many good reasons for their profiting by this favora- ble occasion. It was then that Montelsolem rose and, not able to control his emotions, cried out between sobs, "My brothers, I want to be saved; let us hear the voice of God. Follow my ex- ample." His emotion swept the assembly with it, and his example was followed by all those present, with the exception of one who waited several days, but only the better to repair the scandal of his conduct.

Of three who had been absent, one, after having passed a night reflecting seriously, made the best choice that could be made. The second,

not having the fortitude to make a choice, was relieved of his embarrassment by the voluntary retirement of one of his wives. The third con- tributed to the general good in spite of himself, by making it appear how God sometimes pun- ishes, in this world, hardened hearts that refuse to follow His call. Within a short time, either through gambling or by some accident, he lost half his fortune, and though he remained in possession of his two wives, it was only that they might be examples of the excesses of which women are capable, who prefer half the heart of a man to the friendship of God.

From the beginning of the mission, it had been possible to celebrate the Sacred Mysteries under a shelter large enough to accommodate all the catechumens. There they assembled three times daily, either to pray or to hear the word of God. And it was in this retreat, so similar to the place which had sheltered the Holy Infant, that light began to shine through the darkness.

For Midnight Mass this shelter had been adorned with green garlands, the earth covered with mats, and the choir hung with tapestries or images representing the principal mysteries. A little before midnight the firing of muskets announced that the church had just been opened to the piety of these new children of the faith. Waves of worshipers hurried toward the palace of the Infant God and, at the sight of the night suddenly changed into splendid day, they were moved to cry, "Jesus, I give You my heart."

Since baptism was to be administered to the adults on the Feast of the Circumcision, Jan- uary 1, the Feast of Christmas contributed to their preparation. But, as is usual in such cases, the days of grace which preceded this holy ceremony were witnesses to the strongest resist- ance. From the first day, Stellam had opposed the work of God by contradicting the mission- ary or recalling the happy times when, accord- ing to him, one could earn a living through gambling alone. But his attacks had never been more overtly hostile.

One evening, however, Stellam had someone inform the missionary that a Protestant chief had said that thirty men of his sect were going to make the missionary pay dearly for the discrepancies between his words and those of their minister. It was pure invention on his part, and was treated by the supposed author of this news as it deserved. Discovered but not disconcerted, Stellam feigned profound repentance and, to give proof of his devotion to the missionary, he had someone tell him that something was being carried on contrary to the true prayer, that already the superstitious fire had been kindled. This time the information was given with such appearances of great sincerity that the missionary went to see the chief, to discuss with him what might be done to prevent this act of apostasy. He was very properly received. At the words, "So! Let's go quickly," Stellam beat a retreat, making it understood that the affair could be managed better without him than with him. The missionary accordingly left with two young Indians. Arriving at the battlefield, the missionary remonstrated with the Indians, but to the force of reasoning they only opposed the force of inertia in absolute silence. The young Indian companions of the missionary extinguished the fire and the missionary departed. Scarcely had he disappeared when Stellam arrived to relight the torches. He presided over this assembly of apostates and sang with more vigor than ever the diabolic chants of his old cult. But neither his chanting nor his gestures nor anything that his delirious imagination could add were capable of reviving the once imperious power of his manitous.

When reproached for conduct which contrasted so horribly with his words of the night before, he contented himself with answering as he laughed, "When I did it, I didn't think it was wrong, but since you say that I have done wrong, I shall not do it again." Let us hasten to say, to the credit of his relatives, that they were the first to condemn such conduct. For a long time his wife, who was the flower of the catechumens, waited and hoped for his conversion, so that he might be baptized. Two of his sisters, who had been baptized among the first, were remarkable in more than one respect by reason of their virtue. The son of Martha, one of his sisters, was endowed with the qualities most honored among the Indians and was the first of the catechumens to contribute by his zeal to the instruction of the others. To reward him for this, the missionary, at his baptism, gave him the glorious name of Vincent. We hope that one day good example may finally lead this unhappy chief back to his duty.

Next to Vincent, those who distinguished themselves most by their zeal in instructing the other catechumens were the young men. With their help, those with the poorest memories learned all that was prescribed. One of them in a single night learned all the necessary prayers. This is what he did to help himself in this study. He held in his hand as many small sticks as there were words to learn. When he had learned one word, he stuck one of the sticks in the ground; when he had learned the second, he planted the second stick, and so forth. After planting each stick, he began from the beginning again, repeating each time all the words represented by the series of sticks. Thus, by repeating the same words over and over, he succeeded in memorizing them. Naturally the last word learned was the first one to be forgotten, so that one would scarcely have the last words ringing in his ears, before running quickly into the lodge of the examiner, making sure his instructor was with him. The instructor was sometimes the son or the grandson of the reciter, and when memory failed, it was toward the child that the eyes of the older man were turned as if asking for pity. By this procedure, which Heaven blessed, all the prayers had soon been learned by the majority. Then it was a question of making sure about the disposition of heart. To this end: Three days before baptism, in the morning and in the evening, the names of those who had been sufficiently well instructed were called out in the chapel and each one, upon hearing his name, had to show he was present by standing. Then the assembly was informed that if anyone knew any reason why the person named should not receive baptism, he should inform the missionary.

On the last day there was a great council of the chiefs, during which each one was requested to say what he thought. All confirmed the mute testimony of the preceding assemblies. Seventy-nine adults were admitted to baptism on the Feast of the Circumcision. Nothing was omitted which might render the ceremony imposing and, thanks be to God, we have the consolation of being able to say that it was worthy of being witnessed by Heaven.

*Paulin's homeland, site of the
first mission among the Coeur d'Alene's.*

*Father Point himself called this
painting simply "The Land of Raphael."*

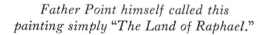

The first announcement in Victor's
country of the existence of the true God.

The land of Ignace.

But what is pleasing to God is not pleasing to the enemy of man. On the very evening of the solemnities we were informed that Stellam, more than ever, had been spreading dire predictions. We were told that, among other unfortunate things, he had said it was good not to be baptized, for baptism, instead of giving life, only brought death. He said that among the Flatheads many had died after having received baptism; that Gabriel, one of the first to be baptized, was on the point of death and that the same fate awaited Étienne. Stellam predicted that many others would suffer identically. Many newly baptized had in fact died during the first year of our mission among the Flatheads. Since both Gabriel and Étienne actually were very ill, there was every reason to fear lest such talk shatter the still-unconfirmed faith of the stragglers. Fortunately, Providence came to our assistance. Étienne and Gabriel had received the last sacraments, proof enough that they were in danger of death. But since both had believed in the twofold power of extreme unction, they were able to be up and about on the day following their reception of this sacrament. Thus the sacrament of the sick did not make men die, and we were able to point out this fact about extreme unction and even more so about baptism. For outside of the two sick men who had been cured almost instantaneously, not one of the old men who had been baptized the year before had ceased enjoying the best of health. Hence, the assertion to the contrary fell with all its weight on its author, not to punish him as he deserved, but to make him finally surrender to the solicitation of grace. From that day on, the contrary chief never dared to speak so disdainfully against the common belief.

At the beginning of January, Stellam left for the grand hunt. The capable hunters, obliged to follow his example, left in the care of the missionary the infirm, the aged, and all who might be a hindrance to them, promising that they would not forget anyone as soon as they had found deer. During their absence, there was nothing more edifying than the conduct of our infirm and our convalescents. "Listen to Father," said a chief, who had just returned from the portals of death. "His word, which is the word of God, is the food of our souls." Then, with a zeal like that of a novice, he would add,

"For my part, I should not mind dying of hunger before the return of the hunters."

At the end of about two weeks the hunters who were forced to listen to the harangues of Stellam were agreed that the Blackrobe ought to be asked to pay them a visit. An Indian was accordingly sent to ask him. As the missionary was eager to know how they now stood with respect to the essential thing, he quickly and willingly accepted their invitation. He had the consolation of finding all, or most, of them of the same mind as they had been at their departure.

The hunt itself was the best means of closing the door to the tempter. The men would set out, without eating, before sunrise, course through the snow the whole day long, return only after nightfall, fasting sometimes until their return, and would add to all this some devout prayers. Lake Pend d'Oreille, together with its environs, offered the most favorable spot both for fishing and hunting. To the south there was an impassable chain of mountains running from east to west, forming an enclosure. To the north, there were gentle slopes, usually abounding in deer. In the middle of this vast amphitheater there was beautiful water, which did not freeze until February. What location could be more desirable for hungry hunters? But here, as on the shores of their lake, God had trials in store for them. "Walk straight before God," the missionary often told them; "you know that He does not love deceitful hearts." And every day, here as elsewhere, the word of God bore fruit.

The most remarkable conversion was that of a medicine man. He was on his way to one of his relatives who had just been seriously wounded as a result of the clumsiness of one of the hunters. The missionary ran to help the injured one. The Indian, who was mounted, offered to share his mount with the Father. And they rode and talked together as friends. When they arrived at the side of the injured man, the Blackrobe did what anyone else would have done in his place. He spared no effort to make himself useful, happy to be able to achieve success. The medicine man, watching everything closely, was so impressed that, thenceforth, he thought only of being converted. He was baptized on the Feast of the Holy Name of Jesus. This conversion, not expected so soon, made such a strong impression on the stragglers, that they decided to visit the Blackrobe, announcing that they, too, desired baptism. They thought, however, that, in view of present inconveniences, it would be more prudent to wait until summer. This was, obviously, only a device of the evil spirit, attempting to prevent them from profiting by the present opportunity, which was most favorable. When the Indians were shown that, by acting in this manner, they were exposing themselves to the danger of missing the most favorable of opportunities, they all decided to profit by it—all, that is, except Stellam. However, his wife, his sisters, his relatives, his former friends, in short, all in the camp who were of good disposition, united in an assault against him. The mercy of God spoke to his heart so insistently that even he finally surrendered. This was undoubtedly a remarkable development, but an embarrassing one for the missionary, charged with admitting only lambs into the divine flock. In view of the opposition, the recent public attacks of the applicant, and of the pretended changes of heart, of which so many examples had been given, it was difficult to credit his new attitude. On the other hand, considering the impelling violence of his character, there was reason to fear the results of a refusal of the favor he solicited with all the appearances of good faith.

It was decided that this favor would not be refused, but that it would be granted under only one condition, namely, public reparation of the scandals of which he had been the author. The would-be convert not only submitted himself to all that was demanded of him. He went further than might have been expected of the very best-disposed man. He gave a speech which drew tears from his audience and then, proceeding to the lodge of the missionary with his medicine sack, he threw it into the fire, saying in the presence of numerous witnesses, "Now I reject you, to obey only the true God."

On Candlemas, in the midst of a perfect calm, Stellam and the other chiefs who had not yet been baptized received the sacrament together with fifty other adults. What was most remarkable, in the course of this second solemn administration, was the zeal of the godfathers and godmothers in repeating to their godchildren what had to be done for a worthy reception of the sacrament. An Indian woman named Louise, about whom we shall have remarkable things to say later, distinguished herself on this occasion by the help she gave to those most in need of assistance. The solemnity of the occasion was broken suddenly by the sobs of a catechumen at the moment the regenerative waters ran over his brow. This was Pierre Ignace, whose emotion communicated itself to the others present.

The goal which we had set ourselves as we met on the great lake of the Coeur d'Alenes had been reached. There was no more doubt relative to the site of the reduction. We took leave in the hope of seeing each other soon. The meeting ended during Holy Week. Before our departure the earth was opened to receive the remains of a child who had died in the robe of his innocence. The child was the son of a medicine man, formerly wicked enough, but become so virtuous since the great transformation of his tribe that on the very day on which Heaven subjected his faith to this harsh trial, he answered the missionary, who strove to console him, by saying, "Today, Father, I know the soul of my son is in Heaven. My heart is happy. I now wish to weep for my own mistakes. When I pray, my heart is strong. I shall pray always." The child, whom we might call the ambassador of our gratitude, was buried on the spot which was the cradle of a new life for a large number of his tribe. On the cross guarding his remains we carved the words *Te Deum laudamus.*

One night, near the middle of Lent, there had arrived at my lodge a man who had traveled twenty miles on snowshoes through thawing weather. He was so old that, as he said, he had already reached manhood when the eldest of the Coeur d'Alenes, now almost a centenarian, was still in his cradle. As soon as he saw me, he cried, "Father, you told me to be baptized before I die. I feel that I shall soon die. This is why I have come to see you." He had come several times before, this good old man, and always for the same purpose. Asked whether he still believed in his old medicine, he answered that he did not, that he had long since abandoned it and would never again take it up.

"What medicine did you formerly have?" I asked.

The village of the Sacred Heart seen from the south.

The village of the Sacred Heart viewed from the west.

The village of the Sacred Heart viewed from the east.

The village of the Sacred Heart seen from the north.

"Wolf medicine," he replied.

"How did you acquire it?"

"I was unable to keep my horses because the wolves were so bad. One day, when I was particularly sad, a wolf passed before me. I said to him, 'Wolf, have mercy on me.' Immediately the wolf replied, 'If you pray to me, the wolves will no longer eat your horses.' I prayed to this wolf. And, sure enough, the wolves no longer ate my horses. This lasted until I knew that it was not good to pray to wolves. Then I stopped praying to mine and wolves began their war again and have now eaten all my horses down to the last one. So what do you think I ought to do? Continue praying well?"

"What do you mean by praying well?"

"Praying as one should."

"What will you do if I baptize you?" I asked.

"I shall continue to pray as you do."

"And your wife? What will she do?"

"She will do whatever I do."

"How do you know that?"

"Recently she said to me, 'Breathe on me, for I am ill.' 'What!' I said to her. 'Do you think that if I breathe on you, you will live a long time? Don't you see, poor old woman, that when one is as old as we are, one should think only of dying well and that to die well it is necessary to have a good prayer?'"

"And what did she answer?"

"That she would do whatever I do."

"Well, then, this is what you will do. You will remain here for several days. I shall instruct you and when you have been instructed, you will go to your wife and tell her what I have taught you. Then, one day, we shall have baptism. From now on you are to call yourself Polycarp."

Not far from the spot where we were, on the banks of a small lake, was a group of Indian families especially difficult to convert by reason of their having been gravely scandalized in point of morals by the apostles of commerce. They had not been in contact with the protectors of the area; but the Lord has His elect everywhere, and when He wishes to call them to Himself, the passage of the Red Sea is there to teach us what is to be done.

There was, near this little camp, a great tree, the highest and thickest in the country. This tree, hollowed out by fire, fell before our very eyes. Near the ruins we erected a cross, which, with the fallen tree, is the symbol of a remarkable occurrence in this solitude. It was there that I experienced the happiness of baptizing our two centenarians, Polycarp and his companion; and—something rare enough to deserve mention also—of adding to their baptism the sacrament of matrimony. For, though they were both free, because they had been married only according to the Indian manner, they did not even think of the possibility of a separation. There, too, in short space of two days, the earth was opened twice to receive the mortal remains of two women taken in the bloom of their age, but with the robe of the baptismal innocence which they had worn only a few hours. Finally, it was there that all our infidels of yesterday, profoundly moved by the great contrasts of life and death, youth and old age, prostrated themselves at the foot of the Tree which has redeemed the world and vowed, in the presence of the Blackrobe, that they would never have any other prayer but his.

We had just celebrated the beautiful Feast of the Annunciation.[60] Already the buds of the trees were swelling. The *kirile*, a charming little bird of this area, could be heard singing, and bustards were descending in flocks on the banks of the lakes.[61] These were certain signs of the return of spring. Everything which assailed our senses opened our hearts. But, at the perspective which opened before us, another great joy filled our souls.

On March 30, 1843, as the chosen people greeted the promised land, so did we greet the land of Gabriel, chosen to be the center of the reduction of the Sacred Heart. Gabriel and Michael were already there, with the strongest and bravest of their men. They worked so strenuously that, on the Friday of Passiontide, the framework of the church was assembled. On the following Thursday, Holy Thursday, the missionary was able to offer the first sacrifice of the Mass in the new chapel, acknowledging all of the favors received by the entire tribe.

While the church was being finished, a Way of the Cross was made. Progress had gone as far as the fourteenth station when the missionary felt a fainting spell overcoming him. Though the weakness was obviously attributable to the fatigues of the day, the Lenten fast and the many obstacles he had encountered on every side, the missionary, believing he was dying, thought only of preparing himself. Since it was Good Friday, about three o'clock, the day, the hour, and the attending circumstances caused him to consider himself most fortunate to have his life terminate at such a moment. . . . But God judged otherwise, for, on Easter Sunday, he was able to celebrate Mass.

What has already been said about the jealous and contrary character of Stellam (named Joseph at his baptism) began to manifest itself sharply because of the preference given to the land of his arch rival. Stellam was the last to arrive. He came, less for the purpose of helping or of encouraging than for that of paralyzing the effort of our workers. In fact, scarcely had he and his twenty useless companions arrived, when he began by saying that their positive intention was to establish themselves nowhere but on his own lands. It was better, he said, to earn a living by gambling, as they used to do, than by working, as they did now. He succeeded in convincing some of the chiefs that their interests were the same as his. From that moment on, some of them remained in league with him. But, not content with the harmful influence he had exercised by his talk, he added to this the greatest of scandals.

On Good Friday the missionary learned that Stellam had left his wife for another, though the wife had conducted herself perfectly since her baptism. The unhappy wretch had furtively joined the object of his passion. But public indignation ran so high that Stellam gave semblance of repenting, promising to repair his faults, after his return from the root harvest, by working like the others in the interest of the reduction. He did return, but too late and only to cause new discord. He complained that his part of the root harvest had not been given him and demanded, as compensation, things which he knew could not be given him, thus crowning his odious and ridiculous behavior.

On the day on which the tribe dispersed to hunt provisions of roots, the wretch, under pretext of distant relationship to a man dead five years, was shameless enough to take, in broad daylight, three horses belonging to the heir of the deceased. These horses had been foaled by a mare which had been the only inheritance in this case.

When Stellam had arrived in the land of the Spokanes, where roots were to be gathered, he opened his lodge to all the gamblers in the country. First, he contented himself with watching the games; then he took part himself. Having lost his rifle, he flew at the winner in such a rage that, if his brother had not thrown himself between them, he would have stuck the winner with an arrow he held in his hand. Not content with singing the praises of gambling, he was shameless enough to eulogize polygamy also, maintaining that, instead of being an evil, it was a great good, that the minister of the Nez-Percés had said so, and so on.[62] To what extremities will not jealousy and hatred carry the man who has entered on the road of apostasy! But these excesses of evil, with God's help and through the prayers of Martha, the sister of the great sinner, produced good. Stellam appeared confused within himself and disposed to do everything to make us forget these scandals. Some days before, another lamb, no less bewildered, but somewhat less given to scandalous conduct, had returned to the fold. And, in spite of scandals and difficulties of all kinds, the work on the reduction continued to progress.

During the period from the first day of the meeting until the separation this is what was accomplished: The church had been finished; seed had been sown; each one had received his own parcel of land; and public fields for the entire tribe had been set aside. So much for the material side. There were, besides the Angelus, prayers before meals, prayers of thanksgiving, four or five hymns, examination of conscience, and, for all, the study of the short catechism. All this was in addition to the ordinary prayers known by heart by a great number. There were also confessions for all in preparation for Holy Communion, which could not take place until after the harvest.

Some progress could be expected. There was, indeed, great and rapid progress, with respect to religious instructions as well as education. Since the latter, which embraced both religion and morals, was most easily grasped by the chiefs and other mature persons, it was the thing most willingly and most often discussed. And because personal authority was joined with

*What could be more desirable to
hungry hunters than a land abounding in deer?*

*A bear, surrounded by hunters, will
sometimes attack one who imprudently comes too close.*

*This Spokane Indian, aged one hundred and four,
walked twenty miles through snow to ask for baptism.*

*A mother, at the grave of her only daughter, urges
another girl to follow the good example of the deceased child.*

force of example, there resulted such general enthusiasm that even those who were most given to inertia were forced to follow along.

It is a fact that, since that time until the writing of these lines [so spoke Father Point in April, 1845], that is, four or five months after this period, I knew of no single instance in which a serious sin was committed in the village of the Sacred Heart. If there were venial transgressions, they were so well repaired that the public good perhaps suffered less than it would have had no such transgressions occurred. I have witnessed fathers and mothers who sometimes made long trips to come and acknowledge some slight fault, and this outside of confession, sometimes publicly, and always to demand a penance. Sometimes husbands followed their wives and mothers followed their daughters. They would exaggerate the faults thus admitted, but only to excuse them by saying that they themselves had given occasion for them by their lack of patience or charity. Children imitated their parents. One day a child came and admitted having made a little companion cry by hitting him on the head with a toy, which he bore in his hand. As proof of his repentance, the child handed over the toy, which he valued highly.

It was during these days that the last adults who had not yet received baptism because of lack of preparation or sufficient instruction, made the greatest efforts to merit this favor. Of all those who presented themselves for their first Communion there was not a single one who might have been unworthy. Most of them might even have been proposed as examples to more than one fervent, civilized Christian. What simplicity! What charity! But above all, what faith was in these poor children of the forests! Undoubtedly something of those virtues was necessary for the old men who made themselves the humble pupils of their children and for those children who made themselves the patient instructors of their aged fathers; for the mothers who, after giving to their children the food they refused themselves, spent long evenings breaking with them and with others, the still more needy, the bread of the Divine Word; for the men who, not content with the exacting toil of the day, passed entire nights trying to cram into the head of some poor idiot, or deaf or sick person, the things rigorously required for admission to baptism; for the more intelligent men who refused themselves the pleasure of adding to their knowledge, in order to repeat, not ten or twenty times, but hundreds of times what they had first learned; and, finally, for the chiefs of each tribe who exhorted their people from dawn to dark to weep for their sins, recalling to mind the fires of Hell and the joys of Heaven, the passion of Our Lord, and all the themes which had touched them most.

I spoke of their faith. How simple it is! How pure it is! How confident is the faith of the Indian! The first idea which the missionary impressed on them was that God's benevolence is no less great than his power. What admirable fruits were produced in their souls, not only by the sacraments of baptism, penance and Holy Eucharist, but also by the simple sign of the cross, the use of holy water, the mere sight of a medal. They were told, for example, that extreme unction has the twofold power of purifying the soul and restoring physical health, if God so wishes. They believed in the second effect no less than in the first, and more than once their faith was rewarded by almost instantaneous recoveries.

One day I was informed that an Indian woman, as yet only a catechumen, was ill. I replied that I would go to see her. Thereupon her sister arrived to say that she had died. I hurried to her, in the hope that her sister had been wrong. On my arrival, all those about her repeated that she was dead. To make certain, I tried all possible means, but there was not even the slightest sign of life. I exhorted everyone to pray. Everyone prayed with fervor and I turned again to the sick woman. I pronounced the words of baptism. Whereupon, her lips, until then immobile, tried to express something. Perhaps she understood me. I baptized her; she began to breathe, opened her eyes, sat up on her mat, made the sign of the cross and began speaking, thanking Heaven for the double favor she had just received, for she was convinced that baptism had given life to her soul and restored the life of her body. Perhaps she had only suffered a fainting spell, but even if this were so, as I believe, it is still true that the prayers of these good people were not in vain.

*The best time to shoot deer was
in the autumn just before mating season.*

*Winter hunting was good when the snow
in the mountains was deep enough to cause numbers
of animals to descend to the plains.*

*A little before midnight on Christmas Eve
night's shadows turned into splendid day as the
Coeur d'Alenes' new house of prayer opened for Mass.*

*An illustration identified by the missionary-
artist simply as "The Feast of Corpus Christi."*

*The singing of the hymn "Lauda Sion Salvatorem"
preceded and followed the celebration of what was for an entire tribe
the celebration of their first Holy Communion.*

*During the days assigned for the learning of prayers and
the study of the Catechism the Indians helped one another.*

*A symbolic representation of a desolate widow
beseeching God to have mercy on her, and of a young mother crossing a
dangerous rapid to seek baptism for her newborn child.*

*A sister offers food gathered from trees
in the forest to a younger brother held in the arms of their mother.*

Following a celestial vision a number of Indians
who were seriously ill recovered suddenly and completely.

A heavenly envoy announces the glad
tidings of salvation to the Coeur d'Alenes and commands the devil
to depart from the land.

*Indians, publicly confessing faults,
reveal inadvertently their heroic virtue.*

*The sacrament of penance was often
administered in camp or during a march.*

An Indian woman, apparently dead, showed
signs of life when the formula of baptism was whispered to her.

The recovery of a man who had
received the sacrament of extreme unction demonstrated its
twofold effect of health for body and soul.

*With the help of his parents a dying
three-year-old boy made the sign of the cross.*

*A Great Chief, dying, gives parting advice
to members of his family who surround him.*

*The great council of Nez Percé chiefs,
asked if they wished to become Christians, replied affirmatively.*

*A Blackrobe, with the aid of an interpreter,
explains Christianity to a group of Nez Percés.*

*Heavy rain and contrary winds forced
the missionaries en route to the reduction of the Sacred
Heart to take refuge on shore for three days.*

*The Blackrobes' food supply was almost exhausted when they learned
that a woman was seriously ill on an island three miles away.*

*There was a small Indian camp on the island in
Lake Coeur d'Alene where the dying woman and others were
baptized during the missionaries' six-day visit.*

*The grave of the Indian woman
became a blessed spot on The Isle of Salvation.*

ILE DU SALUT

Several days later, an Indian came to tell me, "Father, my little daughter is dying. Since yesterday she has eaten nothing."

"Has your daughter a medal of the Blessed Virgin?"

"No."

"Here is one. Place it around her neck and ask the Blessed Virgin to cure her."

All was done as instructed. The child took to its mother's breast again, fell into a peaceful sleep and returned to health, so soon and so completely, that no one who had seen her dying could doubt for a moment that her recovery was due to the protection which had been invoked.

Another indication of the Indians' faith is the custom they have of making the sign of the cross, not only at the beginning and at the end of their principal actions, but also whenever they take their calumet to smoke or lean over a stream to quench their thirst. They teach their children to make this sign, even before they are able to articulate words. I saw two young parents lean over the crib of their only son, who was dying, to prompt him to make the sign of the cross. The poor infant, scarcely three years old, made every effort to give them this consolation. Another scene, no less touching, was that of a young woman, seated near the grave of her only daughter, speaking with a little girl for whom she had stood godmother on the preceding evening.

"Look, child," she said, pointing to the grave, "see how happy one is to die when one has been baptized. You shall go to find my little Clemence, who is now in Heaven."

There was in the tone and in the expression of the pious mother, something so calm that it seemed she already partook of the happiness of which she spoke. These virtuous acts multiplied by the hundreds as the time for the reception of Holy Communion approached. The weeks before the Feast of the Immaculate Conception were devoted to the necessary preparation.

To render our Coeur d'Alenes pleasing to God, we had, on our arrival in their land, placed them, in a very special manner, under the protection of the Sacred Heart of Jesus. Since their first meeting in the village which bore that revered name, they had not ceased to join us in invoking it with confidence in all of their needs. We happily acknowledge that this is the source of all the changes which consoled us so much. We have seen what the Coeur d'Alenes had been and what they continued to be during the first winter we passed with them. Today, thanks to the divine benevolence which has blessed their good will, what a difference is found! Speaking only of what transpired on All Saints' Day and on Christmas, what edifying things we were able to witness! At the end of October, over a hundred families were gathered in the vicinity of the church to the construction of which almost all had contributed in one way or another. To see these poor little thatched huts huddled around the chapel brought to one's mind the pelican in the desert,[63] especially since the Indians were there to receive their first Holy Communion.

A goodly number of the Coeur d'Alenes had, by this time, acquired a certain degree of religious instruction, but most of them, particularly the old people, still left much to be desired. The missionary had only two months left in which to instruct them. At the end of that time, the winter hunt, so essential to their living, would begin. Consequently, the missionary was obliged to give his instructions in as abbreviated a form as possible.

We have remarked before that the Indian hardly ever forgets what he has once seen, and if he associates some idea with what he has seen, this idea always recurs to him when the object with which it is associated is placed before him. Hence, his tendency to express all his ideas by images and his facility for speaking by means of signs. It was upon this gift that the instructor based his entire system of instruction, and he was not sorry he did so. He made pictures which represented, by means of various hieroglyphic forms, what is necessary to believe to be saved, what one had to do, and so on. Then, with a long pointer in hand, he explained each one of these truths and tried, through the interpreter, to bring the explanation within the comprehension of the least intelligent. This was repeated, first, by the interpreter at the end of the meeting; second, by the parents in the individual lodges; third, in the public addresses of the chiefs; fourth, at the opening of the following meeting by the missionary himself, in order to rectify whatever defects might have crept into the presentation by the others. There was unity in the plan, clarity of explanation, insistence on the principal points, and everyone sought to follow the instructions.

Should I say that, during these days of sanctification, the instructions were more frequent, the prayers longer, the confessions more complete? No, this would have been impossible. But it is true that everything was done in a manner to edify angels and men. This will not surprise you when you learn that to my feeble efforts was joined all the zeal of Father Joset, who had just completed his third year as a missionary.[64] Still, in spite of the general disposition of which I have just spoken, it was not without some apprehension that it was decided to admit to Holy Communion certain souls whose intelligence was somewhat limited. But for these, as well as for the others, the effect of the sacrament was so perceptible that I would reproach myself today if I had done otherwise.

During the last two days of the retreat, the young people of both sexes competed with one another in adorning the church.[65] It was, indeed, a small church, and a poor one; but I have no doubt that it would have seemed rich if one realized that at the very limits of American civilization there were only two such churches, one among the Flatheads and another among the Pend d'Oreilles.

On December 8, we arrived at the moment of the Lord's triumph. The stars were still gleaming brightly when the words of the song, *Lauda Sion Salvatorem*, were heard ringing out. An entire Indian tribe, until now silent in their lodges, moved, silently and devoutly, to the church, now no longer merely the house of prayer, but in very truth the throne of the Heart of Jesus. The august sacrifice began and the Indians attended with rapt devotion. One would say that each member of the congregation was listening intently to the innermost promptings of his soul, the better to hear the inner voice speaking to them. They were so deeply devout that the priest spoke only a few words to them before they approached to receive Communion. Thereafter, they were so absorbed in their own contemplations, that the missionary, fearing to

impede the work of God, left his neophytes to their own devices. Afterwards, there was the recitation of a few prayers and, at the end, the singing of the *Lauda Sion*, repeated in chorus. High Mass, sung about ten o'clock, and the consecration of all to the Blessed Virgin in the afternoon, were noteworthy for the continuation of the sentiments which had filled the Indians' souls in the morning. In the evening, renewal of vows took place.[66] At the same time, twelve new converts were baptized. The ceremony was preceeded by an instruction, reminding all of their solemn obligations and suggesting to them means to persevere in their good intentions. All recited thrice an act of the love of God, so devoutly that one might have said that they were responding to the triple question of the Saviour as did once the Prince of the Apostles. After an expression of their sentiments, so simple, unanimous and true, their eyes turned piously toward the altar where the Blessed Sacrament was exposed. Now they seemed to say with St. Augustine, "O Beauty always old and always new, our love has, indeed, been tardy, but we will love you always." Finally, as a seal to their promises and a crown to the graces they had received, the Benediction of the Blessed Sacrament ended a day so rich with spiritual values that it was a day too short for all

OVERLEAF

left

This picture of a barge being towed was probably painted by an Indian boy who was so interested in Father Point's artistic work that the missionary gave him some drawing material to see what he could do with it.

right

This drawing of the interior of a steamboat and of a calumet ceremony was also the work of an Indian.

No. 3 — vue d'un fort — ouvrage et chartred —

1809

of them. Thus, the moments following the singing of the *Vivat Jesus* were moments of regret, and each one was scarcely able to tear himself away from the church.

At the end of November, 1845, ten chiefs or notables of the nation of the Nez Percés presented themselves at the reduction of the Sacred Heart to be instructed. They had been half civilized by Protestantism; that is, they were more difficult to lead to the true faith than the idolaters themselves. But, since they appeared disgusted with everything having to do with Protestantism, we thought that our instruction might not be useless to them. And though, from a material point of view, we were at this time quite indigent, they remained with us for ten days. After passing the day either listening to our explanations or translating the Catholic prayers into their own language, they would spend the evening reciting to one another, in order to impress the prayers on their memories. This exercise sometimes extended far into the night, so that with respect to knowledge there was nothing lacking of what was rigorously required for their admission into the true fold. But we judged it prudent to postpone for some months the fulfillment of their desires, assuming of course that their conduct remained in accord with their promises. Besides, they did not have their wives with them. So it was to be expected that, upon returning to their camps, they would be exposed to many an assault against their present intentions.

We learned later that in each of their camps there came into use two kinds of prayers, one according to the Protestant manner for those who remained Protestant, and another according to the Catholic manner for our visitors and their families or friends who had decided to be converted with them. Since the latter are the

most influential and most esteemed in every respect, there is reason to hope that soon all will walk in the right way.

The Indian rarely sheds tears because he regards them as a sign of weakness unworthy of a man. Nevertheless, one day when I was explaining to them, by means of an interpreter, the Stations of the Cross, of which they had images before them, the oldest of my auditors, whom I had baptized in the Flathead camp during my first winter hunt, and the youngest of the catechumens could not hold back their tears. "What!" said the latter, sobbing, "the Great Chief of Heaven has suffered this for us! Ah! Until now I have had two hearts, but I am finished with that. Now I wish to have only one heart."

It was toward the end of autumn, 1845. Father S——— and I had left the reduction of St. Ignace for that of the Sacred Heart.[67] After paddling for two days, we still had some thirty miles of water to cover. The wind was contrary and the shore, along which we paddled, became so steep that, if we had been obliged to disembark, we could have found no foothold. Consequently, we postponed the rest of the voyage until the next day. But the next day the wind was still contrary and there continued a succession of showers which, during the night, had soaked us to the skin. Still another day and the rain had ceased, but the wind remained the same, and for four hungry mouths there were only three spoonfuls of flour, with only water for seasoning. What was to be done? We tried to retrace our route, but scarcely had we made a mile when the wind, growing more contrary than ever, blew us back to our starting point. The only avenue of escape from our impasse was an inhabited island on the horizon of the lake. But to traverse the three miles separating us from this island we had only a bark canoe so small that to get all our baggage into it and ourselves, too, it was necessary for some to kneel and others to stand erect, while the equipment was arranged as well as possible either to ballast or to permit steering of the frail craft. Besides, even during good weather, it is difficult to make such a long passage without the appearance of a leak. Now we had against us the whitecaps which were piling ever higher,

facing:
An Indian artist's conception of a fort, of wagons, and of workers.

and the sometimes abrupt movements of the paddlers forced us to struggle against them. Without giving explicit consideration to the laws of physics, each one asked himself how much would be required to displace the center of gravity. But since there was neither any choice nor any time to lose, all agreed that we had to attempt the crossing. To lend force to this decision everyone began to disencumber himself of the provisions.

As our Indians drank their meager beverage and measured with their eyes the distance separating us from the first lodge rising above the horizon, they informed us that on the island there was an old Indian woman dangerously ill. Then, of course, there could be no more hesitation. Evidently God was closing all other means of emerging from our predicament for the very purpose of saving this poor soul. So all of us, without tarrying any further, hastened over to the canoe. But even only a few feet from shore the waves became so menacing that our two paddlers, courageous and strong as they were, turned to ask us what they should do. Our answer was, "Do as you wish!" How these words were understood by them I don't know, but it is a fact that from that moment, with arms straining and heads lowered, they attacked the waves, cutting through them as if all Heaven had called out to them, "Courage! Forward!" Still, this did not prevent a voice coming up from the bottom of the flimsy craft to ask whether we would soon be there, especially when the sides of the canoe began to push in and out more than ever. Yes, we would soon be there, we replied, but how long this "soon"

seemed to everybody! At length we did arrive. And the sick woman? She was in very serious condition, we were told. I hastened to her and my arrival was timely indeed, for two hours later her soul, regenerated by the sacramental waters, entered—so we had reason to hope—the house of its eternal happiness.

Six more days spent on this land blessed by such a holy death added to what had already been accomplished ten baptisms of adults and three marriages. On the seventh day, when the entire island had become Christianized, with the winds at our back and our provisions once more replenished, we took advantage of the opportunity to continue on our way, after both the Fathers and the new children of the Faith had expressed their hope of seeing each other again where there shall be no more separations.

For an hour all went well. We had already passed the spot where, eight days earlier, we had been forced to call a halt. Suddenly, the wind and the waves attacked us so violently that we thought we would never survive. But *Modicae fidei! Quid timidi estis?* [68] At that moment, we heard a shot, and, immediately, there appeared a deer followed by some hunters who were our friends. That development ended our fears as well as our fast. That evening, at the reduction of the Sacred Heart, we gathered around a warm fire, recounted our adventures, and thanked God for His care of us during our short excursion. I enjoy recalling these events and, it seems to me, others might find some pleasure in reading about them. This is why I take the liberty of recounting two or three similar experiences.

facing:
The exterior and interior of a kitchen with which the native artist was undoubtedly familiar.

ON THE ELEVENTH of October, accompanied by an interpreter, I entered the lodge of the grand chief, who greeted me as a good friend.[69] On the previous evening, he had given me a magnificent robe embroidered with porcupine quills. Though surrounded by other lodges rivaling his in size, the chief's was conspicuous, even from a distance, for on this day a standard had been hoisted to mark an unusual occasion. The grand chief probably owed the majestic name he bore to the eagle represented on the standard. A few moments after our entry, the chief's lodge became the sanctuary where all the chiefs of the [Blackfoot] empire and the great officials of the Crown, ranged in a circle, listened to the *Veni Creator*. After this, we showed them the pictures of the Stations of the Cross. My interpreter was a little half-breed Gros Ventre, who knew the Blackfoot tongue very imperfectly.[70] I know not whether my explanations were properly translated, but the brightly colored pictures, aided perhaps by an interior voice, held the attention of my audience.

As we were about to leave, they brought in their sick. The most common malady of the Gros Ventres is an inflammation of the eyes, caused by their custom of plucking the eyelashes and painting the lids red. To remove the paint, I gave them a few drops of zinc ointment, which they believe to have miraculous healing powers. But how difficult it is to live up to a great reputation! Soon they were calling on me for all of their illnesses, future as well as present, internal as well as external. They even brought me cripples, hoping that I could cure them. Finally I had to tell them that such cases were beyond my power, but it was difficult to convince them. Fortunately, goodness of heart, with which the Gros Ventres are liberally endowed, prevented this situation from arousing in them anything other than disappointment.

On the fifteenth, a war party asked the missionary for letters of recommendation for Fort Crow [*le fort des corbeau*].[71] The party was led by the son of Chief Eagle. That young man was anxious to see the interior of the fort, as his father had done a year before. Since the youth had made me a pair of trimmed mittens, I could hardly refuse his request. Therefore, I wrote to the captain of the fort, asking him not only to receive the party, but to attempt to mediate between the Crows and the Blackfeet. Peace between these two nations would be a great blessing, for each had been trying for years to exterminate the other. Father De Smet had written along the same lines ten weeks before from Camp Victorious among the Flatheads.[72] I know not how the request was received or whether it was communicated to the Indians directly concerned. Members of the Crow tribe, whom I met later, said they knew nothing about it. It may be added that many traders thought that such a peace would be detrimental to commerce.

At the end of November, another party of Gros Ventres, en route to the camp of the Pend d'Oreilles, passed through a camp of the Piegans where I was at the time. Their intentions were entirely peaceful, and so favorable that they made me promise to pay them a visit in a few weeks.

I was accompanied by the interpreter from Fort Louis, an old hand in this country.[73] As we traveled, he showed me here a hill where so many Crows had scalped so many Gros Ventres, there a hollow where an enemy party had forced him to turn back. After these stories, he instructed me in the rules to follow in such cases.

"If you cannot avoid a battle, fight resolutely, because resolution frightens the enemy, who will then let you alone. If you are in a group, and your camp is not too far distant, try to escape to warn the camp. Brigands, you see, are afraid of being recognized for what they are and of receiving, later, what they deserve. They try to appear to be what they are not and this saves your companions. The worst situation is when you are caught. I do not mean being captured by something you can grasp or from which you can escape. I mean being caught by water, fire, the cold, by the night, by hunger, or by sickness. I was once caught by the night, in the middle of a river, on a small block of ice, going adrift at a frightening rate. I promised to have a Mass said in honor of the Blessed Virgin and

102

*The
Flatheads,
Coeur d'Alenes,
and
Blackfeet*

then I jumped. As luck would have it, I landed on the shore."

As we were talking, we dismounted to avoid a too-sharp descent. Finding ourselves at the bottom of a deep ravine, we worked our way to the top, without knowing where we were. To use my companion's expression, we were badly caught. When the sun set, the cold became very severe. Our feet were wet and our horses were exhausted. One can imagine our relief when we spied smoke, then the horses of the Gros Ventres, and finally the camp for which we had been hunting since morning.

This camp, on the shore of a small river, was so well hidden that one was on top of it before seeing it. In the camp, there was a small lodge, distinguished from all the others only by its poor appearance. But in it there was a fire, on which was a kettle, and around it places for us. And as a final touch to our new-found abundance, we met there the very best of the Gros Ventres, a man named the Bearded One. We were introduced then and there. In addition to the beard, which was not customary among the Indians, he wore a hood. But what made him appear to us a true Capuchin was neither the beard nor the hood, but his charity, his modesty, one might almost say, his religious virtues.[74] However that may have been, this excellent Indian, after serving us the best he had from the basement to the loft, took pleasure in collecting around us the best he had in his realm. For, poor as he seemed to be, he was a king and all his subjects, who had the greatest respect for him, listened to his guests as to envoys from Heaven. Since my departure from St. Mary's, I had seen nothing which could warm the heart of a missionary more. After explaining the major purpose of our coming to teach them about the way of Heaven, I summarized, in the following words, what I had resolved to ask them:

1 Would you be happy if the Blackrobes were to come to you to do what they had done among the Flatheads?
2 Would you prevent those with evil intentions from doing them harm?
3 Would you always be friends with the Flatheads?

To the first two questions, the affirmative answer was unanimous. To the third, they remained silent. What might be the reason for such a great change toward the Flatheads? They did not take long to give us the answer. After a pause of some minutes, they related in great detail all that had befallen them on the occasion of a recent visit with the Flatheads.

"With the best of faith," they told us, "we went to the Flatheads' camp to rejoice together over the alliance which had been made. We smoked the calumet, bartered, and so on. But at the moment of our departure, they not only broke several of the bargains that had been made, but also, they forcefully appropriated a rifle and a blanket."

This was obviously a grave accusation. Were the Gros Ventres untruthful? No. Were the Flatheads treacherous? This was even less probable. After a discussion, which was not a long one because it was conducted in good faith, the following facts were established:

1 The accused were not Flatheads, but rather Pend d'Oreilles.
2 These Pend d'Oreilles had been absent at the time of the great peace-making.
3 The Piegans, despite their treaty with the Flatheads, who were the allies of the Pend d'Oreilles, had just plundered the latter in a most reprehensible manner.
4 The Pend d'Oreilles had mistaken the Gros Ventres for Piegans, just as the Gros Ventres had mistaken the Pend d'Oreilles for Flatheads.

103

*The
Flatheads,
Coeur d'Alenes,
and
Blackfeet*

OVERLEAF

left

*The evil effects of dispensing
liquor to an Indian is cleverly
portrayed by one of them.*

right

*An Indian's idea of
various means of transportation
used by traders.*

N°5.   Traite et distribution de liqueurs

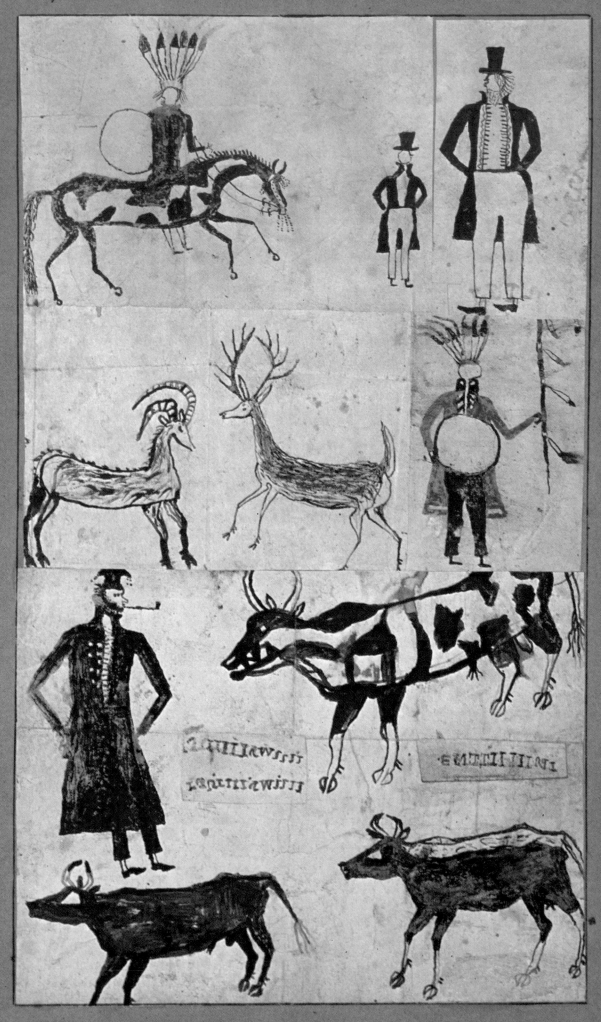

To take eagles, who have a means of escape which the kids and wolves lack, different tactics are required. What does the trapper do? Having laid out his bait, he crouches in his ditch, taking care to have an opening for one of his hands, and proceeds to wait patiently until the eagle swoops down on the bait. When the bird does this, the trapper seizes it by the talons, pulling it toward him violently. Before the bird knows what is happening, its head is smashed against a rock.

110

*The
Flatheads,
Coeur d'Alenes,
and
Blackfeet*

To what use can this dead bird be put? To many important uses. First, the eagle serves the manitou in the beliefs of many Indians. If they kill one, it is mostly to put some of its relics in their medicine sacks. Second, a bone flute is an excellent thing with which to invoke the manitou, and there is nothing better than the tibia of an eagle for making a flute. Thirdly, vanity being a divinity to which the Indians sacrifice no less than other men, the feathers of the eagle, especially those of the tail, are a means par excellence of adorning or ennobling their wearer. There is not an Indian who would not be jealous of such an ornament. The usual place for the feathers is the outer edge of the shield, the end of the lance, the headpiece of the chief; the headdress of the warrior; the hair of the young men and often the tail of their mount.

Generally the Indian loves everything that flutters in the wind. Thus he wears his hair long; his horse's tail and mane are long. He loves to have hides fringed and uses colored ribbons. Every kind of fringe and feather, but especially eagle feathers, please him so much that very often he would not relinquish things of this kind for a whole world full of useful goods. And it must be admitted that in the eyes of a vain man the costume of an Indian riding through camp at full gallop is not without its charm.

But let us return to our Gros Ventres. Toward evening we dismounted at the lodge of one who, next to the chief, was considered the greatest man of the camp. What brought him this honor was that in the eyes of my companions he was reputed to be the best trader; that is, he supplied the most robes for commercial purposes. Besides, he maintained a good lodge. In fact his lodge, which was one of the largest of the camp and distinguished by two medicine

animals at the entrance, contained everything a Blackrobe interpreter could have desired. I was placed in a kind of niche which was so well padded that I believe no similar alcove in a civilized country could have exceeded it in comfort. But how was it that the master hardly turned his gaze toward me? I was asking myself the reason for this cold reception, so out of keeping with the Gros Ventre character, when my host's silhouette, outlined clearly against the lighted portion of the lodge, made me recall a Gros Ventre to whom a few days before I had been unable to give the medicine he desired. At that time I did not know that, when it was a question of medicine and the Gros Ventre, it was much more expedient to give something worthless than to give nothing at all. A coldness caused by this memory was quite excusable, so instead of reproaching him—and without betraying that I had noticed anything—I slipped into his hand some tobacco which would enable him to play the generous host in his lodge. This pleasure which, thanks to the generosity of Fort Louis [Lewis], I was able to accord him without drawing on my already impoverished purse, so changed his attitude toward me that from that moment we were comrades.

Soon the lodge was filled with important men. We smoked the calumet and discussed some important matters. The principal personality of the group, who was the oldest, was called the General. This name had been given to him by the white men because of his prudence and courage, and perhaps also because of a laced coat of which the fort had once made him a present, as sometimes happened in the case of chiefs considered to be above the others. There was no one in the tribe who did not respect him, and he was appointed to give answers to my questions. To the first two questions, which I mentioned above, he answered:

"We have always been good to the whites. How could we now mistreat the Blackrobes? But as for the Flatheads . . ."

At this point the complaints which we have already listed, were renewed, but after the same explanation had been given the same results were achieved, though not without a certain small reservation.

"For," added the wise old man, "I think that, without ceasing to be friends, it would be good if in the future we saw each other only from a respectable distance."

Was this reservation a reasonable one? My experience so far had proven to me only too well that it was difficult indeed for two Indian tribes, which had been enemies for a long time, to stage a reunion without having some imprudent word escape from one side or the other. A single word of this kind was sufficient to rekindle all the fires of discord.

From this I concluded that, if we were to convert the numerous tribe of the Blackfeet, it would be necessary to work on their own terrain and that we should not delude ourselves with the vain hope of a physical rapprochement which would perhaps be the greatest obstacle to a conversion.

At the end of the meeting the old General put a few questions himself.

"Father," he said, "you have asked what we would do if the Blackrobes came to us. But can we be sure that the Blackrobes will come?" This was his chief question. I repeated what Father De Smet had said to one of their men as he was passing through the camp of the Piegans, namely, that if they persevered in their good dispositions and if the chief of the Blackrobes could take charge of some of their children—which there was reason to hope would be possible—I had no doubt that their wishes would be fulfilled.

The next day there were brought to be baptized some of the youngest children who had not yet had the happiness of receiving this sacrament. After the long ceremony, the Father was invited to a feast in the lodge of the medicine man who had been quartered in the Father's lodge while on his way to the Pend d'Oreilles. To show the Father how fondly his hospitality was remembered, the medicine man treated him to a kind of little fruit called beef berries boiled in scrapings of animal skin. Then, what was perhaps a little better, he informed the missionary of his desire to receive baptism, a desire all the more easy to fulfill because his one and only wife was equally desirous of being baptized. But since, in the case of adults, I had made it a rule to proceed very carefully in these matters (and it would have been impossible to instruct them suffi-

ciently well), I was able only to encourage him to persevere.

This accomplished, we resumed our way to the fort, where I hoped to do for some other adults what I had not been able to do for this one. We did not arrive until after dark, having crossed the Missouri on ice. This crossing could be dangerous because the current does not always permit the ice to form solidly. In such cases one usually used a probe to try the ice. In the absence of such an instrument, one does the best he can, which is what we did.

At the mere name of bloody Blackfeet, American travelers have visions of the worst possible things in Hell. A hundred times they have heard travelers preceding them say that these terrible enemies of the whites breathe only pillage and carnage, and this is not without some foundation in truth. But what the travelers do not always add is that the Blackfeet are all this and something else besides. Often they do such things only to avenge similar crimes of which their most outspoken accusers are themselves not always innocent. As for their appearance, it can be said that the Blackfeet do not manifest such horrible dispositions. With most of them, a lofty brow, a well-formed nose and a prominent chin impart to their features something that is not without nobility. They also show excellent breeding.

The tribe is divided into several bands, each one of which has its chief and its own particular

OVERLEAF

left

This three-in-one drawing by an Indian bears the French description: "Engagés—animals—some alphabetical characters."

right

Entitled "Religion and Superstition," this picture is truly unique as an Indian's attempt to convey an abstract idea.

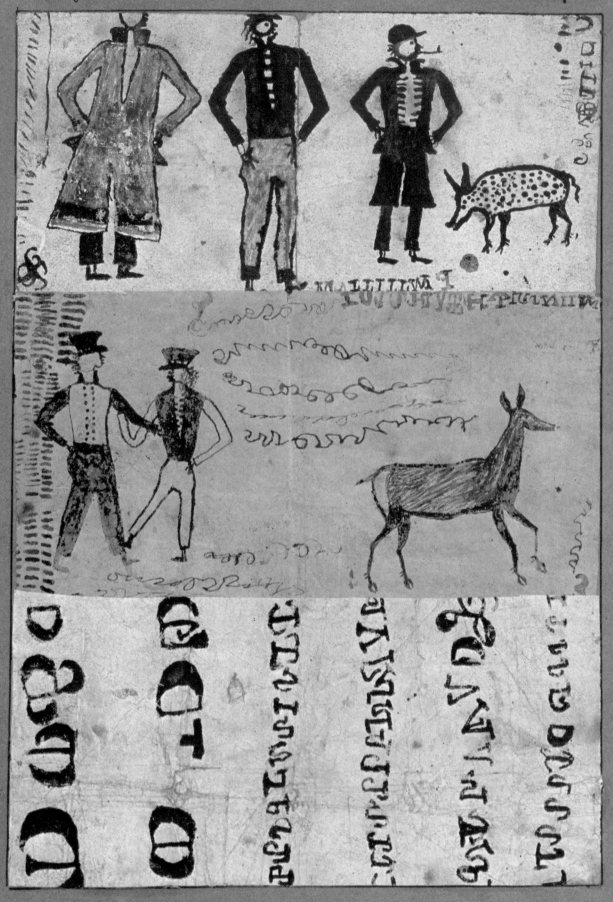

KSISTEKOMINA   N° 22

Ksistekomina

name. The largest group is called the Fish Eaters, not necessarily because they eat more fish than the other Blackfeet, but perhaps, as often happens among the Indians, to commemorate some exceptional circumstance. What was this circumstance for the Fish Eaters? Those I asked about it were not able to tell me.

Here is how I came to have a closer acquaintance with the Fish Eaters. After the autumn hunt, all the hunting expeditions composing the nation of the Blackfeet usually gather, for the purpose of trading, in the vicinity of Fort Louis [Lewis]. At this time the supply boat is abundantly filled with all the things needed for barter. The principal chiefs, having learned that the Blackrobe was there to offer them his services, all made haste to have a look at him. They were almost all in full regalia. Their costumes and visages, each one stranger and more picturesque than the other, would have been truly fine subjects to paint. The Blackrobe profited by the opportunity and made a few sketches. These resemblances were so very much to the taste of the subjects that they showed their appreciation by asking the painter to visit their camps. One of the most insistent belonged to the camp of the Fish Eaters. He was not their first chief, but by reason of his personal qualities and especially of his alliance with the master of the fort, who was married to the oldest of the chief's daughters, he was the most highly esteemed.[75]

I promised him that I would accept his invitation. But on the day when I had intended to fulfill my promise, the whites whom I had asked for an interpreter excused themselves on the grounds that people of this band had recently shown great hostility toward them. However well founded their fear may have been, it was so obviously an obstacle to what I believed were the designs of God that, in the absence of a white man who might accompany me, I turned to a Blackfoot, who spoke, as I also did, enough Flathead to enable me to make the Fish Eaters understand what I had to say to them. He did not dare to refuse my request on the spot, but when we had crossed the river, he lacked the courage to go farther, assuring me that the night before a man of the tribe [of Fish Eaters], armed with a huge knife, had broken into his lodge to kill his wife, a half-breed. Thus, to my

great disappointment, I had to postpone my project. But the postponement was not for long.

Toward the month of December, Panarquinima, our visitor, reappeared at Fort Louis [Fort Lewis]. And about this time the fort's chief interpreter was to go to his camp, and to several others, to deliver for his master a message which would be of interest to all. To complete this good fortune, the master of the fort and the interpreter felt that my presence would be in their interest. I hastened to take advantage of this opportunity and believing that our visitor was still of the same mind, I said to him, "I shall accompany you."

"If you wish," was his reply.

"Tell me what you think," I said. "If I go to your camp, it will only be to give pleasure to your people. If you think they do not care to see me, I shall not go."

"Get your horses," was his reply.

We left, and after three or four hours of trotting and galloping, we were introduced to the lodge of Panarquinima by Panarquinima himself. This was done in about the same manner as we had conversed, that is, rather coolly. Our host was displeased. Later on we shall see why.

The lodge was equipped with everything it needed to be the lodge of a grand chief and medicine man of the first rank. Between the fireplace in the middle of the enclosure and the place farthest from the door, which was that of the master, there were a large crescent, a very elegant metal perfuming pan, all the material needed for the calumet, a basin full of water to quench the thirst of the smokers and, to make this more convenient, a goblet floating on the surface of the water. Above all this there was a richly decorated medicine calumet, a kind of scepter with a little bell on it, a feather bonnet, some boxes, arms, and receptacles of every sort.

facing:
Unfortunately Father
Point did not translate this
Indian letter, written in 1842.

116

*The
Flatheads,
Coeur d'Alenes,
and
Blackfeet*

At the back of the lodge, opposite the opening, there was a bed of rich furs. To the right there was an elbow rest formed by a tripod. Beneath the tripod there was the living symbol of vigilance and nearby, the symbol of fidelity. That is, to the right and to the left of the chief were a cock and a dog. The cock alone had the right to pass between the chief and the fireplace, for this space was sacred. When the chief had taken his place, the Blackrobe humbly took the one which seemed most in keeping with his position. But as he did so, he had the misfortune to avail himself of the cock's exclusive privilege, and this so shocked the interpreter, who knew the chief's susceptibility on this point, that he could not help drawing the Blackrobe's attention to it. The chief, however, acted as if he had noticed nothing.

As the camp was fasting and would depart the next day, there was no time to lose. After a light repast, the liquid portion of which, taken freshly from a spring, was neither agreeable nor abundant, the important men were convened. When they arrived, the women of the lodge disappeared. The calumet was prepared in silence, lighted according to the rules of custom and passed from mouth to mouth until it had arrived at its starting point, where it was laid aside. I announced that I had something to say. Having every reason in the world for not wishing to offend anyone under these circumstances, I did what I could to say only what was pleasing. After thanking the assembly for having evinced a desire to see the missionary and to hear the word of the Great Spirit, I spoke of the advantages which would result from peace with the Flatheads and of the still greater advantages of establishing in their territory a reduction similar to that of St. Mary's. In such a situation, when the audience approves of what is said, its members, in a kindly manner, say, "Ai, Ai." At the end of my address not a single sound was uttered in answer.

At length Panarquinima turned imperiously to the interpreter and said with authority, "But what the Blackrobe tells us is the truth. How is it that he tells the truth when the truth has never come from the mouth of a single white man?"

"It is very true," answered the interpreter humbly, somewhat disconcerted by the question. "It is true that there are many white men who lie. But the Blackrobes are not like them. No one has ever reproached them even for the smallest lie."

"If this is so," replied the chief, "it is good."

Then he turned to the Blackrobe, assuming a little less haughty attitude. "Blackrobe," he said, "since you are not lying when you say that you love the redskins no less than the whites, and the Blackfeet no less than the Flatheads, if you wish to come into our lands, you are welcome. We shall be the friends of the Flatheads. If anyone should try to harm you, there will be someone there to defend you."

God holds all hearts in His hands. May He be forever blessed! This time the whole assembly voiced its approval, and the following day, before the middle of the morning, more than one hundred baptisms had been administered. All the lodges had already been dismantled. The mothers, who had waited until the eleventh hour of the day to procure for their children what they regarded as the greatest happiness, brought them to be baptized in the open air. The cold was so intense that the regenerative water, even as it ran from their brows, froze between the fingers of the missionary. With what fervor these poor Indian women showed their gratitude! They repeated their "Ai, Ai" so tenderly that even the hardest of hearts would have been softened.

As we were leaving this budding church, which had been begun in such a marvelous manner, we heard sobs coming from a neighboring lodge, the only one, I believe, which still stood. The death of an old idolater was being mourned. I had not been notified that he was so near to the end. The grief I felt at not having been able to help him cast a shadow over the joy I felt at having helped so large a number of others in spite of my unworthiness. Honor and glory to God alone!

Was Panarquinima converted on this occasion? In part, yes, but not entirely. He was too much attached to his medicine, and up to that time he had reaped too many honors by means of it, to renounce it all at once. And despite his natural good sense in many of the inconsequential things of life, such was the dominion of the Prince of Darkness over him that he carried his extravagant credulity so far as to believe the little black and yellow bird, whose winged carcass he wore on the top of his head, was nothing more or less than the master of life. He also believed that there was a place on a nearby island from which emerged the most beautiful bison in as large numbers and in the same manner as plants grow out of the earth. He also believed that in a heap of iron, which had somehow been brought into his country, there was a virtue which produced the most beautiful horses. To humble a spirit so proud of its imagined powers and thus to lead him to the light of the Gospel, there had to be one of those strokes of divine justice which always brings conviction. This grace was not to be lacking.

Toward the month of February our ambitious Panarquinima, wishing to add something to his great name, led a large war party against the Assiniboines.[76] He forgot nothing in preparing for the success of an enterprise so glorious in his mind. But what he imagined to be appropriate was a sacrifice to the sun on an unprecedented scale. Beautiful calumets, prize blankets, hides, cloth of various colors—nothing was spared. And what happened? Our glorious hero, assisted by his cohorts, in one night stole ninety horses from the Assiniboines while the latter were asleep. But the following night the vanquished staged a surprise attack on the conquerors and not only recovered their property, but pursued the thieves so relentlessly that they forced them to abandon their own equipment, including arms, robes, flags, calumets, medicine sacks, and so on. In spite of their speed, many of the refugees returned to their camp with frozen extremities. And how many did not return at all! But what was more important to Panarquinima than all the victories he had hoped for was a new conviction, namely, that to be victorious it is necessary to have recourse to a power other than the one which shines only during the day or the one which shines only during the night. This conviction came to him as a result of his campaign. Thus, when he reappeared before the Blackrobe, he had no difficulty in promising that he would have nothing more to do with the honors that had been accorded him. To prove this he handed over to the missionary the so-called master of life, which had served him as a crown, and indicated that he wanted to be of the true prayer. May God give him grace not to fall again into his error.

Much-needed game was sometimes on the other side of a steep hill.

Climbing was often difficult for both man and beast.

I I I

Hunting the Buffalo

On the subject of hunting Father Point's records are extremely detailed.
He explains how large- and small-scale hunts were conducted. He describes scouting
for game, how the kill was utilized, how an unlucky Indian could share in the take, and
the women's part in drying the meat and curing the hides.
Since the missionary accompanied the Indians on several winter and summer hunts,
he speaks with considerable authority on this vital phase of Indian life.

THE ANIMAL to which many writers give the name buffalo—a name used by the English—is the bison of the naturalists. The French call it the ox, just as they call the antelope the kid, or the buttes of Missouri and Nebraska names such as a house, a citadel. So, too, the French gave the Chinooks, the Piegans, and the Salish such names as Coeur d'Alenes, Blackfeet, and Flatheads. Though some of these expressions seem somewhat strange, they are, nevertheless, correct, if not in the literal sense, then certainly in the figurative one. Thus, figuratively, the Piegans could be called Blackfeet because they were given this name when they were walking far from the path of righteousness. The Chinooks could be called Coeur d'Alenes because tenderness of heart was wanting in their character. But, in the case of the Salish, there is nothing in either their appearance or their intellectual and moral qualities which could justify the very singular name of Flatheads, unless one assumes that the Chinooks, who actually did follow the barbaric practice of flattening the still tender heads of their children, at one time constituted one nation with the Flatheads. But this is improbable, since the Chinooks lived on the Pacific coast while the Flatheads lived in the Rocky Mountains.[77] The distance between their customs and languages was probably just as great as that between the places they inhabited. If this supposition is true, what explanation would remain for the fact that the Chinooks, in spite of their horrible practice which is still continued, have preserved their primitive name while the Flatheads have lost theirs?

What is a bison? The bison resembles the lion in its mane, the camel in its hump, the hippopotamus or the rhinoceros in its tail and the skin of its quarters, and the bull in its horns and legs. Its black horns are short and it has a long beard of coarse hair. A forelock, also of coarse hair, hangs loosely between the horns as far down as the eyes. Its breast is broad; its rump, slender; its tail, thick and short; its legs, stout and turned outward. A hump of long russet hair rises on its shoulders. The rest of its body is covered with black wool. It has a ferocious appearance, but it is really gentle. The largest are found between the Missouri and the Mississippi. They grow to about half the size of an elephant.

Though the female is smaller than the male and less ferocious in appearance, she nevertheless surpasses the male when it is necessary to defend her young, attacking as many as a dozen wolves at a time with admirable courage. But in the opinion of the hunter there is a quality which surpasses even the heroism, and that is the delicacy of the flesh of the cow. Thus, when a hunter returns from the chase, one should not ask him if it is a bull that he is bringing back. This question alone would mark the inquirer as a stranger to the country and still more to the art of hunting. In terms of this art—and this should be remembered—the female is more noble than the male.

The flesh of the buffalo can take the place of all other foods. As with bread, one never tires of it. In the field, the hunter lives off of the cuts that cannot be preserved or which are not worth the trouble of preserving. The loins are daily bread during the closed season. The tongues and the humps furnish feasts for great occasions. From the marrow and the scraps of meat is made a kind of cheese, which is the provision of the traveler. Even the entrails and the brains are put to use. To what use can the rest be put? The hides are made into robes, tents, packs, shields, bridles, saddles, stirrups, and thongs of all kinds. The horns are made into vessels, spoons, powder horns, bows, and sheaths. The tail is used to make whips and various ornaments. The hair is made into *essuies cabrasses* and cloth.[78] The bladder is used to make receptacles for liquids, grease, medicine, and paint. The bones are made into cutting and agricultural instruments and little bones into osselets of all kinds for games, cults, and so on. And if wood should happen to be scarce, the buffalo droppings can be used as a substitute in making fires. In fact this manure is so necessary a factor in sacrifices to a manitou that without it even the strongest smoke of the sacrificial fire would be disagreeable to him.

The buffalo is for the Indian, at least insofar as he is superstitious, something more than manna in the dessert. Hence, all his efforts are bent toward procuring the buffalo. I almost said that all his desires are directed toward the buffalo. For there is no fatigue he will not endure, no enemy he will not defy, no form of death he will not face to get the great beasts. This is proven by the fact that the Flatheads have gone into Blackfoot territory to hunt.

Are these animals numerous? "They are so numerous," wrote Chateau-Briant [sic] in the account of his travels in America at the end of the last century, "that when they migrate, it sometimes takes several days for a herd to pass, like an immense army. Their movement can be heard from a distance of miles and the trembling of the earth can be felt."[79] But today their number has so diminished that in 1842 the hunting camp with which I was traveling had to march twenty-four days before finding any trace of a herd. I am speaking here for the Rocky Mountain region where they are most abundant. Whence this great falling off in number? It is a result of the campaign of extermination carried on by American commerce. And what do Indians receive in compensation? Only things which destroy men and serve to enslave women. I am speaking of the introduction of liquor, which degrades the natives more than ever, and of vices and diseases formerly unknown in the wilderness.

There is only one means of preventing, if not the demoralization, at least the annihilation of these poor peoples already so reduced numerically from what they were at the beginning of this century. Is it the continuation of trade in its present form? Is it the preaching of error by Protestant missionaries? Is it mere material aid from the Government? Experience has given abundant proof that none of these means will suffice. I repeat that there is only one means and this is to make of them good and true Christians. That is what we are trying to achieve with the help of God, as will be evident from the notes which follow.

THE BUFFALO HUNT IN GENERAL

Finding the Animals

ARRIVED IN COUNTRY where it is hoped that buffalo may be found, the camp halts and the chief sends out scouts. There is no time to lose, for it is essential to see without being seen either by the animals or, what is even more important, by enemy war parties. When buffalo are discovered, and the enemy fails to appear, the scout returns hastily. As soon as he is in sight of the camp, he opens his robe wide and lifts his rifle into the air to indicate that game has been discovered. At this sign the whole camp rejoices in proportion to the length of their fast, which has often lasted several weeks. The scout arrives, takes his seat in silence, and the calumet is passed to him. After solemnly inhaling a puff, he tells what he has seen. The chief then stands among the lodges and solemnly announces: "My children, let us thank the Great Spirit, for game has been discovered. Prepare your arms and your best horses, et cetera. We shall leave at such and such a time." Talk is resumed, children jump about; even the dogs and horses, growing restless, seem to sense what is about to take place. The hunters prepare their weapons, the women prepare their kettles, and the children make ready their knives and spoons. All this is quickly accomplished, for the whole thing is conducted much the same way as at the time of our first parents.

At the beginning of the autumn hunt the only well-fed beings in the camp are the horses. They are too valuable and too badly needed not to be carefully looked after. The dogs are pitifully lean, but never better disposed to run down small game. Woe to the wolf that ventures from the woods when they are around; in ten minutes all that will remain of him will be the skin. When, instead of a wolf, it is a deer or a goat, the pursuit is no less hot, but the profit is not all theirs. On the return from the hunt the horses and dogs are just as dissimilar as before, but now the leanness and fatness have changed places. This is caused by the difference in pasture and in the nature of their activities.

Manner of Stalking the Animals

As in all kinds of hunting, buffalo should be stalked as carefully as possible. The slightest noise will stampede the herd. Caution must be exercised by the hunters, if not lest they be seen, at least, lest they be recognized. For hunting on a small scale, a cap with long ears is worn and the hunter crawls on all fours so that the herd will notice nothing but what appears to be an animal just like themselves. But for a running hunt on a large scale, this is what is done: After the hunters have knelt and recited their prayers, they mount and, taking advantage of the most favorable natural concealment, advance as noiselessly as possible in order to come up in the face of the wind. The very breath of the hunters would suffice to stampede the herd, which would be a poor victory indeed. When the hunters have arrived at a point where they have the wind in their faces, three things are sufficient for the Indians to reach their prey, namely, the formation of a straight line, the signal from their chief, and the full gallop of their horses. If they have to gallop only five or six minutes to reach their prey, they have very favorable chances.

Manner of Attacking

The running hunt is an attack to the death. The animal belongs to the first one who hits him. To strike first is not only a gain; it is an honor, and just as in the Indian wars, the first

A Blackfoot conveyance called a travois *is an ingenious device of many uses.*

*When not transporting heavy loads,
the* travois *can serve as a ladder for erecting lodges.*

Among the tasks left almost exclusively to women
were those of preparing, curing, and even of transporting buffalo hides.

A friendly party of Gros Ventres passed through a
Piegan encampment during Father Point's stay with the latter group.

shock is the rudest. In an instant pell-mell ensues. During the summer hunt, this first scene, which is the most interesting, is obscured by a cloud of dust so dense that none of the detail can be distinguished. But in the winter, the horses and the horsemen, the bulls and the cows and the calves, the wolves, the rifles and bows and arrows, the game falling or fleeing— all are outlined so vividly against the white of the snow that one would really have to have the soul of a St. Francis Borgia not to look on with bulging eyes.[80]

Soon there is a complete rout. Columns of fleeing animals can be seen to detach themselves from the main herd, some pounding off in one direction, others in another; some in a straight line, others in curved formation. Some flee uphill, some downhill, depending on the accidents of terrain. All the columns are headed by the more alert or robust as leaders, not making a stand against the danger, but fleeing as swiftly as possible. For the skillful hunter this is the moment for making his choice of game. If the number of animals is large, everyone makes haste to do this. But the hunters are all respectful, one to another. One never finishes what another has begun. If an animal has been wounded, but not mortally, the horseman maneuvers until he can deal the death blow most effectively. If the animal has been wounded mortally, the hunter pursues it calmly, knowing that it will soon fall. To seek to hasten its death would be the height of imprudence, for there have been cases in which the animal, with hardly a breath of life left, still found enough strength to avenge its blood. The bison is just as formidable at the moment of death as it is fearful of the hunter under normal circumstances. When one of the animals stops, exhausted, the prudent hunter always keeps a respectful distance. There is nothing more majestic than the fall of a bison. It seems that to redeem itself from the shame it has suffered, it holds out to the bitter end without betraying any sign of weakness.

When the buffalo has finally fallen, the hunter does not tarry to skin it, but goes immediately in hot pursuit of a second, a third, and so on, just as long as the vigor of his horse can respond to his own ardor. Men have been known to dispatch as many as fifteen without

once dismounting from their horses. Some, called *fareaux*, sometimes hit several without even reducing the speed of their horses.[81] And, what may appear incredible, they sometimes hit three with the same arrow, drawing it out after each strike and sending it after another fleeing buffalo. I once saw an Iroquois who had sent an arrow clear through a buffalo and, with that single shot, killed a second buffalo running alongside the first one. The same man, when pursued by a huge buffalo, saved himself by plunging his knife into its heart. But let us save these details for the following chapters.

It is evident that the honor and profit of the hunter depend no less on the vigor of the horse, the quality of the weapon, and the strength of one's arm than on the skill of the hunter himself. The best horse is one which edges up closest to the buffalo without taking fright. In hunting terminology this tactic is called "sticking to the animal." For the ordinary hunter, the best weapon is the bow. For the superior hunter, the best weapon is the rifle. With this, one hunter can do on the run what another can do only while standing still.

Trapping the Buffalo

For those who have no horse or who have only a poor one, there remains one resource. They choose a level plot of ground, elevated abruptly above another plot, and set up two rows of posts forming a triangle with its base at the point where the steep drop occurs and its apex at some distance. At the apex of the triangle an opening is left, large enough to allow a man to squeeze through but too narrow to permit a buffalo to escape. This done, the man who is to pass through this opening approaches the herd on all fours, dressed in a buffalo skin, with horns mounted on his head. The herd, seeing him approach in this disguise, is at first somewhat astonished, for, after all, even if he does have a skin and horns like they do, his carriage is that of a quite extraordinary animal. But stupidity always wins out among fools; the stupid herd, blindly following its new guide, descends with him into the enclosure. Only the guide emerges, and he then has the game boxed in.

If you have not the means of building an enclosure, but have a number of companions, place some of them in a blind alley or in some other recess, and send the rest to look for the herd with instructions to drive them in your direction by beating drums. Then, proceeding on the principle that fleeing animals will always try to cross your path, instead of advancing precipitously and noisily, you move at a gentle gallop, directing your course so that it is parallel with the ambush, and you can be sure that the entire fleeing herd will fall into it. When, instead of this kind of terrain, you have at your disposal the steep banks of a river, attack the herd from the rear and, in place of the gentle gallop, direct your course precipitously toward the cliff and yell at the top of your voice. You will see the entire herd, down to its last member, jump over the edge. But this butchery is a hunt to extermination.

A word now on the small-scale hunt. It is usually done on foot and cannot be accomplished by a large number of hunters. It requires less exertion and less courage, but more skill and patience, than the large-scale hunt. When a herd of buffalo has been discovered, the first thing to do is to advance cautiously, taking care to conceal your identity. When you have arrived within rifle or arrow range, place yourself in some recess or behind some bush and from there take stock of the relative positions. Choose the females, marking out the fattest and the oldest, and see if among them there is one which leads the entire herd. In a large herd there is almost always a female leader, and she is accordingly called the queen. When you have discovered her, aim carefully, for if she falls, you will see the entire herd group itself around her, manifesting nothing but amazement. Recharge your rifle, or better, if you are not far distant, take another arrow, but don't hurry. Wait until the herd has calmed down. Then shoot again, and continue in this way until you have bagged a sufficient number.

Dressing the Kill

Immediately after the hunt the animals are dressed, that is skinned, and the tongues, humps, legs, and all parts that may serve some

purpose are removed. For a good hunter this is a matter of twenty or thirty minutes' work. This is done during large-scale as well as during small-scale hunts. If your camp is nearby and there are others who can help you, take advantage of this. If the camp is far distant and you have only your horse or even only your shoulders, take what you can carry of the choicest cuts and return with as many persons and as many times as are necessary to recover the rest. In the meantime place your hat, your shirt, or some other object over the pile you wish to preserve. This will serve as a scarecrow. Don't forget to scatter on the spot a few pinches of gunpowder. Whatever might be attracted by your catch has an aversion to this kind of thing.

This is what is done when the animals are scarce, as I was told by a very expert hunter. If they are plentiful and provisions are in good supply, less trouble is taken. Only the tongues and the humps are saved, for there is never an overabundance of these. The rest is abandoned to the wolves. It was thus that my hunter friend revealed to me all the secrets of his art. He was blind in the right eye, but was able to aim so accurately with the other that in one day he killed twenty cows and in less than one month over a hundred deer. One day, while I was present, an enormous buffalo charged, horns lowered, through the lodges of the camp. Manuel, my hunter friend, spied him and with his first arrow wounded him mortally and with his second stretched him out.

Return from the Great Hunt

When the horse has become exhausted and the herd has disappeared, the hunter retraces his steps to collect his game. And it is really astonishing with what facility he recognizes it. If you wish to know, he can even tell where he wounded it and where he left it. But what is very admirable, under circumstances ordinarily so critical both for the modesty and for the probity of the ordinary hunter, is the absolute absence of any kind of wrangling among the hunters. During the total of five or six hundred days, when I followed the Indians on their hunting expeditions, I learned of not a

*The flower of the camass plant is a beautiful blue,
which makes the plain where it grows abundantly resemble a lake. Its root,
roasted and preserved, is a valuable source of food.*

*A by-product of summer hunts was the variety
of fruit that could be gathered along the way.*

*A chance encounter with sworn enemies
was one of the constant hazards of travel in the
Rocky Mountain territory.*

*A Nez Percé family takes to the trail, perhaps to find
a new food supply.*

single instance in which the shadow of a quarrel arose on this point. There is nothing worth quarreling about, they say. If, for lack of a good mount or of skill, a hunter is unable to provide for his family, he will follow, at a short distance, a hunter better endowed or more lucky than he. If this hunter speaks to him first, it is a sign that he wishes to give him something. If this hunter has nothing to say to the one following him, the poor man has nothing to say either, but promises himself that another day he will follow another hunter. Perhaps he adds that this one whom he has just followed in vain had better never follow him.

On returning to the lodges, the next task is one for the women. On them devolves the responsibility for the second dressing of the game. Postponing the more time-consuming tasks, such as the drying of the meat, the dressing of the skins, the making of packs, and so on, they quickly hang their kettles over the fire and refresh the hunter, who sleeps, smokes, or jests, depending on whether he has company and tobacco, or lacks these things.

ACTIVITIES ON THE DAY AFTER THE HUNT

THE MEN SLEEP while the women dry the meat and dress the hides. In the winter, the meat is cooked by suspending it over the fire. In summer, this is done by letting it dry in the sun. Dressing the hides is what one calls the operation of scraping off the flesh [still adhering to the hide] by means of an instrument shaped like a mason's chisel, but manipulated like a short pickax. The first step in this process is that of stretching the hide on pegs driven into the ground, but in such a manner as to avoid having the hide touch the ground. The second step is the scraping process described above. In the third step, the whole hide is rubbed with the brains taken from a buffalo skull. The fourth step is to soak the hide in warm water for about a half hour. In the fifth step, the hide is suspended from a cord about as high as a man can reach and then scraped with a stone until the desired degree of flexibility is attained. In the sixth step, the irregularity caused by the hump is eliminated by cutting the hide in such a way that the remaining parts can be perfectly united. At this point, some tribes cut away only what is superfluous. Others cut the whole hide into two parts and then, after the edges have been made even, join the pieces by means of stout sinews taken from the carcass of a deer. The hides which are to be used for making lodges or for clothing, except the robe, are stripped clean of hair. For these purposes, as well as for making packs, hides with the softest hair are chosen. These will usually be hides from animals killed in the summer. The best hides, those taken in winter, are reserved for making robes.

If good appearance is to be combined with utility, then the hide is once more stretched out on the frame like a piece of cloth to be embroidered. By means of a kind of chisel of wood or bone, dipped into a glue made of scrapings and colored according to desire, symmetrical lines are deeply impressed into the hide. These lines are ineffaceable. In the same manner are painted the luxurious panniers which the more elegant individuals suspend from the sides of their saddles. Finally, if one wishes to carry elegance and luxury as far as they will go, one adds to the painting and the carving embroidery work in glass beads or in porcupine quills; the seams and borders are adorned with hair, bristles and fringes of all kinds hung heavily with deer teeth, the whole often weighing several pounds. But all this extra work is done during the closed season.

The largest task after the making of packs is the making of the lodges. A single lodge sometimes requires fifteen or twenty hides. Lodges are designated by the number of skins used in their making just as we describe houses by their number of stories or windows. For the food provisions, which come first of all, this is the order followed. First of all the *plats-côtés* are put aside for immediate use.[82] They are prepared by roasting. Also used immediately are the bony parts of the hump, which are boiled, and the stomach, which is cut into strips and either boiled or roasted. The choice cuts, capable of being preserved, such as the tongue or the top of the hump, are kept for festive occasions. The pieces destined to serve as daily provisions are first cut into slices and either dried or smoked, and then beaten with a wooden mallet, to make them tender or to enable them to be packed more closely in the packing boxes. Thus stored away, they can be preserved for months or even years and may be eaten either raw or cooked.

As for the non-meat diet, one can add fat to it in the form of fillets, called in the language of the country "remains." It is said that one does not eat his bread without butter. If you have a cake of wheat mixed with marrow, the best fat in the world, then you have something with which to regale your friends. The first-class gourmets—that is factors at the forts, the traders and the bigwigs of the forts and trading posts—crown their repasts with a dish of beef berries mixed with cream and sugar. But the Indians' taste is simpler. The only seasoning they know is a good appetite and when there is a dessert, they have it first as we do soup, or as wine was drunk in olden times.

*Hunting
the Buffalo*

*Two gaily bedecked Indians
identified by the artist only as "A Kansa and a Crow."*

*The Bannocks, portrayed above, were
members of one of the smaller tribes in the Rocky Mountain foothills.*

The guardians of the calumet are especially
honored members of a tribe.

This picture of an admirable
Gros Ventre family contains a self-portrait of Father Point.

*The interior of a chief's lodge
faithfully reproducing in color items elsewhere described in words.*

*A closer view of some of the things to be seen
in a chief's lodge, including the dog and the cock.*

At one point in the savages'
"practice of medicine" the fire which had been extinguished is rekindled
and the previous milling about subsides.

Understandably the missionaries
regarded the medicine man's antics as "Black Magic."

*A dance called the "Mad Dog"
was ceremoniously performed during a festival visit.*

*The horse that carries the calumet on the march
is exempt from all other use and she who leads him is the
most honored woman of the tribe.*

Maceration was one form of torment practiced under diabolical influence.

Most Indians were firm believers in signs and portents.

*Although the dogs
help to procure game for food, the profit is not all theirs.*

*Buffalo must be carefully stalked
because it is easy to cause a herd to stampede.*

*When a herd has been sighted,
the scout quickly returns to camp, his gun raised in the air as a sign
that buffalo have been discovered.*

*At the announcement of the sighting of game
the whole camp rejoiced.*

*Prior to the coming of the missionaries
no hunting or fishing expedition was undertaken until its leader had invoked
the assistance of his manitous.*

*One medicine man admitted that a power
greater than his own—that of the Blackrobe—prevented him
from working his magic.*

*Before a large-scale running hunt
those who were to participate knelt and recited their prayers.*

*With the wind in their faces the Indian hunters
awaited a signal from their chief to set their horses at full gallop.*

The best horse
was one which edged up closest to the buffalo without taking fright.

For the ordinary hunter the best weapon was the bow.

The running hunt was usually carried to the point of extermination.

For the superior hunter, the best weapon was the rifle.

*If an animal had been wounded mortally,
the hunters pursued it, knowing it would soon fall.*

There is nothing more majestic than the fall of a bison.

*Tormenting a wounded buffalo
could be risky, but Indian children sometimes did it.*

*A buffalo with scarcely a breath
of life left still found strength to avenge its blood.*

*During the great hunt
columns of frightened animals detach themselves from the main herd
and flee in different directions.*

*In the evening, hunters gathered together
for conversation and to smoke the calumet around the fire.*

Winter and Summer Hunts
with the Flatheads, the Coeur d'Alenes,
and the Blackfeet

In this portion of his manuscript, Father Point emphasizes his apostolic work during winter and summer hunts. He also describes chance encounters with hostile tribes. One is impressed with the bitter hardships he experienced and it is clear that his influence increased because of the grace with which he endured them. Throughout this section one can see Nicolas Point becoming the experienced missionary, who knew when to speak and when to keep silent. Because of his genuine affection for his Indian companions, they come alive in both vivid words and colorful paintings.

*A Winter Hunt
with the Flatheads:
December 29
to April, 1842*

DURING THE MARCH to the hunting grounds, the women are in charge of the baggage. To keep the pack animals together and moving forward, they are obliged to run up and down along the line of march. All the while, the women must also care for the children who are too young to fend for themselves. When a pole works loose, or a horse stumbles or becomes mired or loses his load, the women must dismount and take care of the problem. Dismounting is, in itself, complicated by the fact that the saddles are raised, front and back, by a sort of platform more than a foot high. When the company reaches a campsite, the women are obliged to erect the lodges, cut the wood, and prepare the food. They must do this in spite of fatigue or injuries or illness or even increases in their families. But, remarkably, during the entire course of the hunt, a period of three months, not a single one of them showed any impatience.

*Animals less mammoth
than the buffalo were sometimes trapped in a pit.*

*Animals identified by the artist
as "antelopes" were sometimes the objects of small-scale hunts.*

After the women, the grand chief has the most responsibility on his shoulders. He must lead the group, choose the campsites, show to everyone an example of courage and vigilance. The heads of families stand guard at night and hunt during the day. The young people pass their time doing nothing and at night they enjoy undisturbed sleep. The little children eat and amuse themselves from morning to night. Strangely, they never seem to quarrel.

On the evening of the first day, Paulin, the chief of the expedition, had the floor. He recounted the things of his youth in a natural, modest, and gay fashion. Among other curious events, he spoke of the first appearance of the white man in his land, of the mission of the Great Ignatius to St. Louis, and so on.

During the night of December 29–30 we began to sleep on the snow for the first time. The sky was obscured, the winds moaned through the pines of the forest. In a little lodge near that of the missionary could be heard the sobs of a young woman and her child who had seen the one dearest to them in the world laid to rest in his grave. How worthy is the sorrow that wants no witnesses but God and the night!

On December 30, toward sunset, the camp gathered about the chief. Upon arriving in enemy territory, the lodges were arranged in circular cordons, and the most valuable things placed in the center. Until then each one could pitch his lodge where he wished. All that was valuable and all who were ailing were located near the lodge of the Blackrobe. In the evening there was community praying. The chiefs asked to be informed of the arrival of feast days, for, as they said, it was their desire that everything during their travels be conducted as at St. Mary's. These were regulations for ordinary days: After prayers, there was singing before and after an instruction. Before leaving for the hunt in the morning, and before retiring to rest in the evening, three Hail Marys were recited. In spite of the cold, which was very intense during the whole of the hunt, these regulations were faithfully observed. Besides that, they recited the rosary devoutly every day, and every evening the children came to the missionary's lodge for catechism and singing lessons. Often the priest was surrounded by a crowd of elders listening to their children recite. Fitted in between the prayers and the childrens' catechism lessons was a time devoted exclusively to the men, thanks to the missionary's supply of tobacco.

It is commonly known that among the Indians the calumet, the symbol of amity, is still the principal instrument of the cult. Formerly, the Flatheads would not have failed to offer the first fruits to the Sun and the Earth and they would have considered themselves blameworthy, indeed, if, in passing the sacred calumet from one to the other they failed in even the slightest proper ceremonial detail. But now all they attempt while smoking is to maintain with decorum the rules of civility. Usage requires that the youngest prepare the tobacco. He always mixes in with it a kind of small leaf, called by the Indians *kinnikinnik*, which enters into the composition of the calumet's contents only for the purpose of tempering its force or, even more important, of making the principal component stretch further.[83] It is for the most honorable member of the group to light the calumet thus prepared, and his neighbor offers him fire for this purpose. Once lighted, the calumet makes the rounds, going from right to left. Each smoker contents himself with two or three inhalations. These inhalations vary according to the manners of the smoker. The elegant ones exhale the smoke through the nose; or, if they exhale it through the mouth, it must be in such a manner that the smoke comes out diagonally. Smoking time is during conversations. The speech of the Indian under these circumstances has something solemn about it. He gives each word the proper intonation and the words are always accompanied by a gesture. His gestures are so thoroughly in accord with his thought that, with their help and the help of a few conventional signs, persons speaking an entirely different language can understand each other. I have seen Indians engage in long conversations of this kind without missing anything that they desired to communicate to each other. This talent has been acquired and perfected as a result of the need for speaking with people whose language they do not know.

When the Indians are among their equals, or when their superiors set them the example, their conversation is sometimes intermixed with little jokes. The Flathead rarely laughs out loud, but

*Bears are naturally ferocious
and very dangerous, but a good hunter does not fear them.*

*Hungry dogs were fearless dogs,
even to the point of attacking an animal many times their size.*

*When an eagle swooped down
on the bait laid for it, the trapper, crouching in the ditch, seized it
by the talons.*

*Wolves, always gluttons,
liked their food prepared, which made it easy to lure them to a trap
baited with a carcass.*

his smile has something at the same time naïve and spiritual. What usually excites them most is the memory of old practices in the worship of their manitous or the recollection of how awkward they were when they tried out the implements of civilization.

"The first time I saw a rifle," the old chief told me, "I wanted to put it to use before I had learned how to handle it. To get a better aim, instead of resting the stock against my shoulder, I supported it against the thing in the middle of my face. I pulled the trigger. Alas! My poor nose." He ended his little story with a smile.

Sometimes it is good to permit oneself a little pleasantry to erase the frown from the face of an Indian. One should do this rarely and the humorous remark should be an adroit one, otherwise the Indians, who are like children, too readily lose their respect [for the missionary]. Besides, the Flathead, who is naturally a shrewd observer, can jest with finesse. It is necessary to be clever at repartee if you do not wish to be bested.

On the evening of December 30, Titiche Loutso, surnamed the Bravest of the Brave, recounted with a simplicity very admirable in a man of his character, a remarkable event that had occurred just recently. It concerned the apparition of the Blessed Virgin on Christmas Eve, to an orphan of the tribe, an event which has already been mentioned elsewhere. Loutso had left St. Mary's without having had the courage to make the sacrifice required to merit reception of baptism. He needed more than ordinary grace and what he recounted was the beginning of this grace. With what wisdom does divine goodness dispense its favors!

On December 31, there was good news. The grand chief of the Nez Percés had the interpreter tell the missionary:

"For a long time I have desired to be baptized, but since you never said anything to me, I thought you did not love me. This is why I have remained silent so long."

"You were good, old, and a great chief. This is why I have waited, convinced that you needed no one but yourself to help you to decide."

This answer satisfied him. The Feast of the Three Kings was set as the day for his bap-

tism.[84] He was to be named Charlemagne, a name that suited him in every respect, for he was great in stature, in courage, and in authority.

On January 1, at daybreak, there was a salvo of artillery. The chief and his company paid a visit to the missionary. Throughout the entire camp visits were exchanged. There were handshakes given in sign of friendship. Everyone appeared happy.

Since January 3 was the day on which the camp was to be joined by the Pend d'Oreilles, it was desired that the missionary be mounted on a white horse. There was some talk of arranging for a rifle salute. The chiefs and the braves were at the head of the [marching] column. Not far from the gorge, called Hell Gate because of the numerous massacres it had witnessed, the march was held up by a river. The ice on the river had to be broken, for it was not strong enough to support a crossing on foot. When the crossing had been made, I asked whether we would soon see the Pend d'Oreilles. The reply was that they were already with us. In fact, as I turned around I found myself face to face with the four red plumes worn by their grand chief. He was giving me his hand. He and the other Pend d'Oreille chiefs assembled at my lodge. Not a single Flathead chief joined us. It was evident that, contrary to custom and especially to my expectations, their hearts were not in harmony.

The Feast of the Three Kings was approaching and I worked for an understanding between the Flatheads and the Pend d'Oreilles. With this end in view, couplets composed in honor of the new Magi were set to the most joyful music possible. But it was useless. The Orphic lyre would have been impotent under these circumstances, for faces remained as cold as ever. It seemed no one wanted to be in harmony with anything but the winter, which had given a grayish cast to this day and was more severe than usual. Nevertheless, on the Feast of the Three Kings, I baptized, in addition to Charlemagne himself and two of his friends among the Nez Percés, fifteen other Indians, fourteen of whom were Pend d'Oreilles. Their chief, Selpisto, said that, as for him, it would be whenever I might wish. Since there was no impediment on the marital side—for he had only one wife, and he was, moreover, sufficiently well instructed—I decided that he should be one of the first magi of the West. But as soon as I enrolled him at the head of the catechumens, he began getting schismatic ideas. A Flathead, who happened to be in his proximity, heard him say, "If we leave the Flatheads, the Blackrobe will follow us."

On what he based such an assumption I could not even begin to know. But it could be traced to some rumors spread by a mischief-making stranger who wished to sow dissension between the Flatheads and Pend d'Oreilles. And this explained the unfriendly atmosphere about which we have spoken and the differences which were still to arise in the course of the hunt.

Early in the morning of January 11, Selpisto informed me that it was his plan and, he assured me, the plan of all the Pend d'Oreilles to separate from the Flatheads, because the old chief, Smoire, who was unfortunately the leader of the camp this year, allowed nothing to be done except as he wished it. No less pained than surprised at a decision which destroyed my highest hopes, I hastily called together all the chiefs in order to make evident to them how inconvenient such a course would be. (I would not do this now, for very good reasons which I did not know at that time.) In spite of my remonstrances, and of the word given me by the Pend d'Oreilles, the camp had hardly been struck and its march resumed when Selpisto left with his people. With the exception of several families, he was followed by all the Pend d'Oreilles, Coeur d'Alenes, Spokanes, Coutanes, and so on.

On January 16, the Feast of the Holy Name of Jesus, two new catechism classes were organized, one for the families of the Pend d'Oreilles still remaining with us, the other for a large party of Nez Percés who had just joined us. As it was winter, and we could meet only in the evenings, we had to have a shelter. A satisfactory one was made from two lodges placed at our disposal by the grand chief of the Nez Percés, who had been baptized on the Feast of the Three Kings. In this double lodge, which formed a poor enough little chapel, the proclamation of the Gospel was begun by the translation of the Apostles' Creed.

On January 18, the Feast of St. Peter's Chair at Rome, there was a great fall of snow and the first burial of a baptized child.[85] God, when He wishes and in the manner most pleasing to Him, sustains our weakness. There was something about this triple coincidence—I don't know what—which gladdened the heart. In spite of all the great obstacles, I never felt more courage to work at the instruction of my catechumens.

On January 19, the Blackfeet visited us during the night. The next day a party of Flatheads met and spoke with them, but they were mutually too suspicious to shake hands. The Flatheads had reason for their reserve. The following night seven of their horses disappeared. The interpreter, who was one of those affected by the raid, almost lost his head. What was most inconvenient for the missionary was that he lost this man's services at the very moment when frequent instruction would have been so useful. Added to this loss was also something bordering on calamity. Many of the men had only very little meat left. For the pack animals there remained only a few blades of grass hidden beneath the snow and for the dogs there remained only prairie wolves. Consequently, the dogs spared nothing that smelled of animal. Leather receptacles, saddles, stirrups, things that had only the smell of leather about them, became prey to their rapacity. Several times during the night I woke with a start to repel the attacks of a huge white dog looking for something to eat at the bottom of a packing case I was using for a pillow.

It is when food is scarcest that the hunt is most interesting to observe. Neither dogs nor hunters are ever more vigilant, more industrious, more alert, more courageous. At the first scent of game the dogs begin to yelp, and dogs, children, horses, hunters, all make a dash for the prey. This is only a faint suggestion of what happens when a large herd is discovered. Then a thousand cries ring through the air, and the hunters prepare for the chase with the same ardor as famished defenders of a fortress for the taking of a convoy of provisions.

On January 22, which is the Mary Sralralt of the Flatheads—that is, the day especially consecrated to Mary, the patroness of their reduction—we were swimming in abundance. Each hunter, on this day, killed three and four cows.

A warrior, fully armed, was a formidable sight to behold.

Women warriors proved themselves rivals of the men in courage.

*When hostile Indians
were encountered, a hunting party sometimes became a war party.*

Passing through enemy territory, a leader prepared his men for combat.

What rejoicing in the camp! This is no cause for astonishment, for they are hungry and for the Indian the female buffalo is virtually the best food on this earth.

The buffalo, as has been shown above, is a veritable treasure for the Indian. Hence it is toward the procuring of just this that Indians direct all their marchings, their occupations, their industry, almost all their desires. For this there is no fatigue they will not endure, no kind of death they will not defy. This innate proclivity attaches them so solidly to the nomadic life that only after long and arduous work could one succeed in making them enjoy the fruits of civilization.

On January 25, people began straggling back to camp. First there was the old Blackfoot chief, long a guest of the Flatheads, recently baptized and still as fervent as at the beginning. He had left to find some of his tribesmen, in order to bring them to the Blackrobe so that they might be converted. But during the seventeen days in which he had searched over mountain and through valley, he found no occasion to approach his people as a friend. The only advantage we gained from his hazardous undertaking was the knowledge that the Pend d'Oreilles were not far from us. One day, however, this man was to render us important services.

The interpreter, who had left the camp in pursuit of the raiders, had not been able to overtake them, much less recover his horse. He finally resigned himself to coming back to the missionary and we again began instructing our catechumens.

On January 31 we found ourselves in terrain recently grazed bare by buffalo. Fresh tracks gave evidence that they were not far away and that there was a great number of them. In fact, that evening the campsite became a theater in which could be seen, down to the minutest detail, all the principal scenes of the great hunt. Here was an enormous buffalo, mortally wounded but still fleeing before a hunter in hot pursuit. There was another, halted in its tracks, but still erect, seemingly concerned only with the manner in which it ought to die. Still another lay stretched out on the ground, awaiting only the final operation by the hunter.

Meanwhile the women went about putting up the tents. Suddenly there was a great noise. The mothers fled in all directions, dragging with them whatever children they could grab. Carried along with the others, a chief shouted commands which I couldn't understand. What caused this turmoil was a buffalo charging through the camp. But the animal was soon far away, carrying twenty arrows which had found their mark. Many of its companions were fleeing in all directions, and hunters were edging up to them on their horses. We watched them in the last rays of the disappearing sun. As the evening shadows gathered, nearby gorges swallowed up buffaloes, dogs, and hunters.

Soon all was obscurity and silence. All that could be seen were the stars. All that could be heard was the wind sighing through the cedars on the mountain. The yelping of the dogs died in the distance. The wolves began to howl. It was the hour of illusions. The rumor was spread about that the hunters had become lost; that Blackfeet had been seen prowling in the vicinity; that perhaps the men had been massacred. Mothers began to wail and children to ask where their fathers were. Finally, the hunters, young and old, did return, and there was rejoicing. They were laden with the best of game. Hope, fear, uncertainty, tumult, calm, noise, silence, losing one's way, returning, terror, hilarity, destitution, plenty—all this we had witnessed within the space of a few hours. If it is contrasts one wants, one should go hunting with the Indians, in the wintertime and in the Rocky Mountains.

On February 1 the temperature was pleasant, the sky was cloudless and the sun was brilliant. It is true that instruction of the catechumens had been going on only since the Feast of the Holy Name of Jesus. But for nine days now prayers had been added to the instruction and She whom one never invokes in vain had so well prepared their hearts that it would have been in defiance of divine mercy to have made wait any longer those for whom the winter hunt almost always meant war. While the finishing touches were being given to the preparation of those who were seeking baptism, the baptized children were bringing in greenery and the girls were making garlands to decorate the altar. The youths were preparing the illumination. Thus everything seemed to be contributing to make of the Feast of the Purification a day doubly great. The Powers of Darkness appeared to be jealous, for during the night preceeding, though the sky was perfectly clear, the force of the wind was such that the lodges had to be anchored to withstand it. Later we shall see how this is done.

On February 2, as soon as day broke, there was a great calm and the rays of the sun, two hours later, had so tempered the cold of night that it was a pleasure for all the camp to meet around the altar. Four children, chosen from four different tribes, were choirboys. Little Paul, the favorite of the Queen of Angels, had the first place. The catechumens were arranged in a semicircle in front of the priest. The first ceremony was the blessing of the candles.

There was present an old man, over eighty, whose lined face reminded one of the ancient patriarchs. The whiteness of his hair, a rare thing among the Indians, was whiter than the bank of snow on which he was seated. Though he was completely blind, he had come from a place more than twenty days' distant. He had made that long journey to ask for baptism, not only for himself, but for his children and grand children. Viewing him with the eyes of faith, who could have helped putting into his mouth the consoling words, "Nunc dimittis"? Toward the middle of the day, fifteen adults, chosen from the five tribes, were enrolled among the true children of God. A large medal had been promised to the catechumen who should be first to learn all of his prayers. He who earned it was a Spokane named Jean, a true apostle to his whole family.

We are still in the early days of the winter hunt, which is a dangerous period for soul and body. The intense cold, the fatigue, the nature of the occupations, the enforced idleness following work, the ample food following a long period of want, the mingling with different tribes, the recounting of adventures, and sometimes the presence of lewd women; all of these experiences tend to favor crass nature at the expense of grace. What could be done to forestall such an unfortunate development? Call together, as often as possible, those who ran the greatest danger, refresh their memories of the great and numerous favors they have received from Heaven, place them under the special protection of the Blessed Virgin; in a word, lay the foundations for a pious association of children of Mary. This, it seemed to us, was the surest and easiest means of assuring their perseverance. At any rate, it was the means we decided on in the evening of February 2.

On February ——,[86] a Sunday, there was a strong wind; the sky was overcast; there was an icy cold, no pasturage for the horses, and the buffalo had been frightened away by the Nez Percés. The cold was intense, the barrenness was depressing, and the snow was troublesome. But yesterday's rest had been a blessing and today we were marching in the name of the Lord. Confidence! Toward midday, we reached the summit of a high mountain. What a change! The sun shone, the cold was less intense, and we had before us an extensive plain. On this plain was good pasture where there were groups of buffalo. The camp halted; the hunters assembled and knelt to invoke the help of their patron. They then set out, and before the sun sank they had taken one hundred fifty buffalo. It must be admitted that if this hunt was not miraculous, it at least resembled very much the catch of fishes which was miraculous. Peter had cast his net in the name of the Lord and caught one hundred fifty-three fishes. The Flatheads had observed Sunday in the name of the Lord and bagged one hundred fifty-three buffalo, a wonderful catch. It was also a hunt wonderful to behold.

There is no hunt without accidents, but those which occurred on this one only served to increase the joy and the gratefulness of the hunters. For example, on one occasion three falls were caused by a single collision, that of a buffalo, that of the horse following it, and that of the hunter mounted on this horse. But acting more promptly and adroitly than is usual at such a juncture, the hunter, before the others had risen, aimed his shot so well that of the fallen three only two arose, to take along the carcass of the third. Another time a cow, to avenge its wounds, turned so fiercely on its aggressor that the horse, frightened by this maneuver, threw its rider. The rider had just risen to his knees when the infuriated beast

Converted Indians added prayers to the customary harangue before a battle.

A woman warrior's swift about-face left the enemy stupefied.

*Victorious warriors, following
a battle, dressed in their finest garb and rode, chanting triumphantly.*

The procession of the calumet was part of the formal victory celebration.

rushed at him with lowered horns. The hunter seized the buffalo by the horns and held her down until he had found a means of escaping from a contest which was so unequal.

A young dandy, to enhance the elegance of his horse, had braided its tail. Now it came about that, while he was fleeing before a cow he had wounded, she approached so close to the horse that one of her horns became entangled in its braided tail. The buffalo, apparently fearing it had been ensnared, began to pull away, and the horse did the same thing. Both pulled so energetically in opposite directions that it is easy to divine which of the two contestants came away the loser.

On February 9 there was distribution of ashes.[87] What do these signify? I tried to explain their meaning to the poor Indians, but there was in our midst something which spoke more clearly. This was the body of a young man carried away by death in the prime of his youth.

During the night of February 9–10, the old Blackfoot chief addressed a harangue to his tribesmen, whom he suspected of prowling about in the vicinity. He had been doing this almost every night since his return. This time his words were heard, for after a calumet had been placed at the edge of camp, a Blackfoot delegation presented itself before the Flatheads, saying that their companions would come to smoke with the Flatheads if this was agreeable. When the Flatheads had acquiesced, a dozen of them, accompanied by the missionary and by old Chief Nicolas, went to meet the visitors. About ten in the morning, Indian chants could be heard coming from a dark defile whose entrance was lighted by the sun. Very soon the brigands of the mountains appeared. What bitter memories must have been awakened by their appearance! But generosity fosters pardon, and the Flatheads thought only of receiving, in friendship, those who had raided them most mercilessly. Hands were shaken in sign of reconciliation, a dance was held, the calumet was smoked in the missionary's lodge, and then there was conversation, just as if relations had always been friendly.

All the visitors were invited to spend the night in the best lodges of the camp. With such guests in our midst, it seemed we had no more to fear from the Blackfeet, and I went to sleep with greater sense of security than before. But what was my surprise when I learned on awakening that a Blackfoot had been killed as he was leaving camp with four stolen horses. Fortunately for our guests, the raider was not of their group. Instead of holding them responsible for something they had not done, and which had been punished already in an altogether fitting manner, the Flatheads granted the visitors permission to bury the dead man. But our guests, either wishing to show disapproval of his conduct or because they feared reprisals, hastily took their leave, abandoning the dead man to the wild animals. A small present, given them as they departed, was enough to prove to them that the spirit of reprisal is not the spirit of the children of God. This was to bear fruit in the future.

On February 13 we received momentous news. The Pends d'Oreilles, from whom we were separated only by a mountain, had just scalped thirty Blackfeet. It was a Coeur d'Alene who brought us the details.

"The Pend d'Oreilles," he said, "had suffered from a shortage of food since they separated from the Flatheads. Three Pend d'Oreilles (among whom was the son of Chief Kous Kous Kaemi) and I went scouting to see if we could not find at least something to alleviate our shortage. We arrived at the summit of a mountain to find not animals but a war party of Blackfeet. We pursued them, killing their chief, and managed to corner them in a ravine in which they had entrenched themselves. Fortunately for us the shots had been heard by the camp and all the Pend d'Oreilles warriors rode out, led by Kuiliy, a young Pend d'Oreille woman renowned for intrepidity on the field of battle. They pounced on the Blackfeet we had cornered. One of the Blackfeet cried out in fright, 'Let us escape!' 'No,' replied another, 'We have come out to fight, and we have to fight now.' 'My children,' added one of the oldest of them, 'this is the end, but we must defend ourselves to the death.' Within a few minutes death had taken its toll. Except for four of them who escaped through the bushes, they were mercilessly slaughtered. Only four of the Pend d'Oreilles were wounded, though they had to expose themselves to almost point-blank fire to reach their enemy."

Some days later I saw, not without horror, the thickly strewn remains of these unfortunates. Birds of prey and animals had left only the bones.

On February 13 the camp of the Pend d'Oreilles was espied on the slope of the mountain to our right. Smoire, who saw it, struck off to the left, where we camped. The Pend d'Oreilles were only three or four miles away from us. The missionary thought it his duty to pay them a visit. They were so pleased at this that the next day they came to rejoin the Flatheads, with the intentions of receiving instruction for themselves and their families. This development was all the more advantageous because the hunt was drawing to a close and they had only begun to lay in provisions.

Three days ago Smoire had said we would remain here for fifteen days. Today he announced that camp would be struck in the morning of the following day, to start the return trek. The next day, sure enough, he was on the way back, amusing himself for two days in a spot where there was not a trace of buffalo. Selpisto, who was more fortunate, informed the Pend d'Oreilles who were in the camp and the Flatheads themselves that he was surrounded by buffaloes and that in two or three days he had killed so many that he did not know any more what he would do with them. He invited them to come and share his good fortune. Kous Kous Kaemi, chief of the Pend d'Oreilles, and the Flatheads were of the opinion that they should accept the invitation.

We set out for Selpisto's camp. To reach it we had over three miles to go. The sun was still high. But Smoire wanted to make a halt, and he camped on a low-lying spot where several horses became mired up to their bellies. Yet Smoire made it understood that he would not budge from there until the hunt had been ended.

"My horses are gaunt," he said. "If they give out on the way, the Pend d'Oreilles will not give me any others."

"I should not like to leave the Father," said Kous Kous Kaemi in turn, "but I have ten children to feed and almost no more meat to give them. If, therefore, Smoire refuses to accede to the general wish, I shall be forced to leave him." But there were two or three catechism lessons every day to prepare his people for baptism and we had just begun a novena to St. Francis Xavier to the end that the approaching harvest might not be abandoned to the birds of the sky.

To bring all these interests into harmony, the missionary announced that he would spend a few days in Selpisto's camp, giving assurance that he would return before the Flatheads started back for St. Mary's. Michael declared that, wherever the Blackrobe went, he also went. The whole Flathead camp felt the same way and everyone, including Smoire himself, was forced to follow the crowd and strike camp.

The arrival of the missionary in Selpisto's camp was an occasion for great rejoicing there. But just at the moment when everyone felt all their prayers had been answered, there came an Indian with a pale and rugged visage, to announce, with all the calm of profound sadness, that Smoire, accompanied by about twenty lodges, had deserted. This news saddened the Flatheads who had already arrived, but only served to add to the joy of the Pend d'Oreilles. Selpisto sent to the lodge of the missionary more choice cuts of meat than would have been needed for royal feasts for many a day, and hastened to procure for him a great number of catechumens. This was an excellent opportunity for the missionary, who quickly arranged for several catechism classes, public recitation of prayers learned, examinations on the most important questions, and distribution of prizes. Already the catechumens were demanding that, while they were waiting to be baptized, they be given French names. What prospect could have been more promising? But on March 7 everything was upset. The interpreter informed the missionary that there was a rumor about that he would soon leave Selpisto's camp and that Selpisto, furious over this development, was preparing to depart. In fact, the whole camp was beginning to take down their lodges. Kous Kous Kaemi and Michael, who had wind of what was transpiring, asked the missionary what he intended to do. The missionary replied that he would follow them. But they were of the

*The undulating movements of the prized
eagle-plume headdress harmonized with the dance and the music.*

*Even elderly women
abandoned their supporting staffs and joined the scalp dance celebrating
victory in battle.*

*A clumsy attempt to assassinate
Pierre George was revealed by the accidental discharge of a rifle.*

*As Indians courageously
rushed to the defense of Pierre George, the camp resembled an armed
fortress under surprise attack.*

opinion that it was necessary to leave Sel-pisto.

Then Selpisto himself arrived on the scene, more astonished and perturbed than any of the others at what was going on. The interpreter, visibly at a loss for words, tried to explain the matter, but from his sorry explanation it became most evident that the whole deplorable affair was a figment of his own poor imagination. Selpisto, more convinced than anyone else that this was the case, retired without saying anything. The interpreter staged a disappearing act. The missionary quietly awaited further developments. There was an air of uncertainty throughout the entire camp, an anxiety impossible to define. People were going to and fro, some leaving the camp, some returning to it. A long file of pack animals, having taken to the road in pursuit of Smoire, was now retracing its steps. The leaders seemed not to know which way to turn. Many Indians of all the diverse tribes grouped themselves quietly around the Blackrobe. As for him, he sat with his chin resting in his hand, awaiting in silence the end of this mysterious scene.

When he saw that almost everybody was on his side, he rose and, with no little surprise, saw Selpisto, with a violent gesture, signal to him to follow. The missionary, taken aback by this invitation, made him understand that he could not accept it, that his duty required him to be with the Flatheads, that he had just renewed his promise to them to remain with them, as was proven by the presence of some of their warriors bringing his horse to him and of the son of Kous Kous Kaemi, who had joined them. Then after extending his hand affectionately to Selpisto he broke away, considerably shaken. Meanwhile, what was happening in the Flathead camp?

When I arrived at their camp, I learned that an agreement had been reached between the Flatheads and the Pend d'Oreilles to the effect that Kous Kous Kaemi, grand chief of the latter, was acknowledged chief of the two tribes until the end of the hunt. This arrangement, which I have always regarded as a political *chef d'oeuvre* under the existing circumstance, gave me the key to a great many things, all more or less exonerating Smoire. As for the interpreter, who had had time to reflect, he appeared,

accompanied by several estimable Flatheads. This time he had come to offer his services. Since I had no choice, and since I placed less price on my self-esteem than on the good which I was unfortunately unable to do without the help of his tongue, I gave him to understand that I would remember only his services if he, in turn, would do his utmost to help me repair the loss of time. This he promised and both of us set about our tasks.

Winter in the Rocky Mountains is far from being as rigorous as it is in the same latitude on the Atlantic coast. The temperature is usually so stable that sickness, especially colds, is very rare. But sometimes, when fresh snow falls and there is a high wind, the snow is changed into powder that can be very dangerous. One day we were so violently assailed by it that the poor missionary who was accompanying the hunting camp would have fallen victim to it had not friendly hands and a fire, lighted in spite of the storm, come to his assistance at the moment he was about to fall from his horse. Another danger, slightly less serious but longer lasting, is snow blindness, caused by the high wind and the reflection of the sunlight from the white snow. The eyes are so painfully affected by it that for several days they are unable to stand any light at all. The remedy for this is snow converted into steam by means of rocks heated red in a fire. The steam is applied to the open eyes.

These little trials are inherent in the very nature of the winter hunt. It might perhaps be useful to indicate what some of the others are, if only to convince those who regard hunting as a pleasure rather than an apostolic work. This is not to mention the ills of others which the missionary, willy-nilly, must himself feel by reason of the great confidence that all have in his ability and in his compassion. He has to suffer inconveniences over which the Indians only laugh, or which they don't even think about, such as going without bread, coffee, salt, sugar, clean linen, and so on.

Traveling is done on horseback, despite cold, wind, ravines, valleys, and mountains. Frequent falls are unavoidable, in spite of the finest horsemanship imaginable. Sleep is often interrupted and is liable to become eternal as the result of a visit of some Blackfeet. There is constant cohabitation with thousands and thousands of individuals of the school of Epictetus.

All this is a part of the daily trials of the missionary and the only effective remedy against them is a good dose of patience. Add to them ignorance of the language, being far away from one's own country, civilization, friends, and perhaps it will seem that altogether the conveniences and inconveniences bear no faint resemblance to what we call the cross of the Apostles.

A word now on the consolations. On March 12 we had the consolation of being able to offer fifteen baptisms of adults, solidly instructed and perfectly disposed, as a bouquet to St. Ignatius and St. Francis Xavier. On Holy Thursday there were nine more, and four on the day before Easter. These, together with the fifty-two already administered, made eighty regenerations. About sixty adults had been baptized during the hunt.

Back at Hell Gate, the place where three months earlier we had met the Pend d'Oreilles, everyone made an effort to remove the estrangement caused, as we have seen, by fears and hopes, whose motive had been more than pardonable. Smoire placed the missionary's lodge between his own and that of Kous Kous Kaemi, undoubtedly to demontsrate to him that accord had forever taken the place of the spirit of contradiction which he had only too well maintained during the first two thirds of the hunt. Touched by this sign of attention and still more by what he had seen and heard on the subject of religion, Kous Kous Kaemi did not wish to depart without coming, at the head of his people, to give witness of his gratitude.

"Though I have not laid by any provisions," he told the missionary, "I am very happy that I went on this hunt. But I should be happier still if you would finish, among my people, what you began during the hunt."

This said, he took the missionary's hand with all the signs of respectful affection and did this several times, contrary to the custom of the Indians. Selpisto thought it best not to appear, but, to prove that his absence was not to be attributed to any blameworthy sentiments, he had a person in his confidence tell the missionary that the finest day in his life would always remain the one on which he had had an interview of several hours with the missionary.

That evening the missionary and the Flatheads were reunited in the chapel of St. Mary's, singing for the first time the *Regina coeli*. One may judge how happy we were to hear this singing, which is in every respect so capable of gladdening hearts.

The Summer Hunt with the Flatheads

The summer hunt differs from that during the winter in the diversity of the game sought, in the variety of occupations, and, if I may be permitted to speak so, in the theatrical scenery. This last is no less attractive than that during the winter. Since Easter, our dear converts had been witnesses to religious ceremonies highly capable of elevating their thoughts to Heaven. They had followed, with enthusiasm, the exercises of the month of Mary. At the end of that beautiful month, in honor of their patroness, they had elevated a monument of gratitude on the very spot where Mary had deigned to appear to one of their children. On the Feast of Pentecost, a hundred of them made their first Holy Communion. On the Feast of the Sacred Heart, all had assisted at the Procession of the Blessed Sacrament. Thus, toward mid-July, the usual time for their summer hunt, they were still aglow with their initial fervor. They asked the Blackrobe to accompany them on the hunt lest they lose their devotion during the distracting period ahead.

The theater was to be the same, but to arrive at it, the Flatheads followed another route, ascending the course of a river. While the nation was on the march, each of the various lodges would live, in part, on the plant called bitterroot, which thrived only on the river banks and which gave the river its name.

There is nothing more grandiose than a chain of mountains—the variety of their gigantic shapes, the majesty of their snow-covered summits, the bluish tint in the distance. The great number of small streams, the murmuring of the waves, the singing of the birds, the cries of joy of the children at the sight of some fruit, the accelerated gallop of the horses at the passage

*An Indian who had stolen some horses
escaped punishment when he returned them and asked to be baptized.*

*Three Indians escaped from captivity
by singing their enemies to sleep with hymns.*

This head-on attack
was the prelude to the simultaneous death of two braves.

Constantin, a Great Chief, truly converted,
mercifully pardoned those who had massacred his two sons.

of some tawny beast, the absence of fatigue and of want and, better than all these things together, the presence of a people, superior in every respect—all this seemed to contribute to making the Blackrobe's mission almost a pleasure.

It was necessary to elevate souls to the contemplation of another kind of beauty. To this end, the daily instructions turned on the march of the people of God in the desert. These instructions were given after morning and evening prayers and were repeated by the grand chief in the evenings or sometimes early in the morning. Thus all those who had made their first Communion remained worthy of repeating it many times during the hunt. On [the Feast of] St. Ignatius, the flower of the horsemen, led by the grand chief Victor and the little chief Michael, two Indians of great renown if there ever were any, could be seen approaching the Communion rail in honor of our saint.[88]

After marching for fifteen days between magnificent mountains where there were only deer, bighorns, or goats to test the agility of the hunters, we saw open before us a vast plain on the edge of which four male buffalo were tranquilly passing. Males are not as good as females for the table. During this season the males are fat and live apart from the females. But these four were not disdained, and soon, to the great joy of the hunters, they became the means whereby the camp broke its buffalo-meat fast. On this plain, called Peter's Cave, there was an abundance of camass. The flower of this plant is a beautiful blue in color and makes the plain on which it abounds look like a lake. The flower of the bitterroot, has shades of rose. The roots differ greatly in shape. The bitterroot's is long and odd-looking. That of the camass is like that of an onion, which it also resembles in the disposition of its layers inside.

The bitterroot is indeed so bitter to the taste that a civilized mouth can scarcely bear it. The root of the camass tastes something like a prune and a chestnut. It is eaten with pleasure, but its digestion is accompanied by very disagreeable effects for those who do not like strong odors or the sound that accompanies them. The root is gathered by means of a stick with a claw on one end, giving it the appearance of a shoemaker's hammer. While the left hand grasps the stick, which is like the handle of the hammer, the right hand thrusts the claw into the earth and extracts the root with as much rapidity as skill. This work is relegated to the women, being carried on from sunrise to four o'clock in the afternoon. To preserve the bitterroot it has only to be dried in the sun. But to preserve the camass, and above all to make it palatable, it must be cooked. To do this you dig in the earth a circular hole a few inches in depth and with a diameter about equal to that of an ordinary wagon wheel. This done, you fill the hole with wood, which you burn until you have a bed of glowing embers. On this bed of embers you spread stones and over the stones a layer of earth. On the layer of earth you spread the roots and over the roots a second layer of earth. On this you place a sufficiently large quantity of wood to maintain a fire for thirty or forty hours. When all this has been done, you have a food which can be preserved for years. But, to succeed, a great deal of care, skill, and experience is required. Hence, success at this undertaking is a mark of distinction for the women.

The cooking of moss, called in some countries Spanish bread, proceeds in the same manner. But the Flathead never has recourse to such mean fare. He prefers, in case of a famine, to eat the pellicle found between the bark and the wood of certain trees.

There was in the area in which we found ourselves a variety of edible roots. There was a small white carrot of excellent flavor and a potato which would, perhaps, differ little from ours if it were cultivated. But since it never reaches a size exceeding two or three centimeters in diameter and is fairly scarce, it is for the Indian a treasure that remains buried. The other species, introduced by our brothers, replaces it abundantly.

The large animals still showed themselves only on the edge of a forest, too thick to be easily penetrated. While waiting for better game, the hunters amused themselves pursuing antelope, which appeared here and there on the way. This pretty animal, called *cabri* (kid or goat) by the French *voyageurs*, resembles the roe deer in shape and size. But the antler of the male, which has only two prongs, is smaller, and its coat, like that of the stag, is white on the rump and belly. When it goes through the woods, its ordinary gait is an elegant little trot. From time to time, it stops in its tracks, turns toward the hunter and examines him curiously. This is the moment to fire. If the hunter misses his shot, the animal darts away like an arrow. But in a moment he stops again to get a better look at the hunter. The hunter, who knows its weakness, attracts it by waving a brilliantly colored object. The poor animal, drawn on by this bait, comes closer. But its curiosity causes its death.

Occasionally there can be seen a kind of sheep, called bighorn because of its relatively large horns which curve downward so that the tips are near its mouth. In quality, the flesh of the bighorn is next to that of the buffalo. Then come the hind, the roe deer, and antelope, and finally the white ram. I must add, too, the elk which, in the quality of its meat, is almost the equal of the buffalo. The snout of those noble animals, like the hump of the buffalo, is one of the choicest of morsels.

On August 2 we camped in a spot where the kingdom of nature offered all the very best to fulfill our needs. There were limpid waters, currant bushes, and a large number of deer. Everyone knows that the deer, in spite of its size, is by nature very timid. To bewilder the deer a few shots fired in the air suffice. Frightened by what it hears, it seeks to flee, but fearing to encounter its enemy in whatever direction it flees, it turns around and around, and stops. Even if there should be hundreds of them, they follow this same tactic until they are exhausted. It is then that the hunting is good, and the deer fall to the last one.

The best time to shoot the deer is just before the rut. With male animals of other kinds this also holds true. But the length of time the male is with its mate varies considerably. In this regard, one cannot but admire Providence. If it were not this way, many fawns, unable to take care of themselves before the cold season, would perish miserably. The mating season of the buffalo is from June until September; that of the antelope and the deer is from September until November; that of the roe deer from November to December; for the bighorn from December to January. For the white sheep it is from about Christmas time until February.

The site on which we camped was able to offer for our table dishes of each one of these animals. But as the deer and buffalo seemed bent on bearing most of the expense, the pots were filled with the choicest morsels from these animals. And, indeed, they were so at the very moment the news was spread that Father De Smet, who had been alone for three months, was approaching, scarcely a hundred paces from the camp. Sure enough, several minutes later he was in the midst of the hunters, all the more welcome because the scarcity of powder and tobacco was beginning to make itself felt. The generous distribution which was made added to everybody's joy. Everything continued to get better up to the Feast of the Assumption.

This beautiful feast was the anniversary of our first meeting with the Flatheads at Fort Hall. The site of our camp was the spot where, the winter before, one hundred fifty-three cows had fallen before our hunters. It was there, too, that the Flatheads had received the first friendly visit from the Blackfeet. These were all so many reasons for celebrating the Feast of the Assumption with all the ceremony possible. During Holy Mass, which was sung, Father De Smet distributed Holy Communion to a great number of the faithful. Needless to say the day was spent joyfully in prayer and pious conversation. But evening brought with it a good deal of sadness, for Father De Smet had resolved, for the good of the missions, to make a trip to St. Louis and had chosen this moment as the time of his departure.

We were camped on the banks of a little river called Tobacco Fork. It was so named by reason of the prevalence of a root having the color and shape of a roll of tobacco. Among the blessings I have already mentioned was the routing of one hundred sixty Blackfeet by six Flatheads, which had occurred there. All this recalled to us that God protects His own, but also that it would not be prudent for a traveler, whoever he might be, to venture alone into the defiles separating us from a camp of the Crow Indians, to which Father De Smet wanted to proceed. Hence nine of our best braves offered to accompany him to his destination.

On August 17 our little camp sat on the banks of a small stream whose twists and turns

top left:

*Athanase was one of the bravest
Flathead warriors.*

top right:

*Pierre Jean
became a Flathead chief,
though very young.*

bottom left:

*Placide was noted
as a clever bear hunter.*

top left:

Augustin, a son of
Coeur d'Alene Chief Gabriel.

top right:

Damas,
also a son of Gabriel.

bottom right:

Isidore Natatken, a Coeur d'Alene
medicine man.

over a light kind of earth had made ravines in many places. These were ideal as lairs for all sorts of enemies. The surroundings, magnificent because of the rich vegetation, offered good opportunities for an ambush. Bears were so abundant that our youths killed a dozen of them in less than an hour.

In the evening, the report of a firearm aroused the whole camp. In a lodge adjacent to that of the missionary a poor old widowed mother of two children had received a ball in the throat; it had not left her time even to cry out. Fortunately, since her baptism she had not had a single sin with which to reproach herself and since her first Communion she had not let a single Sunday go by without approaching the Communion rail. Her remains were interred on the banks of the Yellowstone. Fearing lest her grave be profaned, we tried to hide it as best we could from the Blackfeet. I learned later that a Blackfoot, the murderer of this poor woman, was himself killed in retaliation without having time to repent. As for the two little orphans, they found some consolation for their loss in the person of a Flathead chief, if, indeed, there is any consolation for the loss of a mother.

The Yellowstone Mountain derives its title from a large river of that name which empties into the Missouri. It is in the vicinity of this mountain that most animals are ordinarily found and, consequently, most of the Blackfeet. But the great gathering of which we were a part caused both the animals and the Blackfeet to retreat. The Nez Percés, who had already obtained their provisions, were on the way back to their country. The Pend d'Oreilles scouted over the north side, while the Flatheads, under the leadership of Victor, headed toward the east.

Two camps farther on the buffalo began to be in evidence, for the pasturage was good. One of our people was deathly ill. These three reasons prompted us to halt there. While the hunters were beating through a nearby woods, an enormous buffalo emerged and, to escape the death that was in pursuit, jumped into the river. But he had been hit in so many places while on the run, and was so exhausted, that instead of inspiring terror when he mounted the bank, he only caused a great deal of hilarity among the crowd that had colletced. And as a crowning disgrace, he was dispatched by the children.

But there was an attack that was a little more dangerous. Two bears had been seen going into some brush. They were quickly surrounded by the younger hunters. A friendly young Blackfoot, who thought the occasion ripe for showing off his courage, approached too close. The bear, with a single bound, leaped from its cave and clawed so deeply into the arm in which the Indian held his bow that the aggressor who had not had the more prudent courage of a Flathead was finished then and there. His name was Peter. Strangely enough, his comrade, whose name was Paul, found himself several days later in a similar situation and, wishing to show that he knew better how to handle himself, was caught in the same manner. The same result followed.

Several Crow chiefs visited us, accompanied by the elite of their tribe. Quite recently, they had received Father De Smet in their camp and their chief, after hearing the priest speak of the mystery of the Redemption, took the Father's crucifix and pressed it to his heart. To judge from their calumet ceremony, however, their poor souls were certainly still in a profound darkness. To please their manitou it was required, first, that buffalo dung be mixed with the contents of the calumet; second, that the first puffs be offered to the four cardinal points of the compass; third, that the calumet, having made the round of the lodge, be passed again until smoked out. This ceremony is observed so seriously that one would be tempted to laugh if one was not truly sorry to see how far from the truth these poor souls are.

While the Crow chiefs were there, one of our converts died. He was a man still in the prime of life. The funeral was held with a certain amount of pomp, and the singing, the aspersions, and the cross erected over the remains appeared to leave a lively impression on the Indians. May the memory of the Cross especially increase in their hearts the desire to know Him Who alone is the Way, the Truth, and the Life. The next day, after the chiefs' departure, we hastily moved, for we had already been out two months and our fall hunting had not yet begun.

There were in the camp an American, a Scotchman, and two Chawanons, all of them great travelers.[89] But being better acquainted with the road to Hell than with the road to Heaven, their presence was becoming a great scandal, so a friendly warning was given them. This was not sufficient. The Flatheads, who are not fond of pleasantries touching the honor of their women, gave them to understand that they had to leave, and that it would be better for them not to wait until the next day. Before the end of the year, all of them, through divine justice, received the punishment they deserved.

But the Christian God is more ready to grant mercy than punishment. On the very day of departure, the Feast of Our Lady of Sorrows, the camp came across a great herd, and each hunter took two or three of its finest specimens. This was a prelude to the almost umprecedented abundance with which the camp was to overflow.

The next day, after passing the remains of a large Blackfoot village annihilated by smallpox a few years previously, we found to our left an ideal campsite. It was separated from the river by a strip of woods thick enough to conceal the camp from the Blackfeet as well as to conceal hunters from the eyes of the animals covering the plain. Activity here lasted for three days during which the only enemies prowling about the camp were wolves and the bears. But these gluttons, finding plenty with which to satisfy themselves, were heard emitting their cries of delight. In the sharp yelping of the wolves and the low growls of their messmates, a musical ear could distinguish all degrees of sound, from bass to counter-tenor. It was a beautiful kind of horror in its way.

Buffalo meat is the favorite food of these animals, and they can always be found in large numbers in the wake of buffalo herds. If no hunters are present to capture their prey for them, this is how the wolves proceed to get it. They usually attack only the young, but if they do attack a full-grown buffalo, they make sure it is an old one. They try to separate it from the herd and, if there is a steep embankment nearby, they harass it, driving it in that direction until it falls over the edge. Then begins the feast, which does not end until there is nothing left to devour.

All that God does, He does well. It was during this time of repose that the missionary became ill. It was only a short illness, to be sure, but it was sufficiently acute to expiate the natural pleasure one takes in a spectacle as varied as the one unfolding itself before him. The Flatheads were very good to him, but like other Indians, habituated to suffer without complaining, they did not think of feeling sorry for anyone else. Hoping that they could restore my health by means of choice morsels, they brought the best they had, but I had lost my appetite. Fortunately, there was in the camp a Mexican who spoke French. Out of the goodness of his heart, this worthy man, by little attentions and words of encouragement, did me more good than all the medicines, civilized or Indian, could have done. His name was Manuel, and, to judge from what was said of him by those who knew him, he was the master hunter in all the Far West. He had killed as many as forty cows in two days and one hundred fifty deer in a month. He loved to tell me about his many hunting expeditions, and when he had finished, I spoke in turn of the things I loved. What he told me about the great or the small hunts has already been related, or will be, so we will not speak further of it here.

Late in September a deed of justice and mercy was done. A Flathead was caught in a strange position doing something he should not have been doing. An enemy rifle ball broke his leg and forced him, after some days of intense pain, to return to his own camp. Confused, but nevertheless contrite, from then on he repeated, "I now have only one sound leg, but I would rather go to Heaven as I am than walk on two legs along the road to Hell." And, to remove the sight and inconvenience of his useless limb, he cut it and broke it off sharply, in obedience to the word of the Gospel: "If your right hand offends you, cut it off and cast it from you." The pain of the last part of the operation was so great that, in spite of his determination, he lost consciousness.

Today, September 26, the falling snow makes us fear that our return will be difficult, but this does not deter the camp from starting back to St. Mary's. It is so cold that the missionary, who has scarcely recovered, is forced to dismount and run along the ground to keep warm. But soon good weather and good

top left:

*Charlemagne,
a Nez Percé chief,
great in stature, courage,
and authority.*

top right:

*A Pend d'Oreille brave,
companion-in-arms of the Flatheads.*

bottom left:

*The Bearded One,
a Gros-Ventre chief,
a charitable and modest man.*

top left:

A shiftless, useless Nez Percé.

top right:

An admirable young Pend d'Oreille brave.

bottom right:

Eagle, a great chief of the Gros-Ventres.

fortune return, adding still more to our provisions. At almost every step we come across the remains of herds on the move, here a calf, there an old cow, and sometimes enormous bulls that have escaped the slaughter. It is the young boys, sometimes even the girls, who pursue most energetically the smallest, the largest, or the most agile of the fleeing animals.

On September 28, on the summit of a mountain from which one could see a horizon more than a hundred leagues in circumference, after reciting the first Vespers of St. Michael, I made and planted a cross, to take possession, in the name of the Lord, of a land which undoubtedly contained many souls to be saved, for we were in the middle of the Blackfoot country. How ardently did I wish that I might, from this lofty position, make them hear the victorious cry of the great Archangel, *Quis ut Deus.*[90]

Not far from this spot we found another cross from which hung a piece of black cloth. Probably the burial spot of some Catholic, I thought to myself. The Flatheads, better acquainted than I with the beliefs and cults of the country, informed me that poor blind souls who pass this place very often make such an offering, hoping thereby to be able to kill and raid successfully, that is, return from their wars with many scalps and many horses taken from the enemy.

We were in a part of the country where men very seldom came, as was proven by the peaceful existence which the beavers were leading there. They were so unafraid that in one single night three of our people took fifteen of them. The route along which we rode was so steep and dangerous that I thought it would be a miracle if one of us did not tumble down the more than five hundred feet yawning below us. Scarcely had this thought occurred to me when I saw a horse, laden with packs, stumble in such a manner as to place the poor woman riding it in what I was sure was considerable distress. But far from it! Without appearing to be in the least bit impatient or put out, she dismounted in the snow, unloaded the horse, got it onto its feet again, reloaded it, and led it back to its position. The greatest difficulty, as far as the Flathead women are concerned, is not loading packs or leading the horses, but rather finding themselves afoot with their children, as happens only

too often during a hunt in the rugged country in which they must seek their fortune. And even in this very disheartening situation the women betray no signs of discouragement.

Tomorrow is the Feast of the Maternity of the Most Blessed Virgin Mary. On the day after the misionary is to leave the Flatheads to go among the Coeur d'Alenes. Yesterday confessions began, for many would like to communicate before the missionary leaves. Today confessions should be finished, but already the day is declining and we are still marching along the crest of the mountains. Only after a forced march of ten hours do we descend onto the plain. There we find warm weather again. There also flows majestically the Great Fork of the Missouri, whose waters, separating and then joining, form an island. In addition to good pasturage, there are large trees that will protect us from the sun tomorrow and wood with which we can warm ourselves this evening.

A huge fire is lighted before the lodge, which serves also as a chapel, so that during the night the penitents may wait for confession without too much discomfort. The next day, ninety persons approach the Communion rail. In the evening, mothers bring their children to be blessed by the priest, and the final ceremony is the planting of a cross.

It would be difficult to imagine a more beautiful spectacle. On the horizon there is a chain of summits already covered with snow. Below them is a mass of rocks shaded in red, yellow, blue, and everything that autumn has to offer of the richest in color and form. Immediately before us is brush, mixed with the huge trees and a waterfall foaming as it descends into a basin. The leaves rustle in the evening breeze and the sun lights this magnificent panorama with its final rays. This is what you might have admired had you been with us on this day.

Hunting and Fishing among the Coeur d'Alenes. November, 1842, to February, 1843

The Coeur d'Alenes also have their great hunt, but their country, dotted with lakes and interlaced with rivers, abounds in fish no less than in game animals, so they also have their great fishing expeditions. Fishing, like hunting, is done almost the year round. But the great fishing expedition takes place in fall, and the great hunting expedition occurs in the winter.

On November 14, we landed on the straight banks of the Spokane River, at the place where Lake Coeur d'Alene teems with a prodigious number of fish. It is there that the great fishing is ordinarily done. If the catch is to be abundant, it is necessary to erect a barrier made of wicker screens attached to a line of tripods, solidly joined together by traverse poles. Since at that season the cold is beginning to be felt, the task is difficult for the fishermen who must stand in water which is breast-deep. To volunteer for that task is one way to gain popularity. The catch of fish, like the game procured in the hunt, is distributed equally to everyone. Once the netting has been erected, the whole process becomes obviously quite simple. The catch is usually so abundant that canoes are filled and emptied within a space of a few hours. It is in large measure due to the ease with which the Coeur d'Alenes procure the necessities of life that this tribe is noted for its laziness, to say nothing of other vices. This year, the opening of the fishing season and the beginning of the mission took place at the same time. While some were occupied with making their dam, others were cutting trees for a cross and for a house of prayer.

Contrary to the usual procedure of the missionary, we planted the cross first, for with its help we hoped to put to flight all the manitous in the place. As soon as the cross was erected, each one came to kiss it and say, "Jesus, I give You my heart." Meanwhile, the priest chanted and the people repeated in chorus, "*O Crux, ave spes unica.*" Strangely enough, from that day on there were no more of the diabolic visions, heretofore so frequent, nor of the noisy gambling parties which used to go on for days and nights, to the great deteriment of health, purse, and morals. All the uproar of the gamblers and of the manitous, which resembled a Jewish Sabbath more than anything else, was succeeded by the singing of hymns, the recitation of prayers, and instructions in the truths necessary for salvation.

Six days after the erection of the cross, we were able to celebrate Mass in the new temple. Since all of the edifying events of this time with the Coeur d'Alenes have been related elsewhere, to avoid repetition, I shall proceed immediately to describe the celebration of Mass at midnight on Christmas. A little before midnight, a loud rifle discharge which echoed far off in the mountains announced to the Indians of the area that the house of prayer had just opened. At this announcement, waves of worshipers approached and, at the sight of night's shadows turned into splendid day, one of them could not restrain himself from saying over and over in a loud voice what they had been taught when the cross was erected: "Jesus, I give You my heart." Undoubtedly many others echoed the same words, for from this night on the preparation for baptism was the chief concern of the majority. With some who still resisted grace the spirit of the multitude communicated itself so abundantly that no sacrifice was too much for their generosity. On the Feast of the Circumcision a large number of them experienced the happiness of receiving the sacrament of their regeneration.[91] God, it seemed, could deny nothing to the fervor of the prayer, but their catch of fish had never been so poor. Not only had all of them been without meat since the fishing had begun, but many had eaten their last fish. As a result of this austere fast, two old people, who had been among the first baptized, were so sick that it became necessary to administer the last sacraments to them.

What might be the reason for such a cessation of temporal help? The better ones, as is usually the case, said it was because they were still bad. But those who were really bad (and there was unfortunately still a large number of these, who were all the more dangerous for being hypocrites) began to blame the Cross, baptism, and even the prayer of the Black-robes.

"Remember," they said, "the fishing and hunting of other times. Ah! they were successful, because we prayed diligently to our manitous. Now, instead of praying to them, we reject them, and it is for this reason that we now have no food, that our people are falling ill, and two of them are on the point of death."

White Red,
chief of the Bloods.

Buffalo Skinner,
a Blood chief.

*A Piegan woman
with her child.*

*The Indian wife
of the factor,
Mr. Culbertson.*

These and similar accusations were repeated, at first secretly and timidly, but soon so publicly and so freely that they came to the attention of the missionary. As he was just at this juncture engaged in explaining the Ten Commandments, he put special emphasis on the First Commandment, reviewing the events from the fall of our first parents to the temptation of the Lord in the desert. He thus had occasion to stress the severity of the punishment of those who lend ear to the spirit of falsehood, and also to point out the rewards for those who resist this spirit. When these things had been properly understood and the Master of Life and Death had confirmed the priest's words by the almost instantaneous healing of the sick, the missionary concluded with these words:

"You see, it is neither the Cross, nor baptism, nor the prayers of the Blackrobes which bring sickness to those who listen to them. Proof of this is that those who have listened most attentively have returned from the portals of death, precisely because they placed their confidence in the power of our prayers, the Cross, and the sacraments. As for the results of your hunting and fishing, if they have not been what they used to be, or more abundant still, blame no one but yourself. God does not love deceitful hearts, and before God your hearts have been deceitful. On the one hand you have spoken as we speak and on the other you have spoken as the enemy of God and man. But you know what God's punishment is; you may well tremble lest you be so punished. Search your hearts and your lodges to see whether there does not remain something of the old superstitions. And if something does still remain of them, make haste to bring it to me that I may burn it to remove the cause of the misfortunes threatening you."

This exhortation was repeated throughout the tribe by those who were truly devout, and particularly by two girls, daughters of chiefs, whose courageous zeal recalled that of the Apostles. There resulted, by the grace of God, such a compulsion in the hearts that still rebelled that every evening, until the Feast of the Purification, there were brought into the lodge of the missionary, to feed his fire, medicine sacks and remnants of such sacks, an occasional animal tail, feather, deer hoof, or some small bone, up to that time the object of all the confidence due only to the sovereign Lord. This continued until, finally, it was possible to say that the tree of death had been cut out by its very roots. Then did the Cross appear powerful! To give credit to their own sacrilegious practices, the medicine men repeated, with all possible variations, "In a single day one hundred eighty deer were killed." But the worshipers of the Cross could add, "And we, with the help of the Saviour, have killed three hundred in a few hours."

To make more evident what was remarkable about this occurrence, let us enter into some of the details. For a day to be really good for hunting, three conditions must be fulfilled. First, there must be a goodly number of animals. Second, the snow in the mountains must be deep enough to cause the animals to descend onto the plain. Third, the snow on the plains must be soft enough for the animals to sink into it, but still firm enough to support the hunter on his snow shoes. When and how does the snow acquire this consistency? When it is warm enough during the day for the snow on the surface to melt and cold enough at night for this surface to freeze over. It is rare for the first three conditions to coincide, but still more rare for the other two conditions also to be present. But within the memory of the Coeur d'Alenes these conditions had never been as favorable as they were on the Feast of the Purification. On this day, just as it was becoming light, the man in charge of the camp guard looked toward the mountains and saw black bands descending onto the plain from all sides. There were deer, deer, and more deer.

"My brothers," he cried in a stentorian voice, "put on your snowshoes and take your arrows. Here are deer coming in our direction. It is the Great Spirit that sends them to us. Quickly!"

In a few minutes all the hunters had reached the deer and, laying their rifles and bows and arrows aside, they dispatched the deer by taking hold of their antlers and twisting their necks. This method had three advantages. First, it saved time; second, powder was saved; third, the game was not damaged. When the hunt was over, the hunters brought to the missionary a pile of little sticks equal in number to the number of the deer killed. There were six hundred of them, that is, an average of six for

Typical braves in ceremonial dress.

A brave with his wife and daughter.

each hunter. The president of the new society for young people had, alone, taken twelve. Thus, the most pious was the most fortunate. "Ah!" said the most incredulous among them. "Now we see very well that the prayers of the Blackrobes are more powerful than ours. Father, you may baptize us when you wish. Here we are."

That evening, the most feared, because the most evil, of the medicine men entered the lodge of the missionary, threw his medicine sack into the fire and, before a number of witnesses, said, "I am forgetting about you in order to obey now only the word of the true God."

Let us return to our hunters. The game had to be distributed, but in what proportion? This is the rule: The hunter who made the kill has a right to the hide and half the animal, minus head and legs. His nearest neighbors take the rest, minus the legs. The latter belong to the community. The distribution was made in the lodge of the chief, but before proceeding with it, a prayer was said. This was a custom observed even during the reign of idolatry. At the feast which follows the great hunt, the chiefs begin by eating the hearts. Since this is only a symbol of friendship, to which members of the feast attach no superstitious significance, this custom still persists.

On this evening, following such an extraordinary day, the distribution among the mouths that had been hungry so long was made with greater deliberation than usual. But all the honor is due to Him whose beneficent hand had been so visible to all eyes. One may recall the no less remarkable killing of the one hundred fifty-three buffalo in the first winter hunt of the Flatheads. The conclusion, it seems to me, ought to be this: God always hears prayers when they are humble and persevering, and always in a manner best suited to confirm the faith and increase the devotion of those who invoke His aid.

The hunt, which has just been described, was, in the design of God, something altogether extraordinary. In the ordinary great hunt, the first thing to do is to form a circle, more or less extended, according to the number participating. When the circle has to be enlarged, little pieces of animal skin are substituted for men. These pieces of skin are suspended from branches, and, according to the Coeur d'Alenes, achieve the same effect, by their appearance or their odor, as do the cries and gestures of the hunters. When the circle is tight enough to permit the game to be shot with accuracy, everyone fires at will. But this method is not without its dangers. Sometimes it happens that the arrow or rifle ball, passing through or over the animal, finds another target. During one hunt at which I was present a rifle ball lodged in the body of an unfortunate hunter. In such cases the Blackrobe has no little trouble on his hands. And there are many such cases. This ought to console those who see in an Indian hunt only a series of exercises ideally suited to favor nature at the expense of grace.

The best location for hunting is one where there is a gentle descent toward a lake whose high banks present an insurmountable obstacle to the flight of the game. The Coeur d'Alenes had such a site, during the first days of January. But the hunt there was just like the fishing had been at the beginning of the mission, that is, less productive than in preceding years. The plain where the six hundred deer were killed was open on all sides. To reach the game the circling tactic, the use of rifles, and even arrows would have been useless. The conclusion is that to remove the great obstacle to the conversion of the most obstinate, the hand of God had to become visible. And just as on the occasion of the killing of the one hundred fifty-three buffalo, which we have compared to the miraculous catch of fishes of St. Peter, so here did the hand of God manifest itself in a manner perfectly suited to the minds and needs of these poor people, who could imagine nothing superior to good fishing and, above all, good hunting.

Is there an abundance of game in the Coeur d'Alene country? Perhaps nowhere does so small an area contain such a variety. Next to the roe deer, these are the most common: the deer, the elk, the mountain lion, the carcajou, the white sheep, the bighorn, the goat, the wolf, the fox, the wildcat, the polecat, the hare, the otter, the weasel, the badger, the mink, the marten, the fisher, the beaver, the muskrat, a large variety of mouse-colored rats, squirrels, field mice, not to mention four or five varieties of bear. Of the birds, there are the calumet bird, (which has the same importance as the eagle), the swan, the crane, the pelican, the bittern, the bustard, the snipe, the thrush, the duck, the teal, the magpie, the crow, the swallow, the green woodpecker, the hawk, the turtledove, the fishing bird, many varieties of aquatic birds and others unknown in Europe.

Fish are abundant in lakes, rivers, and small streams. I will not speak here of the mosquito or of the other insects harmful to man. One is devoured by them during certain seasons. Nor will I speak of the serpents which are present in large numbers. In a single day I chased two out of my bed. Fortunately, rattlesnakes are rare there.

What a vast collection of animals! And, sad to say, probably not one of them has not at some time received homage from the Coeur d'Alenes. The most celebrated ones in the history of their medicine are the bear, the deer, and the calumet bird. The most curious of all is perhaps the wolverine. This animal, which is only as large as an ordinary sheep, has many features in common with the bear. Like the bear, it climbs to the tops of the tallest trees, and it has, in the muscles of its paws and neck, such prodigious strength that it has been seen to carry off whole deer and to climb, bearing animals larger than itself. Next to the roe deer, the animals most hunted by the Coeur d'Alenes are deer and the bear.

Bear hunting is seldom undertaken on a large scale because this animal is rarely found in large numbers. It is naturally ferocious and very dangerous, but the good hunter does not fear it. I call a hunter good who combines strength and courage with skill. I saw a Coeur d'Alene who possessed all these qualifications to such degree that before he had reached the age of forty he had killed more than one hundred bears. A goodly number of these had been of the most ferocious variety.

The Second Winter Hunt with the Flatheads: January to April, 1844

The Flatheads had been baptized now for a period of three years. Twice every day, during that period, they had heard the word of God and had put it into practice. It is not surpris-

ing, therefore, that religion had become a part of most of them and that some had attained the heights of devotion which produce saints. More mistrustful of themselves than ever as they left for their hunt, they felt a need for adding three new invocations to their pious practices. The invocations were: "St. Michael, pray for us; St. Raphael, pray for us; St. Hubert, pray for us." These three were chosen because they had learned that St. Michael was the protector of the brave; St. Raphael, the guide of travelers; and St. Hubert, the patron of hunters. They were well aware that during the hunt they would have need of heavenly protection. Besides their morning and evening prayers, always followed by an instruction and singing, there was Mass, as often as possible, in the missionary's lodge. The Angelus and the rosary were recited in the other lodges.

On the march, in spite of the intense cold, which added immensely to the other difficulties, there was not a sign of discord, discontentment, or impatience. Yet it was only after twenty-four days of painful and hungry marching that the news was finally spread that there was a herd of buffalo in the area. When the camp had proceeded to the place, they found there other hunters who, like themselves, were nearer to extreme want than to abundance. Just a short time before, a group of Pend d'Oreilles had pulled the bodies of some buffalo cows out of the Missouri River. The animals had drowned while attempting to cross the river on the ice which had broken under their weight. The unlikelihood of such an incident recurring obliged the Flatheads either to go hungry or to invade the Blackfoot country to find game. The latter alternative was chosen.

For four days the Flatheads rode over the face of the land, finding a great deal of snow but no game. On Wednesday of Ember Week the missionary advised the camp that this would be the proper time for addressing prayers to Heaven, asking divine help in their dire need for food.[92] "But," warned the missionary, "if you wish God to answer your prayers, you must promise to use His gifts only to serve Him better." Listening to the priest respectfully, they disposed themselves to pray. The very next day it was announced that many herds of

top left:

*The son of
Blackfoot Chief Eagle.*

top right:

*Another portrait
of Chief Eagle, a Blackfoot.*

bottom left:

*High priest
of the Mad Dog ritual.*

top left:
A brave
in ceremonial dress.

top right:
A young hunter.

bottom right:
A calumet bearer.

top left:
A bear skinner.
top right:
A soldier.
bottom left:
A man of importance.

There
by the
that w
party
the Li
fact w
becaus
seemed
tions.
gaining
horses
that we
was no
wait th
ahead.
At tha
inform
They r
nied by
Dur
to a N
danger
no less
first q
news?"
"We
Crows.
"Are
"The

Whi
that I
baptize
who for
with us
ceremor
the roa
hard rio
which I
of the F
lay the
of the I
forts, d
other.
successi
projecti
cations.
did so, t
ered sor
in our
warrior

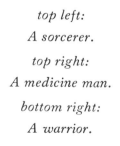

top left:
A sorcerer.
top right:
A medicine man.
bottom right:
A warrior.

top left:
The father of a family.
top right:
A young dandy.
bottom left:
The storyteller.

top left:
A visitor.

top right:
A flatterer.

bottom right:
An old comrade.

One of them, seeing what was in the wind, as soon as he was within earshot, cried out, "The Blackrobes are coming and with them the Nez Percés and the Pend d'Oreilles."

At this cry, the Crows hesitated, and their chiefs, knowing better than the others what they had to fear, shouted, "*Amaraba, amaraba!*" which means, "Off with you." To their commands they added vigorous blows with the rod, so that even the most obstinate were obliged to retreat without striking another blow. The Crow word *amaraba* had been repeated so often that even the Flathead children were still repeating it when we arrived.

The Flatheads spent the night thanking Heaven for such a happy outcome. But the next day the Crows, having undoubtedly learned that the re-enforcements had not arrived, stole thirty horses in plain daylight, right from under the noses of the Flatheads. And, as when an innocent person is mistakenly punished in place of the guilty, nothing more was required to rekindle the fires of war. Toward ten o'clock in the morning, in the midst of a cloud of dust, the Crows came at full gallop, under the false impression that nothing could stand in the face of the suddenness of their attack. But the Flatheads, forseeing such an effort, were waiting in solid formation, ranged in a line outside of the camp.

When the attackers were within rifle range, Titiche Loutso, surnamed the Bravest of the Brave, after making the little vanguard pray, rose up and said, "My friends, if God wishes that we be victors, we shall be victors. If He does not, then may His will be done. Meanwhile, courage!"

He and his men then opened fire so effectively that the Crows immediately changed their plan of attack into a boastful display of horsemanship which only served to tire their horses. Victor, observing this, cried, "Now, my children, forward!" Each of the Flathead warriors rode so skillfully that the enemy horsemen were forced to retreat more than two miles from the point of attack. Nevertheless, taking courage in numbers, the Crows came up for the attack time after time. This lasted until evening.

During the fighting the youngest of the warriors displayed a fearlessness which astonished the elders. Several women rivaled the bravest of the men in courage. In the midst of the fray an elderly woman, hatchet in hand, hurled herself so violently between her son, whose horse was tiring, and a Crow on the point of reaching him, that the pursuer, despite his giant stature, judged it prudent to move away. Another younger woman went about on the battlefield gathering up arrows for those of her warriors who had run out of them. Another, who had advanced too far in pursuit of the enemy, made such a swift about face, at the very moment several arms were outstretched to grab her, that she galloped back to her own lines leaving the enemy stupefied. Still another, after having spent some time pursuing several Crows, returned saying, "I thought these great talkers were men, but I was wrong. They are not even worth pursuing."

Indian fights are very similar to a *jeu de barres*, and for this reason last a long time without spilling much blood.[98] Thus, instead of saying, "We shall fight," they say, "We shall have sport." In this fight, which lasted nine hours, there were only ten killed and fourteen wounded, all on the side of the Crows, with the single exception of a Nez Percé. Why had this one man been killed? In answer to this question, the people of the Little Robe replied that it was because he had not made the sign of the cross before going into battle.

On leaving the field of battle, which had become for seventy-six of their members the cradle of a new life, the Little Robe warriors ranged themselves in an extended line. Behind them came some distinguished women, led by the woman calumet bearer. All of them, both men and women, were dressed in their finest garb. The costume of the chief was red. Everyone carried a green branch in his hand and, at intervals, there were flags of various colors and shapes. As the phalanx started to march, the triumphal chant began, accompanied by the drums. The high voices of the women mingled pleasingly with the bass voices of the men. Each phrase ended in a sharp cry of joy. Excited by the warlike music, the horses advanced proudly along the river, the banks of which resembled the towers and fortresses of medieval times.

When the multitude arrived at camp, there was talk of holding a scalp dance. As the sun was still smiling down with all of its force, they held their meeting in a place where great trees afforded a pleasant, deep shade. These old giant trees served as a grandstand for the spectators who formed a vast audience. Those not lucky enough to find place in the trees or in the first row, watched from horseback behind the others. The same horse sometimes offered vantage point for two people, one sitting in the usual fashion and another standing erect, with his hands resting on the shoulders of his seated companion. In the middle of the natural arena, women were dancing. Off to one side were the musicians whose instruments were piercing whistles and drums, beaten more or less rapidly depending on the nature of the presentation. Among the dancers were members from every lodge. Some carried the weapons which had contributed to victory; others were rigged out grotesquely, wearing outlandish costumes or ornaments of honor. These fantastic decorations were never once taken off. The choicest costumes were those which combined with bizarre form and brilliance of color a system of rattles or bells of many tones. But in the eyes of the Indian nothing could compare with the headdress made of eagle plumes and purple bands. The truth is that the undulating movements of such headgear harmonized with those of the dance and the music, having about them something magical, not always found amid the luxuries of civilization.

Perhaps for the first time crowns of greenery or green branches had taken the place of bloody scalps. Hence this dance, which is, in any event, more religious than profane, offered nothing the least bit offensive or painful. The particular characteristic of the dance was a little hop, more or less lively, depending on the tempo set by the drum or by the chant. The drum was beaten only by the great men, but the chant, which was the soul of the occasion, was participated in by all. From time to time, to break the monotony of the chant, the sharper sound of the whistles could be heard. If, in spite of this stimulation, the action appeared to be slowing down, to liven it, there were harangues accompanied by great gestures, by burlesque grimaces, and by broken cries produced by striking the mouth with the hand.

All this could be seen in our dance. We even saw old women who, to achieve greater effect, abandoned the staffs with which they were supporting their trembling hops, and swung their arms about with all the force they could muster, leaping until they were exhausted. As the movement was a circular one, and the dancers tended to approach the center, it would happen that the circle became too tight and even little hops were no longer possible. Then the dancers would turn about, reform their circle, and begin again with renewed vigor.

After the dance ceremony came the procession of the calumet, which went in a circle to the left until it had reached its point of departure. This procession was made up of three officiating priestesses of distinction, led by a high and powerful personage whose function was to control the speed of the group. The principal priestess was in the middle, bearing the calumet. The one to her right carried a fan, and the third, to her left, bore a kind of cymbal. The whole thing together seemed to express the thought that *peace, concord, and harmony ought to be the fruits of victory.*

On September 9, the north wind, which was blowing into our faces, became so sharp that, in spite of our desire to hurry, we were obliged to call a halt sooner than usual. In the evening a Nez Percé accompanied by three Blackfeet, entered the camp. This Nez Percé presented himself as a great friend of the white men, almost believing himself to be white because, instead of plucking his beard as the Indians do, he shaved it as we do. The youngest of his companions, whose features were most interesting, had lost his parents so early that he did not remember them. His mother, who had been carrying him in her arms when she was captured by the Blackfeet, died a few days later. Whereupon, his father, becoming the mortal enemy of his new masters, virtually ceased to exist for him. But the orphan was adopted by an Indian woman who wished to be a mother to him and who, until just recently, had, indeed, been one. She had just told him, the young man said, that she was not really his mother and that his father, who was in our camp, would be glad to see him. The father, touched by what he learned, but still unconvinced, remembered that his child had a pronounced birth mark. He looked for the mark and so assured himself that this was indeed his son.

A professional liar and importunate beggar.   *A trader who earns his living by barter.*

The following scene took place in the Black-robe's lodge: "I am very rich in horses," said the father, in an effort to attach his son to him. "The fastest horse in the tribe is mine and I will give it to you."

"My father, I should be very happy to follow you," replied the young man, "but only after I have introduced the Blackrobe to my adoptive country."

This was such an exceptional remark that Father De Smet gave the youth permission to visit our lodge whenever he might wish to do so. But many days later the young man assured us that the Nez Percé chief was not his father. Others told us that the supposedly touching scene had been faked only in the hope of swindling the Nez Percé out of a good horse.

With good reason the Nez Percés disliked the Blackfeet. In spite of the esteem in which the Flatheads held the Little Robe people, the Nez Percés conducted themselves so poorly toward them that, if on two or three occasions they did not take leave of the Flatheads, it was only because of the missionaries. On the tenth, when the Nez Percés announced that they were going to leave us, everybody rejoiced. But scarcely had they gone a mile when, justly fearing an encounter with the Crows, they thought only of retracing their steps. This made the Little Robe people, and consequently also the missionaries, decide to say adieu to the Flathead camp. The Flatheads had given sufficient proof that they did not fear war. But they loved peace and everything that might contribute to maintaining it. Thus, as they gave us their hands, perhaps for the last time, it was easy to see that this separation was costing them a great deal. A goodly number of them conducted us for some distance. To spend still one more night with us, five or six of them accompanied us as far as our campsite. The void caused by the absence of our best converts and the recollection of what the Blackfeet were still like contributed to making us gloomy. Also, while skirting the chain of mountains that lay to our left, it seemed to us that the masses of desolate rock, whose ghostly configurations were multiplied by the heavy shadows as we marched along, were the openings of so many caverns ready to spew forth at us all the brigands of the country.

En route, one of the distinguished horsemen fell from his mount and our efforts to revive him were unavailing. He was the first baptized of his nation, a chief who, for five years, had been preparing the way in his country for the preaching of the Gospel. He was a warrior who, in the last battle, had been a prodigy of valor; a Christian who, only the night before, had rejoiced in the hope that his fondest prayers were about to be answered. In a word, it was Nicolas, our precursor, who had fallen at the very moment we were setting foot in his country. What a tragedy for us, for his tribe, and for his son, who was our interpreter! Ordinarily the Blackfeet express their grief in cries and by inflicting on themselves more or less serious wounds. But Sata, this good son, remembering that his father and he had become the servants of a Master who regards sacrifices of the heart more highly than any others, recommended to his wife and his children that they forget the cries, the tears, and the useless blood in order the better to help their dear departed ascend into Heaven. They all passed the night in prayer. At the funeral, Sata himself, whose heart was almost failing him, pronounced the eulogy of his father. Scarcely had the mortal remains descended into the grave when it was announced that the great tribe of the Piegans, the tribe of Nicolas himself, was advancing to meet us.

*Autumn Hunt
with the Blackfeet:
September 12
to November 23, 1846*

On September 12, 1846, with our hearts half sad and half joyful, we struck camp to join the Piegans. In the evening, a troop of buffalo approached us on the run, a certain sign that they were being pursued. As the hunters approached the buffalo and were on the point of descending on them, at a signal from their chief, all the hunters, without exception, dismounted from their horses and knelt to invoke the protection of the Queen of Heaven. For the first time, the Blackfeet were on their knees at the feet of the Blessed Virgin, whom they recognized, as did the Flatheads, as the Mother

Two portraits of people in the upper Missouri country, not identified by name.

When Father Point discovered that Indians,
like many other people, enjoyed anything that
extolled their persons, he tried to portray the most sterling
characteristics of their great men.

of God and their own mother. How could we find words to express what we felt at that moment? And Her protection, which we never invoke in vain was, indeed, not lacking. The hunters arose, mounted their hoses, and swept down on the black column which was approaching. With the greatest of ease, they took the animals. It was, thus, in the midst of rejoicing that the tribe of Little Robe and the Piegans met.

The hunters returned; the great news was announced; fires were lighted and a royal feast was spread. In the lodge of the Blackrobe—and may no one be scandalized—there was a very entertaining evening. Yesterday, it is true, the camp had been grief-stricken. But today everyone was joyful. Thus does the Indian pass, in the twinkling of an eye, from sentiments of sorrow to the most lively gaiety. Who had the floor in our group? A Blackfoot whose originality is limitless. In the middle of his *bon mots*, however, he said such sensible things that it would be difficult to decide whether his wisdom was not greater than his gaiety. Here are some of his observations.

"When we arrived in the camp of the Flatheads," he said, "we had plenty of meat, but the Flatheads, as well as the Nez Percés, had none. We invited them to our lodges as friends and, as is the custom, we gave them something to eat. Since it was said that they ate differently from others, I watched to see how it would be done. Here is what I saw. The Flatheads, before placing anything in their mouths, sit quietly, lower their eyes, make the sign of the cross and then say a prayer. Then, and only then, do they eat. With the Nez Percés it didn't go this way. In fact, they did the exact opposite. As soon as we proffered them a morsel they gobbled it up, like dogs, and that was all there was to it. Let's see what they do on the day of God, I thought to myself, as I watched them. On this day, as on the others, the Nez Percés were working, but at what? They were combing their hair, painting their faces, putting on their fine garments, looking at themselves in their mirrors. Then after they had admired themselves, they went out to let the others see them. But the Flatheads were not doing any of these things. On that day they remained quietly in their lodges, thinking only of how they might pray well or speak well. And on the day of the battle with the Crows you could see very well which ones were the braver."

Then, beginning to speak about himself, this man, who was really brave, said nothing of his great deeds, but spoke only of his faults.

"Formerly, and even today," he said, "there are two things I like very much, the gambling of the Blackfeet and the firewater of the whites. But now that I have learned that these things are evil, just see if I touch them."

Since the baptism of his children, he had repeatedly said that he had left the evil to take only the good.

When Sata, whose father had recently died, came to visit us a third time, the following conversation took place:

"What news, good Sata?"

"For two nights I have not been able to close my eyes."

"Why?"

"Because the image of my father is always before me."

"What do you do when you see him?"

"I pray. I wake up my children and they pray with me."

Sata's children are charming. This morning they came into my lodge to warm themselves. Suddenly the oldest one darted out. A few minutes later he returned with a little branch from which cherries were hanging. He presented the branch to his sister Adele, and she in turn presented it to her little sister Marie. Marie, seeing no one else to whom she might pass the branch, ate the cherries, first making the sign of the cross. There was also a little Indian who ate some of them, but in the style of the Nez Percés.

"Did you see that?" Adele asked her brother. "How this one eats cherries?"

Then the group spoke of other things, while warming their hands, just like reasonable persons.

I had a visit from a Piegan who, on March 12, had given me a present out of gratitude for my having asked the Flatheads to spare his life and that of his companions.

"I come to see you," he said, "to tell you that I have not forgotten the promises I made to you. Since that time I have remained the friend of the Flatheads, and I am so now more than ever. I intend to pray as they do."

Very soon, I said to myself, this good Indian will make up for the loss of the good Nicolas. But how inconstant is the will of man and how terrible the judgment of the Lord! On the day the missionary entered this chief's camp to confer baptism on him, he left at the head of a war party against the Assiniboines and, a few days later, he and all his companions fell before the enemy without having a second in which to repent. This death made more than one better-inspired Indian say, "Do not put off until tomorrow the good you can do today."

On the fourteenth, toward ten o'clock in the morning, when the news was spread that the populous tribe of the Piegans was advancing to welcome us, there was great joy in our camp. Everyone dressed in his best. The horsemen mounted their horses, beat their drums, intoned joyous chants, discharged their firearms and, to give their visitors time to prepare themselves according to custom, advanced slowly behind the Blackrobes. The horsemen of the two camps met. The grand chief of the Piegans, out of timidity or modesty, remained behind. Consequently, it was the grand bearer of the calumet who received our first tokens of friendship. In a lively improvisation, an orator evinced discontent bordering on ill humor, complaining of the lack of pomp in the reception of the Blackfeet. Sata, who spoke after him, expressed himself more calmly, but his tone, his gestures and his upward gaze made it evident that he was speaking about his father. This sadness and regret were mingled with the joy and hope.

When the speeches were finished, hands were shaken, and the most distinguished personages ranged themselves about the missionary. The grand chief, recovered from the pardonable sentiments ill becoming his person, advanced toward us and expressed his appreciation for our visit. He was conducted to our lodge where we proceeded to the calumet ceremony. To be lighted, the instrument of peace had to circulate from left to right until it came to a smoker without head covering. When it had been lighted by him, it circulated from mouth to mouth toward the right until it arrived again at the starting point. Then it was handed back

in the opposite direction, this time stopping only before those who wore headgear. Especially with the Blackfeet, the calumet is the most revered instrument of the cult. Its guardians are pontiffs of the nation. The horse that carries it on the march is exempt from all other use and the woman who leads the animal by the bridle is the most honored woman of the tribe.

Tongues had scarcely become unloosed when another visit, one no less solemn than the first, was announced. It was that of the Flatheads.

Never had these gallant warriors of the great wilderness appeared more noble than on that day. While the body of the army, ranged in several frontal lines, advanced with a measured gait, singing their old chants, one of the chiefs, who was numbered among the bravest, circled about at the head in a truly knightly fashion. They were accompanied by the Pend d'Oreilles and the Nez Percés, about whom we have spoken above. We went to meet them, followed by a great number of Blackfeet of all tribes. For, in addition to the people of the Little Robe, who had not quit us, and the Piegans, whom we had just joined, there were also a number of Gros Ventres and Bloods. Soon the frank manner of the Flatheads communicated itself from person to person and all fraternized as if they had never been enemies.

After evening prayers, in which all desires seemed to combine into one—that for perpetual peace—there was a meeting of all the most highly distinguished personages in the lodge of Great Lake, the grand chief of the Piegans. There, all honors were accorded the grand chief of the Flatheads. After thanking the assembly for the benevolence shown toward his nation, Victor spoke first of the peaceful sentiments he entertained for all the Blackfeet without exception. Then he recounted several adventures, all ideally suited to gladden everyone's heart. Finally, he spoke of the last battle with the Crows, not neglecting to recall the sign of the cross and to give all honor for the victory to the God of the Christians. These opportune words were especially remarkable because the date was September 14, the day on which the Church celebrates the Exaltation of the Holy Cross.

On September 16, as the visitors departed, the quarrelsomeness of the Nez Percés rose

*The sole reward of those who came to pose for Father Point
was the pleasure of seeing themselves portrayed among the leaders of their nations,
for the mission treasury had nothing to offer them.*

again and threatened to upset everything. The Flatheads stood up against the troublemakers, at first laughingly, then in dead earnest, administering a few vigorous cane whippings. The Nez Percé chief, taking the part of the mutinous party, armed himself with a pistol to support them. A Flathead chief gave him two whip lashes across the shoulders. Fortunately, friends intervened and the visitors finally separated. The Nez Percés were very much confused over their misadventure and the new friends remained as kindly disposed toward each other as could possibly be wished.

On September 17, when a Nez Percé struck a Flathead woman, he received from another woman the chastisement he so well deserved. On the eighteenth, four others tried some mischief and could only thank the swiftness of their legs for their safety. On the nineteenth, two Crows were killed by two Gros Ventres and five Piegan lodges were hotly pursued by Crees. On the same day several Blackfoot camps assembled in the vicinity of Fort Louis, where we, as well as the provision boat, were awaited. Would this boat bring strong liquor with it? This was the great question of the day. On the twentieth, the Feast of Our Lady of Sorrows, ninety-six children and two aged people were baptized.

On the twenty-first, a few Bloods arrived, having taken twenty-seven horses from the Crows. One of the Bloods, the son of the grand chief, and another, the brother of the chief, gave assurance that if the Blackrobes would visit their camp, they would be welcome. On the twenty-second, an old man of great influence in the Piegan tribe was baptized. He received the name of Ignatius Xavier. Catholic prayers were translated into Blackfoot. On the twenty-fourth, the Feast of Our Lady of Mercy, we left the Piegans to go to Fort Louis. The Little Robe chief, who was accompanying us, was concocting some sinister project, as was evident from his expression and his excited manner as he marched cautiously along. While still a few minutes from Fort Louis, he said, "We are going to see a Blackfoot who has sworn to kill me because, last year, I fired at him to avenge the death of a Nez Percé who had placed himself under my protection. This is what I shall do to heal the wound. I shall offer him a horse. If he accepts, well and good. If he refuses it, then I shall kill him, seeing that if he is not killed by me I shall be killed by him."

What was there to say in such a case? We promised to say a number of Masses in honor of the Blessed Virgin if we succeeded in reconciling the two enemies.

When we had come in sight of the fort, there was a halt for preparations in case of an attack. Rifles were loaded and the battery was ready to fire. Two Indians approached in full gallop to advise the chief of what his enemy had said: "I must kill a Piegan. If it's not the little chief, it will be another."

More determined than ever as a result of this message, the little chief continued on his way and we entered Fort Louis. We asked where the Blackfoot was staying, what his character was, and what his intentions were. He was in a place only five minutes away. He was a difficult character, little disposed to come to any sort of agreement. We sent word that we wished to see him and he answered that we might present ourselves. We did so, together with the little chief and a few others. This warrior's name was Aponista and he passed for the bravest of his tribe, being considered the equivalent of a chief. His lodge, planted in the shadow of great trees, had something imposing about it. We entered and found everywhere evidence of propriety, order, comfort. The fire which illuminated the interior brought even the smallest objects into relief. Around the fire were spread the robes which were to serve as our seats. We were given the places of honor. The others were at our sides according to their rank. Aponista entered last, after letting us wait a few seconds. He was unarmed, but an armed Indian took his station by the door. The calumet was prepared in silence and in silence we smoked. Everybody was waiting. Finally, Father De Smet spoke. What he spoke about may be imagined. When he had finished, the suppliant rose with dignity, approached Aponista, kissed his forehead and covered his shoulders with a magnificent robe decorated with glass beads of various colors. Touched by what he had seen and heard, Aponista, in a tone of repentance rather than of clemency, said, "How could I refuse what is asked of me? Let us forget the unfortunate circumstances which have kept us at odds, and let us henceforth think only of living as brothers."

This reconciliation, made to everyone's satisfaction, will be, we hope, as enduring as it seemed sincere.

On October 18, Father De Smet—accompanied by a twelve-year-old half-breed, who was to be his regular interpreter, and by a thirty-year-old Creole, who had volunteered to serve as interpreter on solemn occasions—set out with the Piegan camp in the hope that, with such good linguistic support, he could work more efficaciously at their instruction. But en route the older one disappeared under pretext of not seeing any animals to hunt.

"But with the help of the younger interpreter," reported Father De Smet, "I succeeded in translating the prayers, which soon came to be recited publicly. After prayers came instruction and, as may well be imagined, the young boy, having no more steadfastness than knowledge, preferred playing truant to acting as interpreter. Add to this the difficulty of making oneself heard by men who had neither the docility nor the constancy of the Flatheads; by women who thought more of the sacrifices with which religion menaced them than of the advantages they might realize; and by children who were impressed only with examples of an immediately sensible nature. Then you will easily understand what the missionary would have given to have the gift of tongues. But, in spite of these obstacles, the prayers were learned by the young people. The principal virtues began to show in the less obtuse spirits and all who had not reached adult age were regenerated in the waters of baptism."

The Blackfeet had some idea of a supreme being and of an afterlife. But these notions were still so obscure that, when one spoke to them of the happiness of Heaven, they asked very seriously whether there were many buffalo in our Heaven, since they thought they were unable to do any kind of good without this. Then, conceiving Heaven as the visible atmosphere, they simply called it "the blue." Thus, the older people, especially the old medicine women, insisted that Heaven was not what we promised it would be.

According to them, what are the goods enjoyed by those who have lived a good life? The pleasures of good meat, of the calumet, of good conversation. And where is the place of these pleasures? In the sand hills that rise up in their country. I have heard an old Piegan tell that, one day, being dead, he found himself in the other life near a lodge in which the old ones were conversing. Not daring to enter without an invitation, he had waited at the door. But since no one had accorded him this civility, he returned to the living, with whom he got along much better.

Almost all the Indian tribes build medicine lodges, that is, temples to their manitous. But these structures, erected usually as the result of some dream, last only as long as the dream. Since anyone is free to dream that he has built a temple, and to believe that the dream is the expression of a sovereign will, everyone is free to build as many as he likes. But since the actual construction involves considerable expense and there are more poor Indians than rich ones, it frequently happens that a good many years pass without a temple being built.

The form of these temples is that of a cone built around a central pole by many long poles joined at the top. Once it has been decided to build a temple, those most devoutly interested in the work go into the forest to choose the principal components. Who will have the honor of striking the first blow of the ax? Men are chosen from among the bravest and women from those without reproach. How can the latter be recognized? By their own witness, ratified by all those assisting. If a single assistant denies the truth of a contention and can support his denial with proof, then the candidate gives her place to another. Once the integrity of the persons involved has been acknowledged, the hatchets do their work. Soon the tree is felled, the branches are removed and the trunk is carried religiously to the spot designated for the construction. It is planted vertically, and the outside poles are arranged in order around it. The frame is covered with foliage; the interior is lined with mats, robes, or pieces of cloth; and rich sacrificial offerings are raised up on the central pole. Buffalo tongues, which are to be distributed to the assistants, are arranged in the form of wreaths and, finally, at the back of the sanctuary a niche is fashioned in which the high priest is to perform. Such are the indispensable preparations of the medicine lodge.

Upon whom are the functions of high priest to devolve? On the one who pays for the construction of the lodge. Who will be the acolytes? Twelve dancers. What color will their garments be? Some white like those of the high priest; others, black. What will be their function? To lead the others in a dance. How long will this dance last? Two, three, and often four days. What rules must be observed during this time? Absolute abstinence from food and drink. If something happens to be eaten or drunk, the solids must be covered with certain herbs and the liquids mixed with a certain powder. Is the dance the only religious exercise? There is also the pantomime, and it is considered the principal ritual. What is its object? The great coups, that is, the most remarkable past feats of arms. Who are the actors? Those who have accomplished these feats. Do they receive rewards for them? They receive, first, a drumbeat corresponding in strength to the merit of the deed; second, something to restore their energy when the pantomime is finished; and, third, the right to change their names.

This last part of the reward is the most honorable one. Each brave may take the name that pleases him. As a rule, however, the manitou designates the name and he is supposed to do so through a dream. On this point [of the ceremony], the more modest and the less superstitious depend on the equity of their friends. This virtue is, of course, exercised in the hope that they will be more liberally rewarded. Usually in these circumstances, the liberality of the man hoping to gain new honor is so prodigal that some have been seen to reserve only bare essentials for themselves. Presents are made by means of a cord, one end being held by the person giving and the other by him who is to receive. The cord is a symbol of the friendship which unites them.

The young men who are present at the ceremony only as spectators, manifest profound humility as the great coups are represented in pantomime. When the ceremony is finished, they may be seen very modestly approaching the seat of the high priest, convinced that in his generos-

ity they too will receive all that is necessary to make them worthy of the honor paid to their elders. At the end, the distribution of buffalo tongues takes place. The first tongue is offered to him who chopped down the medicine tree. And the next is given to the [most respected] woman. The sacred tree will be left standing, as a monument to their religious devotion, until it is reduced to dust.

Perhaps never before did the Blackfeet medicine men talk so much about their prowess as during the days when we spoke of morals and religion. One day, the grand chief, as superstitious as he was brave, sent the son of the grand calumet bearer to visit me. This particular chief had the greatest faith in the power of the calumet. But the young thaumaturge, much less confident than his chief of a power he knew to be only apparent, had to be pressed before he would agree to perform his tricks. For what he was to do was nothing more or less than change the ashes in the fireplace into gunpowder and the coals, which had been raked out, into rifle balls. Finally, persuaded by the insistence of these dupes, he left the lodge mysteriously and returned still more mysteriously equipped with all the paraphernalia necessary for his charlatanism. To mystify his audience, he started by tracing an ellipse in the ashes, and placed in its center his mysterious charcoal. Then, like his brothers in deceit, he stripped to his loin cloth and, raising his long hair over his head, demanded attention.

His audience became more than attentive, when, after having the material he was supposed to transform placed on his left hand, he seized a flute with his right, placed it in his mouth, and raised his head and eyes Heavenward, the better to invoke the power of his manitou. Then, respectfully putting down his instrument of invocation, he placed his right hand over the charcoal in his left, changed the position of his hands so that the right and left were alternately one above the other, moved them about his mouth and hair and, finally, after all this hocus-pocus, without betraying himself, showed to the gaze of the audience the proof of his powers of transformation. But when he was asked to repeat the operation in broad daylight without placing his hands near his body, as he had done so adroitly the first time, he always refused. And this, in spite of an offer of a lump of tobacco equal to the value of a horse. "For the present," he said, "I feel that I do not have the same power." When he was asked why that should be, he replied naïvely, "Because the power of the Blackrobe is greater than mine."

Another medicine man presented himself, promising to do marvelous things. "By the sole power of my breath," he said, "I shall cause a rock to roll toward you, and one so heavy that, if I should wish, it would crush you. I shall throw small pieces of iron into the fire. For each piece you shall hear children crying. I will wrap a buffalo robe around a piece of iron and make a corpse appear where the iron was. If you stand before me, I can make your head turn completely around and remain that way forever. . . ."

The more outlandish the miracles which this charlatan proposed, the easier it was to understand what he was attempting to accomplish. His proposal to hold a seance the next day was accepted, but he appeared only several days later. To our questions, he replied that once he could have done all he had asserted, but now a force greater than his own prevented him from working his magic. And that greater power was the Blackrobe. Whatever the old power of these medicine men may have been, it is certain that their unwilling admissions of helplessness in our presence greatly disposed the Indians to the true prayer. The following facts had the same effect.

An old Piegan had the reputation of being able to revive the dead. I asked him what he did to achieve that result. "I only have this power," he answered, "when a barrel of firewater is placed at my disposal and I am permitted to drink as much of it as I wish."

"How many people have you brought back to life in this way."

"One person."

"Are you absolutely certain that the person was dead?"

"Everybody said so."

"But maybe he had only gone to sleep."

"Ah! I can't say anything about that."

One evening I was called into a lodge where a child was thought to be on the point of death.

I found there an old woman operator breathing on its eyes and whistling into its ears with all her might, convinced that by this means she would cure the child. The child's mother indicated that the woman should let the Blackrobe see the child. The Blackrobe had the child's feet placed in warm water and soon he was kicking away as lively as ever.

A girl complaining of a chest ailment was brought to the Blackrobe by her mother. The girl said that she had learned in a dream that the Blackrobe was the only one who could cure her. In order not to vex her, the Father gave her a powder, very innocent in itself and quite ineffective for such a case. The sick girl took the prescribed dose in great faith and the next day did not feel ill any more. What can be concluded from these occurrences? That most of the miracles attributed to the power of Indian medicine are either purely natural or exist only in the imagination. But are the following of this nature?

An Indian is placed ten feet from a white man named Picard, who holds in his hand a sheathed dagger. The Indian tells him to grip the dagger with all his strength. In spite of his efforts to hold the dagger, it comes out of its sheath, describes a turn, and lodges in the throat of the Indian. A hammer, which is much larger, flies in a similar manner, to some unknown point, and returns to its starting point in some mysterious way. Another makes a shrub shoot up out of the earth and cover itself successively with leaves, flowers, and fruit.

A dead person named the Little Grey Head, asked by a woman concerning the identity of his tribe, answers in a tone of voice that could belong only to him and in such a manner as to prove that he had knowledge of what was actually going on at great distances.

The *accoutoir*, a kind of arm chair in which a storyteller reclines, is smashed by some hidden, irresistible force. And when the end of a calumet is held in the place where the mouth of a dead man is supposed to be, the fire in the bowl can be seen to light up when the supposed puff is taken, just as happens when one really smokes.

On October 28, in the evening, a voice was heard haranguing. At first I listened in silence, but soon cries and sobs could be heard. What was happening? Ten friendly lodges had been riddled with rifle balls by a party of Assiniboines, led by a certain Okoia, to whom the Flatheads, on a similar occasion, had shown mercy. Only a few days ago he had asked the Blackrobe for baptism. Another, who had stolen three horses from the missionary, was killed before he was able to make off with his booty. Another, threatened by the same fate, escaped punishment when he promised that, if he was let off, he would bring back the stolen horses and ask to be baptized. This he actually did. Three Indians of our camp, having been captured by the Assiniboines, escaped on the first night of their captivity by singing their enemy to sleep with the hymns they had learned from the Flatheads.

On the thirty-first, after nightfall, word got around that one of our hunters had fallen into the hands of these same enemies. Warriors ran to their arms; women wailed. The wife of the unfortunate hunter cried, "*Nina, nina. Kimmokit, kimmokit.*" That is, "My Father, my Father, have pity on me, have pity on me." The grand chief, following her example, asked for prayers. Everyone knelt, made the sign of the cross, and prayed with all his heart. Scarcely two hours after the warriors had departed they all returned with the hunter.

This would be the place to speak of scenes of the hunt proper, but since they differ little from those already described, we shall simply indicate what was peculiar to this one.

For richness of vegetation, fitness of temperature, and abundance of game, the most favorable time for hunting is autumn. And this year the season, in all three respects, left nothing to be desired. Hence, there was great rejoicing everywhere, good meat, and a veritable slaughter of animals.

When the take has been considerable, the Blackfeet carry it by means of a kind of vehicle without wheels, which is called a *travois*. It is made of two poles joined about two feet from the upper end, and held to the saddle by means of a thick leather strap. The poles are joined by a crosspiece between the lower end and the rump of the horse. This crosspiece is strong enough to carry double or triple the ordinary load. When not in use on the march, this contrivance serves as a ladder for erecting the lodges, as a buttress to support them, as a platform for drying meat, as a frame for dressing hides, as a bier for showing the dead, and so on.

Why is it that the mountain Indian has not adopted it? Because roads there are narrower and ascents are more abrupt. On narrow roads or paths the contrivance would be altogether useless. As for the steep ascents, the use of the *travois* on them would be very difficult. Even on the most gentle slopes the woman leading the horse has to pull and the man has to push from behind. If this help is not given, the whole load may slide back and sometimes be strewn about, especially when the terrain on which they are traveling slopes just as much sidewise as it does lengthwise. I once saw a horse stop on an almost perpendicular slope on a little rock promontory from which it could move only by making a leap of more than fifty feet. The owner of the horse had no choice other than to lose his horse or make it jump. He therefore made such a racket that fear prompted it to leap. All that happened was that the horse was somewhat stunned after the jump. One does not always come off so easily. In place of a single horse, think of an entire equipage, and, in addition to this, children or infirm people. Then you will understand why this means of travel is used only on the plains. Sometimes a dog may take the place of the horse. But the load and the size of the vehicle must be proportionate to the strength of the poor beast.

In the hunts on the upper Missouri, the most remarkable features are the runs along the river banks, which are sometimes so steep that they become graves for entire herds. In descending the river, we saw mountains of bones in proof of this. This is sheer folly, for misery for the future will result from hunts to extermination still practiced in these parts more than elsewhere! It was said earlier that buffaloes on the run always try to cross the path of the hunter. This is true when the hunter's horse is going at a gentle gallop. But when the pace is accelerated and accompanied by cries and the whistling of rifle balls, then it is every animal for himself and the herd goes wherever it is driven. When the leaders arrive at the edge of the drop, they would no doubt like to stop, but the pressure from behind is too great. The first line jumps, then the second, the third, and so on to the next to the last line. But why do the last animals jump? Because fear does not reason. Another stupid trick of these animals may be seen when they are crossing a river on the ice. They invariably follow the leaders even when the ice begins to break. When they arrive at the other side of the river, if the banks are too steep for them to mount, they would sooner starve than return to the point they have just left. Yes, the buffalo is a most stupid animal. Hence the expression "as stupid as a buffalo."

On November 11, the wife of a Little Robe chief appeared to have died, though some did not think she had actually expired. Since the background of this woman was in her favor, conditional baptism was administered. After the ceremony, when there was no more doubt as to her death, the interpreter, Sata, pronounced her eulogy, extolling the future life in such moving terms that this second death in the tribe contributed no less than the death of Sata's father to disposing the spirit of the people in favor of our sacred beliefs. It was a singular fact that the first graves, above which was to rise the august sign of our redemption, should be those of prominent personalities, a chief and the wife of a chief, and that both should have been taken from among the living at a moment when the greatest blessing had just descended upon the tribe. May this double sacrifice bring down upon the whole Blackfoot nation the grace of a complete conversion.

On November 17, we had an unexpected visit from Pierre George, the grand chief of the Pend d'Oreilles, and Constantin's successor. Selpisto said that before his baptism, Constantin had frequently been victorious over the Blackfeet. For this reason his name and everything associated with him was odious to them. Not long after two of Constantin's sons had been killed by the Blackfeet, one of them, recommended by the Flatheads, came to see him. That Blackfoot was unworthy of sponsorship by the Flatheads because he had only recently killed one of their guests. But because the incident happened during Holy Week, clemency had been accorded him out of respect for Christ's death for sinners.

What would Constantin do? He received the Blackfoot into his lodge and treated him as a friend. When the young men learned what was going on, they rushed into their chief's lodge, determined to wash away, with the blood of the visiting Blackfoot, the crime of those who had massacred Constantin's sons.

Constantin said to them, "Another time I might have consented to your desire, but today I shall not. In giving me the grace of baptism, the God of the true prayer has shown great mercy toward me. I must do for this unhappy man what has been done for me." And not only was the Blackfoot granted his life, but great care was taken to insure his safe return to his own tribe.

To this pardon, the noble chief added, a few months later, a deed of greatness and humility which was still more remarkable. Judging that there was in the nation a man more worthy and more capable than he of bearing the title of grand chief, Constantin resigned his position in favor of another, the same Pierre George who had presented himself to the Piegan camp on November 17.

Instead of being flattered by a visit which was an honor to them, some of the Piegans were irritated because they knew that this visitor would be justified in not feeling entirely pleased with them. Very recently, in spite of Selpisto's mercy toward one of their people and of the calumet which had still more recently been smoked by the chiefs of the two nations, three horses had been stolen from him by some Piegan raiders. And one of these, in place of the death he deserved, had received, as a present from Pierre George, one of his best horses.

The successor of Constantin dismounted at the lodge of the missionary and the great men of the camp presented themselves to pay him their respects. He received them with dignity, smoked the calumet with them, and congratulated them on their good fortune of having a Blackrobe in their midst. He spoke not a word of his horses. But the Blackrobe, who knew what had taken place, after speaking of the advantages of a peace founded on justice, at length turned the talk to robbery and restitution. The gathering uttered approval, but added that, since the culprits had left with their booty, it was impossible to make restitution, at least for the moment. Pierre George's little smile would have told the observer that he had understood. The rest of the day was spent in festive visits, conversations, exchanges of presents, and demonstrations of friendship. Prominent among these demonstrations was the "mad dog" [dance], which was more solemn than usual.

In the evening after prayers there was renewed insistence on the duty of restitution and again general approval of what had been said. But of actual restitution there was not a shadow. A few minutes later rifle reports could be heard, Indians were busily running to and fro, an orator was delivering a forceful harangue. The Blackrobe asked what was going on, but the Piegan grand chief only answered, "Don't go in that direction!" Others were crying "The Pend d'Oreilles! The Pend d'Oreilles!" The firing continued, excitement mounted, and the entire camp was like a fortress surprised by an enemy who did not hesitate to attack.

A little later calm was re-established and the lodge of the missionary was filled with confused Piegans. Pierre George reappeared there, but he was as tranquil as if he had not been involved. But what had just happened? While Pierre George was leaning against a tree, conversing amicably with his nephew, an assassin had crept up under the protection of the shrubbery. It was only when his clumsiness caused his rifle to go off that he was discovered. Thus, it was to aid him on the one hand and defend our guests on the other that so much racket had been made around them. But what God preserves is well preserved. In the midst of all this point-blank firing not a single shot had told. But this protection from Heaven permitted the holders of stolen goods to rest in peace. Our visitors, more sensible of their honor than of their interest, after making every due effort to recover their property, resigned themselves to their loss and thought only of taking the road back to their camp. They had already gone some hundred paces in the execution of this intention when they spied their missing horses. It took only a moment to run up to them and, without asking permission of anybody, to repossess them. Such a brusque recovery of property was, of course, calculated to make the robbers show signs of trying to keep their booty, but three rifles were brought up to firing position so resolutely that order was not disturbed. Thus our three Pend d'Oreilles could return to their people not only as fearless and unimpeachable horsemen, but also without having shed a single drop of blood. Like noble conquerors, they had all the honors of war and all the profits of victory.

Ouest · Nord · Sud · Est

Missouri
De ses sources à son embou-
chure on compte 7000 Kill.
Jusqu'à sa jonction avec le Mis-
sissipi, environ 4600 mètr...
navigable jusq. la riv. Jaune.
Là il est aussi large que la
Tamise à Londres.

1847.

Corbeaux.
Mandanes.
Arikaras.

F^t Pierre

Sioux,
Ponkas

Omahas.
Othos

Cotes · F^t Clay
F^t Louis · F. de l'opposition
Ruines du F. Mackensi
Ruines du F. Ségane

Pieds-noirs · Ruines du F. F.E.C.
Ruine de la maison Mauve
la butte ronde

Roche-jaune
le Steemboat
Island rocher p^r

F^t union
Steemboat Martha
Fort union, vue sud est
Intérieur du fort union

Barthol
Village mandane
Village Arikaras
Buttes carrées
Pêche dans le missouri
Fort Pierre
Intérieur du fort Pierre

F^t Yangton
Butte de médecine

Perspective de la rive droite
Rivière de Ponkas
Vermillion

Butte de l'oiseau noir
Village Mormon 300
La pointe aux Ponkas
Belle vue

La platte · Nebraska

St Joseph

West-port
maison en... missouri
Plan · Westport ou Kansas

Kansas
St LOUIS
Jefferson

Riv. Arkansas

Rivière Rouge

Mississipi. · Ohio

Lac Michigan

Missouri

Rivière rouge

Mississipi

	Voyage sur missouri
	21 Mai
	21 id.
	21 id.
	21 id.
	22 id.
	22 id.
	24
	26 id.
	25 id.
	26 id.
	27 id.
	29 id.
	30 id.
	31 Mai
	25 Juin
	25 id.
	25 id.
	26 id.
	27 id.
	27 id.
	27 id.
	29 id.
	29 id.
	1 Juill.
	1 id.
	2 id.
	2 id.
	3 Juille
	4 id.
	4 id.
	4 id.
	5 id.
	6 s^t id.
	7 id.
	7 id.

Mississipi 5120... si on
on joint son cours avec celui du missouri, il aura
de long 7000 Kil.
à sa jonction avec le Missouri, il est large de 2400 m
Sa largeur ordinaire est de 900 à 1500 mètres
Sa profondeur à sa jonction avec l'Ohio 30 a 40 mèt.
Sa vitesse commune 3 Kil. à l'heure
Vitesse d'un steemboat descendant 19^K, montant 9^K.

7000 Kil.

V

A Stay at Fort Lewis
and a Journey on a Barge Down the Missouri

*Shortly before Father Point's departure from the Rocky Mountains, he helped
to arrange, between the Blackfeet and other tribes, a treaty which enabled white men
who came to the region later to avoid trouble with them. He spent the winter
of 1846–47 at Fort Lewis, and in the spring, having been recalled to Canada, he
started down the Missouri River by barge, on the journey which he here describes.*

FATHER DE SMET and I arrived at Fort Lewis on September 24, 1846.[99] It was the Feast of Our Lady of Mercy. The news we received there was of the best: Father De Smet, obliged to make a trip to St. Louis, would have a good traveling opportunity. I was invited to spend the winter at Fort Lewis. The principal officers at the fort had great respect for the missionaries. There was well-founded hope that at this place all Blackfeet could be immediately contacted. Finally, the sale of liquor had been sternly prohibited by the American government.

On September 25, the supply boat arrived. Since the fort was very low on provisions, there was great joy among all the inhabitants. There was an endless coming and going between the boat and the fort, especially on the part of the little half-breed children, and of their mothers, who were eager to display on their persons part of the luxury of civilization. On the twenty-sixth, articles of trade were displayed in the

facing:
*On this 1847 map Father Point recorded the names
of some of the Indian tribes of the region he
traveled through on his trip down the Missouri
River by barge in the spring of that year;
he also indicated the location of fur-trading posts
along the way. The legends in the upper left-hand
and lower right-hand corners give additional
information about the river and those with which
it connects. Although dates are mentioned at
intervals throughout this portion of the journal,
it is not a day-by-day diary. Its closing sentence
proves Father Point to be above all else the
missionary who had tried so successfully to
help as well as to convert his Indian friends.*

The party was led by the son of Chief Eagle who wished to gain admittance into the fort in the capacity of a brave as his father had done the year before. This young warrior had made me a present of a fine pair of mittens. How could I refuse his request? I accordingly wrote to the captain of the aforementioned fort to ask him not only to receive this party but also to do all he could to have the Crows make peace with the Gros Ventres and their allies, the Blackfeet. Father De Smet had already written in the same vein. Were these letters communicated to the persons concerned? Some Crows later said they had not been. There were some whites who thought that such a peace would be detrimental to trade.

Fort Lewis and a Barge Down the Missouri

FORT LEWIS, which was our point of departure, was built by Mr. Culbertson, as was also the next fort, Fort Clay.[102] It was situated on the right bank of the Missouri in about the center of the Blackfoot country. During the period of high water, that is, from May to July, a steamboat could perhaps have ascended this far. But above this point all navigation became impossible because of five waterfalls within a space of eight miles. During the winter, all navigation is at a virtual standstill because of the ice which freezes to a thickness of two or three feet. This year the thermometer dropped as low as 38 degrees below zero. During the dry season, which lasts from August until freezing time, barges can ascend the river, but only by the efforts of all on board. Rarely does a favorable wind give the crew a chance to rest. In some years a barge runs aground as often as ten or twelve times a day. Then, in addition to the tow line, the crew has to get into the water and heave with their shoulders. All this makes the navigation of these waters so rugged an occupation that the fort of the Blackfeet, which has need of more barges than other forts, must pay more for them.

A common employee is paid from $150 to $280 annually, without counting food, lodging, and heat. The fare is that of the country. Carpenters, blacksmiths, hunters, and all the indispensable craftsmen are better fed and also better paid. In addition to their better salary, the clerks, the principal interpreter, and the traders are admitted to the captain's table. The fort also takes care of feeding the sick and infirm, women and children, visitors, in a word, all the unproductive mouths which usually amount to more than sixty. This is not counting the chiefs who pass through, and sometimes entire war parties who also receive, gratuitously, all the powder they need. I do not include the presents made to the principal traders under penalty of having them carry their merchandise elsewhere. This explains why prices of things are so high, both for the inhabitants of the fort and for the Indians who come there to trade.

In general, the regimen of Fort Lewis (and it is the same in all the forts of the company) appeared to me to have something very pleasant about it. Except for the great effort that must be expended to bring the provision barge up the river, the work, which is usually done only between the two meals is very moderate. If some spend their wages and associate with the Indian in spite of their duties and interests, it is only what they want to do.[103] Nobody obliges them to do so. There is only one reproach that I would feel bound to make to the company in matters of public morals. This concerns the lodging of families. If each legitimately married employee had, as I have reason to hope may someday be the case, his own little separate room, or were at least free to admit only companions with the same tastes as his, I am sure that morals would improve.

I left Fort Lewis on March 19, 1847, which was the day of its funeral, or, rather, of its removal. All portable materials which had gone into its construction were taken thirty miles downstream to the other side of the river. The new site was preferable to the old one under triple aspect of scenic beauty, fertility of the soil, and convenience for trading purposes. Still, in quitting a land in which my heart had struck such deep roots, I could not help sighing as I repeated to myself the words of a celebrated traveler in the catacombs of Rome: "Thus does everything change and pass away here as elsewhere." This is, of course, true for the goods of this world. But what I hope will not pass away are the riches gained for Heaven this year. Those who were present will never forget Christmas, Easter, the baptism of so many persons reconciled to their duties. And the cross which rises in the vicinity will tell future travelers that this land, however desolate it may appear, was a true land of blessings not only for the eight hundred souls regenerated here but as well for all those who heard the voice of the Lord here.

In another place I shall tell what everyone did to promote the visible designs of divine mercy with respect to the Indians. But my heart does not permit me to postpone the thanks I owe them for the kind personal regard shown me during the months I lived among them.[104]

On the twenty-first, about eight o'clock in the morning, we bid adieu to Fort Clay and in a very short time were floating by the auxiliary fort, called Fort Campbell.[105] Those acting in the place of the absent captain saluted our passing with a few rifle shots which we acknowledged by waving our hats. Then we plunged into a solitude so profound that soon we saw only wild animals. But they were in such variety and abundance that our descent had for us perhaps more attraction than the most beautiful promenade civilization could have offered. Within a few hours we saw wolves, antelopes, deer, bighorns, buffalo, bear, eagles, gulls, bustards. As for the denizens of the water, we saw no samples of them until in the evening. Then we saw a catfish, that is, a fish whose three feelers of different lengths on each side of its head give it the appearance of a person with a mustache. By reason of its fine meat it is called a "Missouri salmon." The delicacy of the meat is proportionate to its size and bulk (which sometimes is such that the eyes are eighteen inches apart), and to the depth of the waters it inhabits.

In the midst of these denizens of the water we perceived something which transformed our amazement into compassion. It was a poor dog, abandoned because it was injured as a result of its services to its master. What services can a dog render? It takes the place of a horse and sometimes bears too heavy loads. On the open plains the earth is studded with sharp objects and often injuries are added to fatigue and the poor animal then lags behind. It can only wander about unhappily until it encounters some man or a beast which will put an end to its sufferings. One day, when our faithful Carlo had wandered off in this manner, an Indian sent out to look for him found him on the spot where we had camped the night before. The Indian said he was crying just as a little child cries for its mother when it loses her.

The situation of man gliding over a beautiful river in a boat always has something magical about it, in that the country traversed seems to be moving by on either side. But on certain parts of the Missouri the charm is increased by reason of the real or fictitious beauty displayed on its shores. By fictitious beauty I mean the great landslides created by the depth of its bed, the adjacent land, and the subsiding of its high water. When seen close by they are, it is true, only hideous ravines, obscure holes, hanging ruins or trunks of uprooted trees—in a word, the picture of desolation. But from ever so short a distance these huge masses seem to assume gracious shapes. Colors are blended, the disparate objects melt together, and sometimes effects are produced which it would be impossible to see without shuddering, or being pleased, or lost in admiration, according to the nature of the beings that [seem to] appear, are transformed, and soon vanish. This is a sensible image of the illusions of this world.

OVERLEAF

left

Mr. Culbertson, who built and managed the post at Fort Lewis.

right

Mr. Clark, the clerk at the Fort.

*Fort Lewis
and a Barge
Down the
Missouri*

On May 22, these scenes were anything but uniform. But it is perhaps to this variety that the traveler owes his best impressions. Yesterday their yellowish tint bordering on [black] [106] and the too great proximity of their forms gave them an atmosphere [depressing] to the heart.[107] Today the widening banks of the river permit our gaze to embrace a vast horizon, a more gentle verdure, fresher groves, waters nearer to their source, white mountains shaded in rose, and a great open space which lends some of its blue to the over-somber or over-vivid colors of this vast tableau. All this produces in the soul a joyful effect.

The contrast is the more striking because the dreary aspects, of which I have already spoken, were augmented by a still sadder sight—that of civilization fallen into ruin. I am referring to Fort Mackenzie built by order of Mr. Mackenzie under the direction of Mr. [Kipp],[108] and called Fort Piegan in honor of the Indians of this nation who were the first to form an alliance with them. This was a mark of deference, doing honor no less to the Piegans than to the modesty of the founder. This fort was burned by men who apparently did not know that his intentions were benevolent.[109] Mr. Mackenzie had another one constructed a little higher up [the river]. This one, which received the name the first one should have borne [i.e., Mackenzie], prospered until 1844, when reasons of prudence dictated its transference. Apparently the vicinity of the Judith River, together with the beauty of its environs, overly tempted the persons charged with providing for it. For experience showed that these advantages, and others thought to be available there, did not compensate for the grave inconvenience of being an easy prey to their enemies. The fort, leveled only a year after its construction, was transplanted farther up the river. This was the beginning of Fort Lewis, about which I spoke earlier. But this fort, after having a long career, was soon joined to Fort Clay, then under construction. To omit nothing that ought be included in the present article, I should place between Fort Piegan and Fort Clay the additional fort of 1844 (of the Fox and Livingston Company), which lasted only one spring.

What is to be said of the thousand and one army forts scattered along the banks of the Missouri? They are almost as plentiful as the grass in the fields, but do not last as long, for more often than not rebels destroy what has been built. Thus, in this region, more than anywhere else, in spite of prudence, skill, and long experience, of which qualities there was no lack, there was no permanent dwelling. Fort Mackenzie, which lasted for only twelve years, is cited as a rare example of longevity. But let us honor its ashes, for it was to commerce what Fort Lewis has been to religion.

To give continuity to this journal, I have had to omit the events of the day, ancient history, and some of the monuments which merit attention. I wish to speak of what is called here the Citadel, Pierced Rock, and the Steamboat, which are to the Missouri what the *Maison* and the *Cheminée* are to the Platte, with the difference that the Citadel, instead of being a composition of pure sandstone, is composed of fragments of rock which appear to be the product of some volcanic disturbance. As for the Steamboat, which a missionary would rather call *la Cathedrale*, and Pierced Rock, remarkable only for the hole which pierces it through and through, they, like the odd formations along the Platte, owe their formation to erosion by wind and rain. But there is this difference: sandstone is more durable and, by adding antique tint to picturesque form and the impression of greater durability, presents a more venerable aspect.

Here are the events of the day. Almost under the walls of the fort, a bear was killed by Mr. Culbertson just as it was rearing to attack. There was Louis' hat to be had by anyone caring to go for a swim at the foot of Pierced Rock and its owner wailing, "My poor hat; there it goes up the river!" These are perhaps somewhat inappropriate subjects for the sketching pencil of a missionary. Finally, there was a passably comic Indian story, here given in the style of the day and the country!

"One day when it was raining rather hard a Piegan sought shelter in a cave that went deep into the earth.[110] Hardly had he entered when a Snake entered, too. It was not an animal, this snake, but a human just like us; it was a member of a tribe that goes by that name. But the tribe was not on friendly terms with the Piegans. In a moment the Piegan saw him coming, and you may well imagine how little he was enjoying himself. What was he to do? 'Ah! Comrade!' he said to the Snake. The Snake did not see him. He stopped short and strained his eyes. He had to see! 'Ah, yes! Comrade!' said the Snake. 'You see very well that it is not good for you here,' said the Piegan. 'Go away.' 'I will not go away,' said the Snake. 'I am not so stupid; if I turn around you will kill me.' 'I kill you?' said the Piegan. 'Nothing is further from my thought. But if you are afraid to turn your back on me . . . I didn't tell you to turn around. I told you to go away. You can back up.' 'Ah! That's different,' said the Snake, only too happy to get out of this devil of a hole. Then he went back, back, back, just like a crab, until —oops!—he came to the end, and there he was outside. And the Piegan came out, too, for he was not so stupid, either, as to remain in there. When they were both out, the Piegan again said to the Snake, 'My comrade.' Now there was nothing to keep the Snake from going. 'Go away,' said the Piegan. 'No, you go away,' said the Snake. 'No, you go. . . .' 'No, you go. . . .' They stood there for a long time telling each other to go away. Neither one wished to follow the command of the other. 'Well,' said the Piegan at length, 'I can think of only one thing to tell you, but it is good. If we do not wish to take leave of each other in the ordinary manner, we can do it in another way.' 'How?' asked the Snake. 'Just like we did a short time ago, only better. You backed up, but I didn't because there was no way for me to do so. This time both of us can back up. And then, when we are so far apart—now listen carefully —when we are so far apart that we can't see each other, then we can bid each other good day.' 'Good,' said the other. 'You have brains, you have.' And there they went, backing up and backing up until they were out of sight of each other."

So ends the story.

To end the vigil of so great a day in a more appropriate manner, let us say, in praise of our worthy paddlers, that in the midst of the fatiguing occupation of the trip I heard no one murmur. In spite of the many curious things which the rapidity of our progress opened up before us at each step there was more than one of them who regretted leaving *terra firma*,

thinking of what he would have done with the missionary the next day, as on Easter. But the barges did not halt.[111]

On the twenty-third, Pentecost, the crew at least had the satisfaction of hearing Holy Mass. Half of my cabin was occupied by the altar, so some of our men were on the bank.

On the twenty-fourth, the feast of Our Lady Help of Christians, ice on the river told us that in two nights the temperature had dropped 43 degrees. This change was due to a new air current and the leveling off of the river banks. When the bank advances out into the river, the resulting formation is called a "point." These points are separated more or less by dry strips. From the *Grande Ile* to the Mussel Shell River, that is, within a space of a few miles, they are so close together that as many as twenty-four of them can be counted. On them the animals of the more inoffensive varieties congregate because of the thick shade and the good pasturage. Thus scarcely an hour would pass without our seeing some herd at close range.

To our right we saw the ruins of a house which had been built, during the rigorous winter of 1845, by A. Hamel, present interpreter at Fort Clay. That winter made him decide not to spend another one there. Near there, through the cotton trees on the left bank, could be seen in the distance the blue hues of the Rocky Mountains, otherwise called Wolf Mountains by the Indians, because of the great number of wolves to be found there. Their presence in large numbers indicated an abundance of deer and buffalo, for the wolves usually follow only big game of good quality. The attention of the passengers was fixed with lively interest on the

OVERLEAF

left

Françoise Baptiste Champagne, the mission interpreter, son of Michel.

right

Michel Champagne, the storekeeper at Fort Lewis.

Garde - magazins,

Michel Champagne.

219

*Fort Lewis
and a Barge
Down the
Missouri*

slope of the neighboring shore. A buffalo cow, with her calf, was under attack by a pack of wolves. The barge stopped to give a better view. The hunter jumped ashore and the captain followed him. Wishing to watch the action, I followed the captain. We rounded the hill where the battle was taking place and soon, without being seen ourselves, we saw an interesting demonstration of the courage of a mother in defending her young.

On these banks there were the most beautiful flowers I had seen since our departure. A blue, star-shaped one tinged with rose had clusters delicately arranged around a pyramidal stem which is graced at intervals with two round leaves of diminishing size. Another, similar to the lupine, but more simple, was of a serene yellow with pale green leaves in groups of three like those of the clover. In honor of the feast of the day I called the first one *auxiliame* and the second one *mariane des Pieds-noire*, for I had found it near Fort Lewis right after the passing of winter.

A little farther below was Dry Point, so called because of the whitened tree trunks covering the round. Some were still erect; some had fallen or were being supported by others. This melancholy sight, coming right after the flowers, recalled the paintings of Poussin in which playing shepherds are represented. Near them is a gravestone on which are inscribed the words: "And I was a shepherd, too."

Another sign of human poverty was the remains of a sacrifice offered not long before. The rich furs which had served as the holocaust were still on the platform of branches which had served as an altar. The sacrifice had been made to the sun, by Bloods on their way to war against the Assiniboines.

On the twenty-sixth, we saw before us the round butte which is the halfway mark between the fort of the Blackfeet and that of the Assiniboines. This butte is distinguished from the others by its height and shape. Its flat top gives it the appearance of an overturned vessel. A large tree standing out like a plume to the left shades the summit.

Near the barge we perceived felled trees, trunks stripped of their bark, pieces of wood arranged in mounds, and animals with four large foreteeth, a very flat tail and paws like hands. All this told us we were in beaver country. Everyone knows the industry, the neatness, and the gentle habits of this animal. Thanks to new substitutes for their skins they are beginning to multiply again, and if this continues they will soon be what they once were. This is very probable, for the female produces many young and their lodges protect them from whatever might be a hindrance to breeding.

A fawn was seen on the shore, and the children chased it, caught it and embraced it, wishing to adopt it. But since its mother's milk was failing, it was decided to put it out of its misery.

There was soon a sadder and more grandiose spectacle. This time, not the young, but the lofty and powerful lords of the wilderness that had to undergo fire from all the barges. What would become of them? They were caught between the fire and the inaccessible ramparts of the river. One, struck in the heart, drifted down the river. Some, seeking refuge in a heap of branches, become entangled as in a snare. Some saw safety only in braving the threat of death. The less brave, but nimbler, ones struggle up the high bank. Finally, all that were not dead or mortally wounded disappeared, leaving civilization as mistress of the field of battle.

On the twenty-seventh, there was fog and rain, a kind of mourning of nature, interrupted only by a dismal concert. For there are always some beings who rejoice only at the unhappiness of others, and in this case it was the wolves. The children on the barge, too, had great sport when one of their number got a spanking, which happened often enough.

On the twenty-eighth, we saluted Milk River, which owes its name to the whiteness of its waters, though this color is evident only when the water is low. From the point at which the Milk River joins the Missouri, the latter stream broadens, the mountains fall off into the distance, and the view begins to have something majestic about it. In the evening a nun, that is, a white-headed eagle, killed by our hunter and presented by Mr. Culbertson, had the honor of being painted. The king of the skies is depicted in the spot where he received his fatal wound, that is, under the wall of his stronghold.

On the twenty-ninth, we sighted the nest of an eagle to which attaches a touching memory. At the foot of the tree in which its nest was built, little Josette, oldest daughter of our pilot, had been born eight years before. Several rows of trees, so symmetrically aligned that they might have been planted by a royal gardener, surrounded this nursery. But better by far than their beauty were the piety, the candor, and the happy expression of the child who had been born there. She and her little sister, Marie, did not let a day of the month pass without placing at the feet of the Blessed Virgin the tribute of their piety and their virtuous efforts. They had been the first to crown with flowers the cross now rising on the land of the Blackfeet.

We found more ruins, the remains of a fort built by a dozen men. When the company withdrew, these men wished to enjoy something of Indian life. But either because they could not manage it or because, desiring no other guide but their individual fancy, they had not been able to co-operate, they separated. One of them was killed by the Assiniboines.

On the twenty-ninth, our flotilla almost suffered a serious accident. The wind being stronger than usual, one of our barges was blown against a tree and pierced through both sides. But by dint of rapid work the 360 packs of furs which it contained were unloaded before the water reached them. Out of a hundred barges meeting this kind of fate, so said the pilot, not a single one might be expected to be saved. This accident occurred almost in the same spot where fifteen years before the provision barge had sunk. The loss was estimated at ten thousand dollars, but that was not the worst of it. Since the accident occurred at night, it was possible to see the shore only by flashes of lightning. The barge was borne away by the hurricane winds and several persons who wanted to jump ashore, or who did actually jump, were more or less severely wounded. A Canadian named Benedict was found crushed between the side of the barge and shore; a child of eight years was drowned in its bed, and an Indian woman saved her own life only by jumping into the water. Michel Champagne, then as now pilot of the barge, was hurled ashore by a blow from the rudder. But Heaven protected a man who was to set such good example, and this jump caused

him no injury other than that of bringing vividly to his consciousness the wretchedness of the others. The news of the disaster was carried to Mr. Mackenzie, then the captain of the fort. His reply was that his men should not be set ashore, for he had other equipment for them.[112]

On the thirtieth, there was dialogue between a young passenger and an old pilot:

"Skipper, I think I see to our left, over there above the willows, a white thing in the shape of a sugar loaf. Do you know what it is?"

"It is an Indian pyramid."

"An Indian pyramid! But I have been told that these fellows do not concern themselves with architecture. Well, then, this pyramid must be an exception. Which Indians thought of building it?"

"The Crow."

"The Crow! What an odd name."

"No name could be better chosen."

"But why?"

"Because for their neighbors they are almost always birds of ill omen. They are at war with almost all of them and their wars are almost always wars of extermination."

"And they have erected this monument in memory of some great victory?"

"No. It is said that it was intended to dispose their divinities well toward them."

"In what period of their history do you place its erection?"

"The oldest recollections are only of one thing, and that is of always having seen it there."

"Strange! The nearer we approach to this curious structure the more mysterious it appears to me. The side toward the sun shines like silver."

"But it is not of silver at all. It is, however, made of something almost as durable as silver."

"It is made of marble, then?"

"Not at all. It is neither metal nor even mineral."

"What is it, then?"

"It is made of a kind of branch, which grows like a plant, but which is not a plant. It has roots but does not spring from the earth. It is of animal origin but is never animated. Now, can you guess?"

"There are buffalo around here. Is it perhaps made of their horns?"

*Fort Lewis
and a Barge
Down the
Missouri*

*Augustin Hamel,
interpreter at Fort Clay.*

*Jacques Berger,
a trader who dealt directly
with the Indians.*

A view of Fort Lewis from the south.

Fort Lewis as seen from the north.

"You are almost right. It is made of horns, true, but of horns with many prongs, which is as much as saying that they are not really horns."

"Now I follow you. They are antlers. Am I right?" [Some word play on "*bois*" as signifying both wood and antlers is necessarily omitted here.]

"Precisely."

"Why did the builders of this monument choose such strange materials?"

"Among them the stag is a medicine animal."

"Then this great heap of stag antlers is a religious monument?"

"So it is said."

"And the Indian goes there just as we go on a pilgrimage, and each time deposits his offering there?"

"At least whenever he finds a stag with such a set of antlers. When he does, he does not fail to add it to the others. In this manner the monument has become what we now see. Evidently the first builders laid only the foundation."

"Has no one ever thought of destroying it?"

"It was destroyed in eighteen forty-three."

"By whom?"

"By some whites out on a pleasure party."

"And the Crows have not avenged this deed?"

"Others have avenged it in their place."

On the Feast of the Holy Trinity, thanks be to God and the good dispositions of the crew, I was able to say Holy Mass. The time given to God is never wasted. In spite of threats of a contrary wind the day was almost as good as one might have wished, and the evening was delightful. At least no other evening ever seemed so beautiful to me. As the sun set in a light haze, it exchanged the gold of its fire for the color of rubies. Above it, and outlined sharply against a blue background, a formation of clouds tinged with purple, blue, and violet hung like drapery. A row of beautiful trees cast their shadows to the middle of the river. What was the crew doing in the presence of this rich coloring? While the men drove our barges forward like so many chariots racing for a prize, their wives and children sang hymns in honor of the Queen of Angels. Never had the wilderness heard the like. What person devoted to Mary would not have been moved by this refrain:

Qu'on est heureux sous son empire!
Qu'on coeur pur y trouve d'attraits!
Tout y sessent, tout y respire
L'amour, l'innocence, et la paix.[113]

On the thirty-first, the month of Mary ended and the end of our barge journey was also at hand. At least we thought so, for we would dock in a few miles. But the wind arose, forcing us to call a halt. This offered me another opportunity to observe how a good pilot manages to struggle victoriously against adversity even with an exhausted crew. Our pilot had done this many times.

Here are some of the expressions the pilot used: "Now, men, let's make that point. Keep up your courage. . . . See that snag, don't get stuck on it. . . . Look out for those branches. . . . Make for the shore. . . . Well done; here we are on land. It's all over. . . . Good appetite now."

And the oarsmen certainly did not lack a good appetite. They supped gaily, then lit up their pipes and began to talk about the rest they would enjoy the next day, the cannon shots that they would hear, of the reception to be given, and so on.

On the morrow a magnificent sun rose. To our right were two snow-white peaks. There was a slight wind against us, but it served to cleanse the air rather than to impede our progress. The first cannon shot resounded. A few minutes later the great flag was raised. Artillery pieces answered each other. The bastions came into view. All the occupants of the fort came down to the shore. The barges stopped, greetings and *bon jours* were exchanged. Finally began the handshakes, the gestures of friendship and the manifestations of joy, and so on. All this terminated in a celebration.[114]

I have been among the Indians only seven years, but they have been seven years of missionary work in the closest relationship with them. These give me the right to be interested in everything that concerns them. Having seen in their wilderness, perhaps more than anywhere else, what fruits grace can produce in willing hearts, I have always been happy to recount what I know about them. And today, when they are under attack, I am duty bound to tell what I know about them. This duty is all the more pleasant because its fulfillment is a means of paying honor to my country. I can affirm that if the harvest already reaped cost us efforts, even though consoling, it is, after God, to the French that we are indebted. And, if not to the French of France, then at least to their descendants or to Indians converted by French missionaries. These *voyageurs*, whom Providence scattered throughout these regions, did not, it is true, always conduct themselves in conformity with their faith, but none of them took it upon himself to speak disrespectfully either of his religion, of the priests, or of his country. And since there were those among them who spoke of these things only with the most respectful affection, it was impossible for their sentiments not to be communicated in some measure to their hosts. Hence the surprising confidence the Flatheads and the surrounding tribes manifested in us when we first appeared in their country; the marvelous facility with which they learned to practice their duties and, finally, the admirable fruits spread from the Rocky Mountains to the shore of the Pacific.

The Blackfeet appeared to many to be too far separated from the Kingdom of Heaven to be able to offer such consolation to our ministry. Still we visited them and among them, as elsewhere, we met with a sympathetic attitude. Upon learning what religion had meant for the prosperity of the Flatheads, the women brought their children to be baptized, and many times warriors would not set out on a campaign without first recommending themselves to the prayers of the missionary. Out of the twenty-five or thirty camp leaders who visited us or were visited by us, not one failed to describe his people in terms that served to encourage our zeal. And twelve Indian women at Fort Lewis, whose religion in a short time made them model wives and mothers, gave us proof that with time and patience a minister of the Gospel could accomplish there what we did elsewhere. This very hope was shared by the two Blackfoot forts to such an extent that there was not a man in these establishments who did not encourage it by alms which would have done honor to a prince. And each professed his faith in a manner which would have done honor to the most religious of apologists. Another thing which redounded both to the credit of American impartiality and to the work of which we were the ministers was the fact that Americans of other faiths were the first to suggest a subscription in our favor. What has been said of the Blackfeet can also be remarked about the Crow. I visited only one part of their tribe, the least attractive part, so it is said.

Though the Crows were mortal enemies of the Blackfeet, whose friend I had declared myself to be, it required only a few minutes of conversation to bring them around to the point to which, for the good of humanity, it would be desirable for all warring nations to be brought. Would it not be the same in the case of the Assiniboines if we could speak with them, or if others would do so in our place? We have every reason to believe that it would be, for they, more than the others, are well aware of their needs.

All of this presents more than enough evidence to prove to a reasonable mind that he who would seek, in one way or another, to vilify religion would instigate a horrible war against humanity. Fort Lewis was so well aware of this truth that one of its men, not without reproach in this respect, repented his sins.

Fort Lewis
and a Barge
Down the
Missouri

While cannon boomed
and the American flag fluttered in the wind, fort authorities
advanced to meet their Indian visitors.

The sale of liquor
was strictly forbidden
at the fort, but Indians were eager to obtain other luxury items
that were on display.

Furs ready for shipping were baled by the white traders.

Several men were needed to operate a peltry press.

Fort Campbell
was named in honor of Robert Campbell, a competitor
of the American Fur Company.

Fort McKenzie,
built in 1832 and burned in 1844, was named for Kenneth McKenzie,
president of the Columbia Fur Company.

Mai. Ruine du fort Piegan bâti en 1831 et ab...

Fort Piegan,
built in 1831, was not far
from Fort McKenzie.

Rocher d'environ 130 pieds de haut
appelé la Citadelle

A rock formation about 130 feet high
was known as The Citadel.

*The sacraments of baptism and of marriage
were solemnly administered after the missionaries' arrival
at Fort Lewis.*

*A charming group of Indian women
with their metis children.*

*Felling trees and trimming logs
for dwellings was difficult work in freezing weather.*

*A delightful winter scene which Father Point,
for obvious reasons, entitled "A celestial phenomenon."*

*Fort Lewis
and a Barge
Down the
Missouri*

Le rocher percé.

*The hole made in this rock,
probably by the erosion of wind and rain,
gave it the name Pierced Rock.*

Le Steamboat on Cathédrale

*Another interesting rock formation
was called The Steamboat, but the missionaries
called it The Cathedral.*

Ruine du fort de l'opposition compagnie Fox et Livington, bati
(Mr. Coton agint) en 1844 et laissé un mois après sa
il est encore debout

*Fort Fox and Livingston,
a trading post competing with the American Fur Company,
was abandoned shortly after it was opened.*

ines du fort Effeci F.E.C. bâti par Mr. F. E. Chardon ... en 1º
et laissé en 1846.

*Fort Chardon,
at the junction of the Judith and Missouri rivers,
was abandoned in 1846.*

*When bears were really hungry,
a traveler was not safe.*

*Apparently disarmed by a bear, the hunter
became the hunted.*

One of the beautiful birds of the upper Missouri country
seen by Father Point's keen eye and captured
by his brush.

When Carlo, the mission's faithful dog,
wandered away, an Indian scout found him at the spot
where they had camped the night before.

Fort Lewis
and a Barge
Down the
Missouri

La grande Ile

A sketch of "The Grand Island,"
a few miles from the Mussel Shell River.

La maison Hamel.

The home of Mr. Hamel,
the interpreter at Fort Clay.

Montagnes de roche ou du loup dans le lointain.

*The Indians often called the Rocky Mountains
the Wolf Mountains because so many wolves were found there.*

La pointe seche

*The artist identifies this spot
as Dry Point, so called because of the dying trees.*

*Fort Lewis
and a Barge
Down the
Missouri*

The painting above was called
"Religion," by the missionary-artist; the one
below "Civilization."

A seemingly unfinished view of Fort Lewis.

*Great effort was expended
in bringing the provision barge up the river.*

*Fort Lewis
and a Barge
Down the
Missouri*

*A scene along
the Mussel Shell River.*

*A lone buffalo was sometimes attacked
by a pack of wolves.*

La butte ronde milieu du
Chemin entre le fort des Pieds-noirs
et celui des assiniboines

Round Butte
between the Blackfoot and Assiniboin territories.

vus pris tués ou mis en fu...

Bison being cornered and killed.

Image symbolique de la tempérance et du vice contraire.

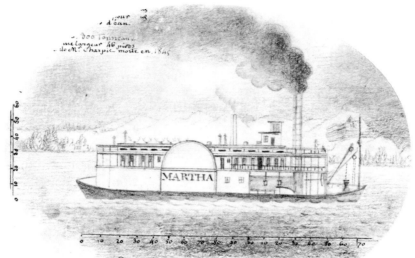

*Steembost de la compagnie americaine
…struit et conduit par le capitaine J. Laberge*

Steamboat Martha
*on which Father Point traveled
from Fort Union to St. Louis.*

*facing:
A symbolic representation of temperance
and its contrary vice.*

*Vue de la rivière au lait
se déchargeant dans le missouri.*

*A view on the Milk River
near the point where it joins the Missouri.*

*Le nid d'aigle terrenatale
de la Petite Josette*

*An eagle returning to its nest
in the tree under which little Josette,
daughter of the pilot, was born.*

Aigle appelé Nonne
de la coeffure blanche

*The white-headed eagle
known as a nun.*

Coupde Sur le Missouri
et naufrage de la barge d'expedition

Shipwreck during a storm.

*Fort Lewis
and a Barge
Down the
Missouri*

Riviere aux trembles.

*Ice began to form on the river
when the temperature dropped sharply
during the night.*

*Le monument sauvage
Pyramide composée de bois de cerfs*

*A pyramid of stag antlers
to which Indians make pilgrimages
as to a religious monument.*

*Stretches of the great river
down which the missionary's barge traveled
deserved to be called muddy.*

*Sunset-tinted mountains
sometimes contained rich veins of coal.*

Fort Lewis and a Barge Down the Missouri

A view of Fort Union from the south.

*Inner court of Fort Union,
at the junction of the Yellowstone
and Missouri rivers.*

Fort Barthot et village des gros-ventres

*Fort Berthold,
a few miles below the confluence of the Little Missouri and the Missouri,
and a Gros Ventre village just outside it.*

*Village Mandane
et dans le lointain celui des Rikaras —*

*Village of the Mandan Indians
in the foreground.*

*Fort Lewis
and a Barge
Down the
Missouri*

*Arikara village
near a fort at the junction of the Grand
and Missouri rivers.*

*A stretch known as Square Butte,
along the Missouri River.*

Fort Pierre

*Fort Lewis
and a Barge
Down the
Missouri*

*Two views of Fort Pierre
at the junction of the Cheyenne
and Missouri rivers.*

Interieure du Fort Piarre

The farm at Fort Pierre.

*Fort Yankton,
one of the many along the Missouri River.*

*A spot identified by Father Point
as Medicine Butte.*

*A view of the right bank
near the Ponca River.*

Fort Lewis
and a Barge
Down the
Missouri

The Ponca River,
which joins the Missouri not far from Yankton.

The Vermillion,
another small river joining the Missouri along the route taken
by the missionary on his way to St. Louis.

Butte of the "black bird."

*Another village sketched by Father Point
during his barge trip down the Missouri.*

*Fort Lewis
and a Barge
Down the
Missouri*

One of many "beautiful views."

*St. Joseph, Missouri,
as Father Point saw it.*

*Weston, Missouri,
another landmark along the way.*

*Fort American
where, presumably, troops were garrisoned.*

*Fort Lewis
and a Barge
Down the
Missouri*

*Chapel and home
of the missionary at Westport.*

*An on-the-spot sketch
of a house being swept away.*

A sketch of the state capitol
at Jefferson City, Missouri,
as Father Point saw it
from the Missouri River.

Convent of the Sacred Heart,
St. Charles, Missouri.

saison; là aussi se promène ma-
jestueusement la grande fourche
du Missouri, dont les eaux venant
à se séparer puis à se rejoindre
forment une île ou se trouve
avec de bons paturages, de grands
arbres qui nous offrent de l'ombre
pour nous garantir demain des
rayons du Soleil et du bois pour
nous rechauffer ce soir.

On allume un grand feu devant
la loge, qui doit servir de chapelle,
afin que pendant la nuit, les pé-
nitens puissent attendre pour la
confession, sans trop d'incommo-
dité. Le lendemain 90 personnes
s'approchent de la S.te table. Dans
la soirée les mères apportent leurs
enfans à la bénédiction du Prêtre,
et le tout se termine par la plan-
tation d'une Croix.

Il serait difficile de s'imaginer
un plus beau spectacle, à l'extré-
mité de l'horison une chaine de
hauts sommets déjà couverts de nei-
je, au second plan un groupe
de rochers nuancés de rouge, de
jaune, de bleu, de tout ce qu'une
belle végétation d'automne peut
offrir de plus riche pour la forme
et les couleurs; sous nos yeux des
arbustes mêlés à de grands arbres,
une cascade qui se précipite en
flots écumants dans un large bas-
sin, la brise du soir agitant le feuil-
lage des environs enfin le soleil
qui éclaire de ces derniers feux
ce magnifique ensemble: voilà
ce que vous auriez admiré avec
nous si vous aviez été présent
à cette fête.

3.me Chasse

chasse et pêche des Cœurs-d'alène

Du 13 9bre 1842 Jusqu'en Février 1843

Sommaire

I

Les Cœurs-d'alène ont aussi leur
grande chasse, mais comme leur pays
semé de lacs et entrecoupé de rivi-
ères ne renferme pas moins de poissons
que d'animaux ils ont aussi leur
grande pêche.

La pêche comme la chasse s'y
fait presque toute l'année; mais
la grande pêche n'a lieu qu'en
automne, comme la grande chasse
qu'en hyver.

Le 14 Novembre nous débarquons
sur la rive droite de la rivière des
Spokanns, précisément là où le grand
lac des Cœurs-d'alène amène une pro-
digieuse quantité de poissons. C'est là
qu'à lieu ordinairement la grande
pêche - Si l'on veut qu'elle soit a-
bondante il faut poser sur une
ligne de trépieds solidement reliés
entre eux par des perches transver-
sales, une barrière composée de
claies d'osier destinée à arrêter les
gros poissons. Comme alors le froid
commence à se faire sentir et que
pour ce travail, il faut se mettre
à l'eau jusqu'à la poitrine, la
tâche n'est pas sans difficulté

Pêche de vaches et de veaux dans le M

*There is a touch of humor in the suggestion
of "fishing for buffalo" as they attempt to escape the hunters
by taking to the water.*

*facing:
A reproduction of a page as it
appeared in the original journal.*

Father Nicolas Point's Manuscript—Its History

JOSEPH P. DONNELLY, S.J.

THE STORY of the progress toward publication of Father Point's precious manuscript, culminating in this incomparably beautiful volume, is a saga meriting inclusion in this rare and valuable work. For the reader to appreciate fully the long and thorny path leading to publication, he should have a somewhat more detailed account of Father Point's last days than that included in the biographical sketch already presented.

In 1847, after Point left the Idaho-Montana area, he spent nearly a year assisting his brother, Father Pierre Point, also a Jesuit, who was in charge of an Indian mission at Sandwich, now Windsor, Ontario. During that year, Nicolas painted a seven-foot-high representation of the Immaculate Conception which, unfortunately, was destroyed long ago when a fire completely consumed the mission church.

In 1848, he was appointed superior of a large Indian mission conducted by the Jesuits on Manitoulin Island, with headquarters at Wikwemikong. There he met with noteworthy success, though he repeatedly requested permission to return to his Indians in the western United States. In 1855, when Father Point suffered a serious breakdown at Sault Sainte Marie, Canada, while on his way to a new assignment at Fort William on Lake Superior, he was directed to return to Sandwich, where it was hoped he could recover.

Nicolas continued working actively with Father Pierre Point until 1859, when the mission establishment at Sandwich became a parish church and was given into the care of the diocesan clergy. In a very touching little biography written by Pierre after his brother's death, we learn that Nicolas had begged in vain to go back to his beloved Flatheads. But his health had been so seriously undermined that he had been retired from active work and went to live at the Jesuit novitiate near Montreal. For that decision, those interested in Nicolas Point's paintings and his journals may be grateful.

Father Point's assignment at the Jesuit novitiate was assistant to the master of novices, a position which required very little of his time. Then it was that, at the insistence of his superior, he organized his journals and numerous paintings into the six manuscript volumes which he called "Recollections of the Rocky Mountains." He had such a humble opinion of the value of his work that he was induced to compile his manuscript only because others convinced him that doing so was, as Pierre Point reports, "for the glory of God and to save the history of the mission for future generations."

Father Point set to work, copying the journals in his beautiful copperplate script onto ledger-sized good rag paper. Each page was so ruled as to form two vertical panels with a space between. At the beginning of each chapter Point embossed a heading, employing a pen with a broad nib so that his looping, cursive script became in itself a small calligraphic work of art. The handwriting of the text in each panel on every page is so beautifully regular and attractive that the day might well come—though may it forever be averted!—when a page of Point's manuscript will be nearly as much a treasure as a page of a medieval manuscript on vellum is today.

When the journal contained a passage for which Point had drawn a picture, at the time the incident originally occurred, he mounted the painting on what we would call kraft board opposite the appropriate portion of the text. Almost all of these illustrations, generally oval-shaped, are enclosed in tastefully conceived borders, often quite elaborate in design. Under nearly every one Point printed, by hand, a title which was usually a phrase from the journal text opposite the picture. The amount of detail included in the paintings is amazing. Happily, his artist's eye caught vital anthropological facts regarding the Indians he drew just before these aborigines discarded their native costumes in favor of dress of European or American manufacture. Point's technique of laying color over color to produce his effects is rather surprising for one who had no training and little or no opportunity to study the works of the great European masters. The perspective achieved in these almost miniature paintings is so excellent that one feels he could walk into a scene. The map of the mission of the Sacred Heart among the Coeur d'Alenes employs a method of presenta-

tion which was not adopted until our own day. Father Point was a particularly able portraitist, and no less skillful in painting animals—except for bears, which almost no artist portrays successfully. His painting of the mission dog, Carlo, is so real that one expects the friendly animal to lick one's hand.

Nicolas Point spent six years, 1859 to 1865, completing his manuscript. When the work was finished, it was assembled, rather amateurishly, into six ledger-sized volumes, which were bound in black buckram. Two sets of leather thongs held each tome securely together, and for each, Father Point composed an elaborate table of contents. He attached small red tabs to each kraft-board sheet so that the pages could be turned with ease.

In the process of preparing his manuscript he certainly had some help from the novices with whom he lived. Undoubtedly those young men were intrigued with the gentle old missionary and his unique work. There is a tradition among French-speaking Canadian Jesuits that Father Point was much beloved by the novices, who were always able to induce him to recount stories of his days as a missionary in the American West. To those young men, Father Point, his pictures, and his stories were as fascinating, we may be sure, as a returnee from Mars would be to any group of young men today. Blackfeet, Flatheads, Coeur d'Alenes—and their folkways —were just as unreal to the young Jesuit novices as Martians would be to a comparable group in our time.

In November, 1865, Father Point went to Quebec. His brother Pierre says that Nicolas was sent there to give him an opportunity to engage in some active work. It was soon discovered, however, that Father Point was not as well as he thought himself to be. He spent most of his days in his room, adding some finishing touches to his manuscript, and teaching small boys their catechism in preparation for the reception of their first Holy Communion. On June 28, 1868, he finished preparing a group of five youngsters for their great day and that was his last apostolic labor. The following day he took to his bed. He lingered until July 4, when he expired peacefully at eight in the evening.

It was fitting that Nicholas Point went to Heaven on the day on which the United States celebrates its acquisition of independence. He had labored long and lovingly in our country for the first Americans. When he died, the canons of the cathedral at Quebec, whose confessor he had been, insisted that his mortal remains be buried in its crypt. Father Point probably would have been greatly disconcerted by such a singular mark of respect and admiration. Father Pierre Point says that the opinion Nicolas had of himself was contained in a short French poem, often quoted by him, which is translated: "I am nothing; I can do nothing; I am worthless." Little did he know how wrong he was!

Since the Jesuits at Quebec, in Point's day, had no college or other extensive institution, Point's manuscript was sent, after his death, to Collège Sainte-Marie, at Montreal, where its founder, Father Felix Martin, himself a historian of real moment, had established an archival depository of material invaluable for the history of the Jesuits and their activity in New France from 1611 to 1675. It is particularly satisfying that, figuratively at least, Father Point's six precious volumes sat for many years cheek by jowl with Father Jacques Marquette's original journal of his voyage down the Mississippi River in 1673. These two Frenchmen had a great deal in common. Each was from northern France and each had a profound understanding of and a great love for Indians. Interest in the publication of the manuscripts of both of these devoted missionaries arose at about the same time.

Toward the end of the nineteenth century, when Reuben Gold Thwaites began publishing his monumental work, the *Jesuit Relations and Allied Documents*, an effort was made by French-speaking Jesuits at Montreal to publish Father Point's manuscripts. Some excerpts from his journals, together with a quite inadequate biography of their author, appeared in a magazine privately circulated among Jesuits. That fact, perhaps, led to an effort to interest the Smithsonian Institution in publishing Father Point's work, including the paintings. Negotiations were discontinued when all parties concerned were advised that not only would the cost of the venture be practically prohibitive but that, further, proper techniques for reproducing the glorious colors simply did not yet exist. We may be grateful that the Smithsonian did not undertake the venture.

Father Point's valuable manuscript reposed peacefully in the archives of Collège Sainte-Marie for four decades, except for one occasion, in the opening years of the twentieth century, when it was lent to the Jesuits working in the area opened to Christianity by Father Point. Though one cannot be certain of the reason, it is quite probable that some Jesuit in that area ambitioned publishing Father Point's work.

In 1935, when Father Gilbert Garraghan, a Jesuit historian and author, was writing his monumental three-volume history of the Jesuits in the Middle United States, the editor of this manuscript assisted him. Like Benjamin Franklin, Father Garraghan wrote an atrocious hand, which I, as his assistant, laboriously learned to decipher. In the course of that composition I was first introduced to Father Point and saw a few of the small pen-and-ink sketches which he had done to illustrate Father Pierre Jean De Smet's *Oregon Missions and Travels over the Rocky Mountains in 1845–46*.

As work on Father Garraghan's volumes progressed, I learned much more about Point, including the existence and location of his precious six-volume manuscript. It became my ambition to bring about somehow the publication of the manuscript which I had, as yet, not seen. Opportunity to examine it occurred by pure chance in 1940 when I was at Montreal for a wholly different reason. As a "visiting fireman" at a historical convention, I called on the archivist of Collège Sainte-Marie, who graciously exhibited his rich storehouse of material pertaining to the Jesuits who had labored so devotedly for the Indians when Canada was a colony of France. When asked what material he possessed from the pen of Father Nicolas Point, the archivist produced a large dusty box containing the priest's beautiful work. Many enjoyable hours of that day were spent leafing through the volumes in a state of constant surprise and delight. It was hard to believe that one little man, completely untrained in artistic techniques, could possibly have produced all these paintings, which told the story of several Indian tribes, depicted their daily lives and customs long before any artist of our West, except George Catlin, had put brush to canvas. Catlin and Point were exact contemporaries. In 1840, the very year in which Point painted his first picture of Indians—some Kansa who visited his mission at Westport—Catlin published his two-volume *Manners, Customs and Condition of the North American Indians*. Once Point's incomparable work had been examined, the idea of publishing it became an uncontrollable obsession.

Innumerable obstacles stood in the path of publication. The Great Depression was not completely a thing of the past. World War II was already affecting the publishing industry, limiting paper and ink supply, and even depriving publishers of the skill of the printing profession. However, I filmed the entire text in black and white and translated the journal portion. With the translation in hand and a few of Point's pictures, very badly reproduced in color, I began seeking a publisher.

Every one approached was enthusiastic about the manuscript until a count was made of the number of paintings. Understandably, each one soon concluded that not only would production costs be nearly astronomical, but each was doubtful whether, even if the project were undertaken, the results would justify the investment. Time after time I was advised to approach wealthy foundations in the hope that one of them would underwrite the venture. But, during the war years and for a long time after, foundations were, perhaps justifiably, interested in social problems rather than in artistic publications. Stubborn by nature and heritage, I continued striving to realize my ambition while the publishing field, after World War II and the unsettled conditions following that disaster, slowly returned to normal levels.

The successful conclusion of the attempt to bring about publication of the Point manuscript has all the earmarks of accident. Loyola University was in the final stages of producing Father Bernard W. Dempsey's *Frontier Wage* when both Father Austin G. Schmidt, Jesuit director of the Press, and Father Dempsey died suddenly on the same day, July 22, 1960. The task of seeing Father Dempsey's book through the last details of publication fell to me and to Father John B. Amberg, Father Schmidt's successor. While completing work on *Frontier Wage*, I sang my oft-repeated song regarding Father Point's manuscript, knowing full well that Loyola University Press would not undertake

the project and expecting nothing more than a mild interest on Father Amberg's part. However, the new director of the Press became a crusader for Father Point. As a result the manuscript was borrowed and each painting was photographed in color by James Chalifoux of Photopress, Inc., Broadview, Illinois. Even that fortunate turn of events might not have effected publication had it not been that, due to their ardent interest, a selection of color transparencies was passed from hand to hand among members of the publishing field. Jack Dwyer of Photopress showed them to Howard Clark of Holt, Rinehart and Winston's International Division, through whom they came to the attention of James R. Lepper, General Production Manager of that firm, and Arthur A. Cohen, Editor in Chief of its General Book Division. How much this book owes to Miss Louella Still of Holt, Rinehart and Winston only the publishers and I will ever know. Their enthusiasm and continued dedication to Father Point and his manuscript equals, if it does not surpass, my own.

This book has been in the process of publication since August, 1964. I expected that Holt, Rinehart and Winston would employ the economical approach of using the color transparencies already available. However, neglecting no effort to reproduce Father Point's pictures with the greatest possible fidelity, their editors started completely fresh from the originals. All illustrations that are not in full color appear as they were drawn in the original journals. Neither time nor money has been spared to present this precious manuscript in all its glory. Many times in the past months I was more than satisfied with work which the publisher rejected. Frequently, in lengthy conferences, I blithely dismissed as unimportant, small errors which Mr. Cohen would not tolerate. Once, during the many months of processing, everything previously done was scrapped and work was started again from the beginning, just to insure that the reader would really have Father Point's manuscript in its original beauty. For the staff of Holt, Rinehart and Winston, this book became a true labor of love, and the results, in my opinion, amply demonstrate the truth of that declaration.

If I were to thank everyone who co-operated

in bringing Father Point's manuscript to the public, this short essay would be much longer than the text of his journals. Those who have had a part in this publication well know my deep gratitude. The greatest source of my satisfaction really is the fact that Nicolas Point's journals and his delightful paintings are finally to receive the plaudits they deserve. The manuscript is not only artistically valuable; it is equally important anthropologically. But most of all, just a year short of a century after his death and one hundred and twenty-seven years after he painted his first picture of an Indian, a whole world will know of Father Nicolas Point's work.

A closing remark from Father Pierre Point's brief biographical sketch of his brother seems in order here. Pierre, obviously feeling that Nicolas merited much more attention than he received in his lifetime, closed with a Latin phrase: *"De Smet Transibat; Point insudabat."* For those who have neglected their Latin, the phrase is translated, perhaps a little too freely, but certainly not unjustly: "De Smet got the credit; Point did the work." If that humble little man, Nicolas Point, ever felt slighted while he was on earth, he will rejoice now, for no one will ever forget him again.

Father Donnelly, S.J.

Father Point's Manuscript —Its History

Pages 1–9

1 The major source of information concerning the life of the Father Nicolas Point is a lengthy biographical note preceding a series of articles in the *Woodstock Letters* XI (1882), 298–321. The unknown author of the sketch tells us that the information presented was gathered from Point's brother, Father Pierre Point, and other Jesuits who knew Nicolas Point. It is not known how many children were in the Point family. One sister became a nun and was sent to Oregon where she worked among the Indians while her brother Nicolas was in the area.

2 Jesuits took over direction of minor seminaries in various dioceses.

3 *See* Walter H. Hill, S.J., "Reminiscences of St. Mary's College, Kentucky," *Woodstock Letters*, XX (1891), 23–37. *See also* Ben J. Webb, *Centenary of Catholicity in Kentucky* (Louisville, 1884), 282.

4 Gilbert J. Garraghan, S.J., *The Jesuits of the Middle United States* (New York, 1938), III, 135.

5 Admittedly, Connelly was a prejudiced witness since Father Point was not only his employer but also his spiritual director. Connelly's letter is in the Jesuit archives at Rome.

Garraghan, *op. cit.* III, 144, 145, gives the complete letter.

6 Father De Smet seems to have thought that Point was from the Vendée. La Roche Jacquelin was the military leader of the Vendeean uprising against the forces of the French Revolution.

7 Besides Point's own account, *see* Gilbert J. Garraghan, S.J., *Catholic Beginnings in Kansas City, Missouri* (Chicago, 1920).

8 *See* Hubert Howe Bancroft, *History of California*, IV (San Francisco, 1886), 265–272. Journals were also kept by John Bidwell, Josiah Belden, Joseph B. Chiles, and Charles Hoffer.

Pages 11–261

1 Father Point's sister was a member of the Congregation of Notre Dame de Namur. A group of these nuns was brought from Belgium by Father De Smet in 1844. A collection of letters written back to Belgium by the nuns has been published. *See* C. B. Bagley, *Early Catholic Missions in Old Oregon* (Seattle,

1932), 2v. *See also Notice sur la territoire et sur la mission de l'Oregon suivie du quelques lettres des soeurs de Notre Dame* (Brussels, 1847). In her *Western Women*, Nancy Wilson Ross devotes one brief chapter to these nuns.

2   The Pend d'Oreilles may have received their name from French traders who thus indicated the Pend d'Oreille custom of decorating their ears. The Pend d'Oreilles are a division of the Kalispel. *See* F. W. Hodge, *Handbook of American Indians North of Mexico*, I (Washington, 1907), 646.

3   Fort Lewis, which Point spells Louis except in his account of his journey down the Missouri on a barge, was located west of the mouth of the Marias River. This trading post of the American Fur Company was named in honor of Meriwether Lewis. *See* H. M. Chittenden, *The American Fur Trade of the Far West* (New York, 1902), III, 963.

4   The Piegans were a division of the Blackfoot nation. *See* Hodge, *op. cit.*, II, 246.

5   Point probably is referring to the decline of the missions among the Flatheads. For a detailed account of this, *see* G. J. Garraghan, S.J., *The Jesuits of the Middle United States* (New York, 1938), II, 375–386.

6   There is some confusion of categories here in Father Point's own text.

7   François Norbert Blanchet (1795–1883), a native of Canada, was sent to the Oregon country in 1838 by the Bishop of Quebec, Joseph Signay. On December 1, 1843, Blanchet was appointed bishop of the long-defunct see of Philadelphia in Asia Minor and Vicar Apostolic of the new vicariate of Oregon (which in Father Point's mind probably means the Columbia River area). Blanchet was consecrated a bishop in Montreal on July 25, 1845. *See* E. V. O'Hara, *Pioneer Catholic History of Oregon* (Portland, 1911), 98.

8   Point assumes that the reader knows the Indians will gather as soon as they smell the calumet. They squat in a circle and smoke the pipe in turn. When the "hero" has had his turn, it is time for him to relate what happened to him. It would have been bad manners for him to speak before that because Indians never conducted any business until the calumet routine was properly completed.

9   The Nez Percés were the most important division of the Shahaptian family, which occupied western Idaho and northeastern Oregon. There seems to be no evidence that they actually pierced their noses, as their name would imply. *See* Hodge, *op. cit.*, II, 65–66.

10 The Red River mentioned here is the river of that name which flows in Minnesota. Point later identifies the Indian as one named Gueri.

11 The Spokanes were a division of the Salish Indians. They dwelt in eastern Washington. *See* Hodge, *op cit.*, II, 1625.

12 "Long knives" was a term used by the Indians to identify Americans in contradistinction to the English.

13 The story of the Flathead delegation to St. Louis is accurately recounted in H. M. Chittenden and A. T. Richardson, *Life, Letters and Travels of Father Pierre-Jean De Smet*, I (New York, 1905), 19–30.

14 Father Gregorio Mengarini, a Jesuit who was born in Rome, was drawn to volunteer for the Oregon mission by Bishop Joseph Rosati of St. Louis, who addressed the students of the Roman College in 1839 while young Mengarini was a student there. Reaching America in 1840, Mengarini went to the Oregon country with De Smet in 1841. After working among the Flatheads for nine years, Mengarini went to Santa Clara, California, where he spent the rest of his life. He died on September 23, 1886. Brother William Clessens, a Belgian, came to America in 1835. A blacksmith by trade, he worked among the Indians until 1891. Brother Charles Huet, also a Belgian, was a carpenter whom De Smet recruited in 1835. Brother Joseph Sprecht (written Specht by Point, whose proper-name spellings are not always historically correct), a German, was a tinner. He died at seventy-six, having worked among the Indians until 1874.

15 Westport, near the present Kansas City, Missouri, was the point of departure for wagon trains going west.

16 The French used the term *métis* to denote a half-breed child. See: J. F. McDermott, *A Glossary of Mississippi Valley French, 1673–1850* (St. Louis, 1941), 103.

17 All Saints' Day is November 1.

18 "Forty Hours" is a term designating a period of particular devotion to the Blessed Sacrament. The period usually extends over three days.

19 The "old soldier of the Empire" was Jean Baptiste De Velder, who had been a grenadier in Napoleon's army. He came to America about 1815. *See* Chittenden and Richardson, *op. cit.*, I, 221.

20 The Kansa was a Sioux tribe which dwelt along the Kansas River. *See* Hodge, *op. cit.*, I, 653.

21 Catholic ecclesiastical artists have frequently portrayed Our Lady of Sorrows with seven swords piercing Her heart.

22 The Osage, a branch of the Sioux, were well known in France at that time because six of them, four men and two women, had been brought to France in 1827 by David Delauney, a Frenchman who had been engaged in the fur trade in St. Louis. At first the group was lionized, especially in France, but soon interest in them waned. They were taken on tour through France, Belgium, Holland, Germany, Switzerland, and Italy. By 1829, Delauney abandoned the poor Indians. Through the generosity of some Parisians and of Bishop Dubourg, who had returned to France and was then bishop of Montauban, the Osages were returned to their own people. *See* G. Foreman, "Our Indian Ambassadors to Europe," *Missouri Historical Society Collections*, V (1928), 109–128.

23 This was Father Herman Aelen who came to America in 1835. Thereafter he spelled his name Allen. *See* Garraghan, *op. cit.*, I, 356.

24 The Kickapoo, Indians of Algonquin stock, slowly drifted from Wisconsin to Kansas. *See* Hodge, *op. cit.*, I, 684.

25 Father Charles Van Quickenborne, a Belgian, born in 1788, came to America in 1817. He was appointed to lead a group of Jesuits to St. Louis where they were to work among the Indians. They reached St. Louis in 1823.

26 "To the Sioux" is an error. Father Van Quickenborne died at Portage des Sioux, a small village near St. Louis.

27 Kenekuk is more commonly spelled Kennekuk. De Smet gives much the same description of this. *See* Chittenden and Richardson, *op. cit.*, III, 1085.

28 The Kickapoo mission, of which Point speaks rather obscurely, was begun by Father Van Quickenborne on June 1, 1836. The site of the mission was a few miles above Leavenworth, Kansas, at the juncture of the Missouri and Salt Creek. The effort was such a signal failure that the mission was closed on May 1, 1841, by Father Point, who then returned to Westport for a few days. *See* Garraghan, *op. cit.*, I, 376–420.

29 The Jesuits on the expedition were Fathers De Smet, Point, and Mengarini and Brothers Clessens, Huet, and Sprecht. Accompanying them were a hunter and two Canadian assistants.

30 St. Francis de Geronimo (1642–1716) was an Italian Jesuit whose apostolic life was spent in Naples. His feast is celebrated on May 11.

31 The Spanish induced the Shawnee to move to the Missouri country in 1793. They moved to Kansas about 1825. *See* Hodge, *op. cit.*, II, 538.

32 This was probably the present Shawnee Mission, Kansas.

33 Thomas Fitzpatrick was known as Tête Blanche and Broken Hand. Each was an Indian designation. Fitzpatrick is said to have had a great mane of white hair. He also had a somewhat deformed hand, due to an old break. He had guided the Marcus Whitman party to Oregon.

34 Benjamin Louis Eulalie de Bonneville was the subject of Washington Irving's *The Adventures of Captain Bonneville.*

35 Father Charles de la Croix was sent by Bishop Dubourg to visit the Osages in 1822. *See* G. J. Garraghan, S.J., *Catholic Beginnings in Kansas City, Missouri* (Chicago, 1920), 23.

36 The Pawnee were spread from the Platte River Valley southward to the Kansas River.

37 *Epinette des prairies* is called, in English, a wild rose.

38 *Turnsol* is the French name for a sunflower.

39 The Cheyenne was a plains tribe of Algonquins whose probable origin was Minnesota. *See* Hodge, *op. cit.*, I, 250.

40 The feast of St. John Francis Regis is celebrated on May 16.

41 This is Luigi Antonio Muratori (1672–1750), whose book, *A Relation of the Missions in Paraguay*, had been read by Father Point.

42 Fort Laramie was near the present site of Laramie, Wyoming.

43 Fort Hall on the Snake River was established in the fall of 1834 by Nathaniel Wyeth, a native of Boston who sought to enter the fur trade, but did not succeed.

44 When Father Point reached Fort Hall it had become a trading post of the Hudson's Bay Company. The chief factor was Francis Ermatinger who had come west in 1824 and married the niece of Dr. John McLoughlin, the most important Hudson's Bay official in the Columbia River region.

45 The *Itinerarium* is a group of psalms recited at the beginning of a journey.

46 The Bannock called themselves Pamaiti. *See* Hodge, *op. cit.*, I, 129.

47 For a discussion of the reduction idea as em-

ployed by De Smet, see J. P. Donnelly, S.J., "Nineteenth Century Jesuit Reductions in the United States," *Mid-America*, XVII (1935), 69–83.

48 The Cree Indians were natives of western Canada.

49 The Angelic Salutation is the prayer "Hail Mary, full of grace . . ."

50 The *Regina coeli* is a prayer in honor of the Blessed Mother. It is said during the Easter season.

51 The "important obligation" was the duty to receive the sacraments of penance and Holy Eucharist during the Easter season.

52 Father Point was the missionary who accompanied the Indians on the winter hunt.

53 The Jesuits had then been among the Indians for about a year. St. Mary's mission among the Flatheads was sufficiently firmly established to allow the missionaries to expand their activities. It was, therefore, decided to send Father Point to open a mission among the Coeur d'Alenes. This new center was given the title of Sacred Heart.

54 The Grand Lake to which Point refers is Lake Coeur d'Alene.

55 Gabriel seems to have been the Cree who met Father De Smet on one of the Jesuit's earlier visits to the country. There is some reason to think that Gabriel may have been one of the Indians who came to St. Louis in 1836. *See* Chittenden and Richardson, *op. cit.*, I, 399–401.

56 The mission of the Sacred Heart was established in Kootenai County, Idaho.

57 Temisposomen is probably a generic term for Indians who were friendly to the French. The word could be a corruption of the Indian word Nipissing.

58 November 13 is the feast of St. Stanislaus Kostka.

59 On the Feast of the Purification candles are blessed before the beginning of the Mass. Hence the name Candlemas.

60 The Feast of the Annunciation is celebrated on March 25.

61 *Kirile* should be translated as curlew. The bustard was, perhaps, a turkey.

62 The Nez Percés had been evangelized originally by the Reverend H. H. Spalding, a Presbyterian minister who started working among them in 1836.

63 The pelican is frequently used in ecclesiastical art to symbolize the Holy Eucharist. The mother pelican will wound herself to allow her young to drink her blood in order to save them from starving. Similarly, Christ is said to have shed His blood to save all men.

64 Father Joseph Joset came to America in 1843 and was sent immediately to the Oregon mission. He remained among the Indians until his death.

65 A retreat is a period spent in silent prayer and recollection.

66 The term "renewal of vows" refers to the custom of repeating the promises made at baptism to live a good Christian life.

67 Father S was De Smet who was in the Oregon mission that year. The reduction of St. Ignace was the mission of St. Ignatius, which is still in existence. It is located near Lewiston, Idaho.

68 *Modicae fidei* is a scriptural quotation which begins "O ye of little faith."

69 Point does not explain that in the fall of 1846 De Smet sent him to Fort Lewis to try to establish a mission there.

70 The Gros Ventres lived along the upper Missouri. They were noted beggars. *See* Hodge, *op. cit.*, I, 508.

71 Fort Crow was Fort Alexander, a trading post of the American Fur Company. It was located on the Yellowstone River.

72 Camp Victorious does not appear to be identifiable.

73 Fort Louis is Fort Lewis.

74 The Capuchins, a religious order of men, use a brown woolen hood as a headdress.

75 Point later identifies the master as Culbertson.

76 The Assiniboines were scattered through the Dakotas and central Canada.

77 The Chinooks dwelt along the Columbia River. *See* Hodge, *op. cit.*, I, 273.

78 *Essuies cabrasses* is translated in English as a halter.

79 The reference is to Vicomte François de Chateaubriand's *Voyages en Amerique, en France et en Italie, 1791–1793* (Paris, 1828–29), 2v.

80 St. Francis Borgia was noted for his gravity and modesty.

81 *Fareaux* may be a corruption of *effrayante*, which, in Mississippi valley patois, meant fearless.

82 *Plats-côtés* indicated the meat on the chest and shoulders of the animal.

83 Probably because of this custom the word *Kinnikinnik* was commonly used by the Indians to denote tobacco.

84 The Feast of the Three Kings is the Feast of Epiphany.

85 This Feast commemorates the transfer of St. Peter's Chair from Antioch to Rome.
86 The date is omitted in the manuscript.
87 Ashes are distributed on the first day of Lent.
88 The Feast of St. Ignatius is celebrated on July 31.
89 Point is using the word Chawanons for Shawnee.
90 *Quis ut Deus* is translated "Who is like unto God."
91 The Feast of the Circumcision is celebrated on January 1.
92 Ember Week is a designation for four periods during the year when penitential fasting is imposed.
93 St. Francis Xavier is called the Apostle of the Indies.
94 Jesuits frequently refer to St. Ignatius Loyola and St. Francis Xavier as "our first Fathers."
95 *Quam speciosi pedes* is a scriptural quotation which begins "How blessed are the feet . . ."
96 Bands within the Blackfoot nation assumed names in honor of a chief or of a memorable event. Since these names were frequently changed, the student can be readily confused. For a discussion of this feature of life among the Blackfeet, *see* J. C. Ewers, *The Blackfeet, Raiders on the Northwestern Plains* (Norman, Oklahoma, 1958), 96–98.
97 The "Catholic Ladder" was a visual aid used by the missionaries to instruct the Indians in the truths of religion. For a reproduction of this see: Bagley, *op. cit.*, II, 119.
98 *Jeu de barres* is a French term meaning mock warfare.
99 Throughout his account of his journey on a barge down the Missouri, Father Point spells the name of the fort "Lewis," though in the earlier portion of his manuscript he spells it "Louis."
100 The Isle of Reconciliation was a name which

Point gave to an island in the river near Fort Lewis.
101 The Fort of the Crows was later destroyed.
102 Here begins Point's *Journey on a Barge on the Missouri*. G. J. Garraghan, S.J. procured a manuscript copy of this account, which Point had sent to the Jesuit general in Rome. Garraghan's translation was published in *Mid-America* XIII (1930–31), 236–254. Point's account, which we include, is the much more complete one.
103 Garraghan translates the word "Indian" as "squaw."
104 Point's account here omits one long paragraph which is in the manuscript used by Garraghan.
105 Fort Campbell was a trading post of the company whose president was Colonel Robert Campbell.
106 In Garraghan's translation the word omitted here is "black."
107 Garraghan's text gives the omitted word as "depressing."
108 In Garraghan's translation, the missing name is given as "Kipp."
109 From Garraghan's text we learn that these were Bloods.
110 The imaginary encounter is not found in Garraghan's translation.
111 At this point Garraghan includes a long story which is not in the manuscript used here.
112 Two paragraphs follow in Garraghan's text which are not found in the manuscript used here.
113 This hymn may be translated:
   Happy is one under Her reign!
   What charms the pure of heart
      find there!
   Everyone feels and breathes
   In love, innocence, and peace.
114 The manuscript used by Garraghan ends at this point.

BIBLIOGRAPHY

Included here are only those books and periodical publications to which reference has been made in the text.

BAGLEY, C. B., *Early Catholic Missions in Old Oregon* (Seattle, 1932), 2v.

BANCROFT, H. H., *History of California* (San Francisco, 1884–1890), 7v.

CHITTENDEN, H. M., *The American Fur Trade of the Far West* (New York, 1902), 3v.
————— and RICHARDSON, A. T., *Life, Letters and Travels of Father Pierre-Jean De Smet* (New York, 1905), 4v.

DE SMET, P. J., *Letters and Sketches*. 1843.
—————, *Oregon Missions and Travels in the Rocky Mountains*. 1847.
—————, *Western Missions and Missionaries, a Series of Letters*. 1863.
—————, *New Indian Sketches*. 1863.

DONNELLY, J. P., S.J., "Nineteenth Century Jesuit Reductions in the United States," *Mid-America*, XVII (1935).

EWERS, J. C., *The Blackfeet, Raiders on the Northwestern Plains* (Norman, Oklahoma, 1958).

FOREMAN, G., "Our Indian Ambassadors to Europe," *Missouri Historical Society Collections* (1928), 5v.

GARRAGHAN, G. J., S.J., *Catholic Beginnings in Kansas City, Missouri* (Chicago, 1920).
—————, *Chapters in Frontier History*. 1934.
—————, *The Jesuits of the Middle United States* (New York, 1938), 3v.
—————, "Journey on a Barge on the Missouri," *Mid-America*, XIII (1930–31), 236–254.

HILL, W. H., S.J., "Reminiscences of St. Mary's College, Kentucky," *Woodstock Letters*, XX (1891), 25–38.

HODGE, F. W., *Handbook of American Indians North of Mexico* (Washington, 1907), 2v.

McDERMOTT, J. F., *A Glossary of Mississippi Valley French, 1673–1850* (St. Louis, 1941).
—————, "De Smet's Illustrator: Father Nicholas Point," *Nebraska History*, XXXIII (1952), 35–40.